Cracking the
AP®

ECONOMICS
MICRO & MACRO EXAMS

2020 Edition

The Staff of The Princeton Review

PrincetonReview.com

Penguin
Random
House

The Princeton Review
110 East 42nd St., 7th Floor
New York, NY 10017
Email: editorialsupport@review.com

Published in the United States by Penguin Random House LLC, New York, and in Canada by Random House of Canada, a division of Penguin Random House Ltd., Toronto.

Terms of Service: The Princeton Review Online Companion Tools ("Student Tools") for retail books are available for only the two most recent editions of that book. Student Tools may be activated only once per eligible book purchased for a total of 24 months of access. Activation of Student Tools more than once per book is in direct violation of these Terms of Service and may result in discontinuation of access to Student Tools Services.

ISBN: 978-0-525-56820-9
eBook ISBN: 978-0-525-56858-2
ISSN: 1546-6914

AP is a trademark registered and owned by the College Board, which is not affiliated with, and does not endorse this product.

The Princeton Review is not affiliated with Princeton University.

Editor: Orion McBean
Production Editor: Wendy Rosen and Lee Elder
Production Artist: Jennifer Chapman
Content Developer: Corinne Dolci

Printed in the United States of America.

10   9   8   7   6   5   4   3   2   1

2020 Edition

Editorial

Rob Franek, Editor-in-Chief
David Soto, Director of Content Development
Stephen Koch, Student Survey Manager
Deborah Weber, Director of Production
Gabriel Berlin, Production Design Manager
Selena Coppock, Managing Editor
Aaron Riccio, Senior Editor
Meave Shelton, Senior Editor
Chris Chimera, Editor
Sarah Litt, Editor
Orion McBean, Editor
Brian Saladino, Editor
Eleanor Green, Editorial Assistant

Penguin Random House Publishing Team

Tom Russell, VP, Publisher
Alison Stoltzfus, Publishing Director
Amanda Yee, Associate Managing Editor
Ellen Reed, Production Manager
Suzanne Lee, Designer

The material in this book is up-to-date at the time of publication. However, changes may have been instituted by the testing body in the test after this book was published.

If there are any important late-breaking developments, changes, or corrections to the materials in this book, we will post that information online in the Student Tools. Register your book and check your Student Tools to see if there are any updates posted there.

Acknowledgments

The Princeton Review would like to give a tremendous thanks to Corinne Dolci for her hard work in revising the 2020 edition. We'd also like to thank our devoted production team for making this book the best it can be.

Contents

Get More (Free) Content
at PrincetonReview.com/cracking

As easy as 1·2·3

1 Go to PrincetonReview.com/cracking and enter the following ISBN for your book:
9780525568209

2 Answer a few simple questions to set up an exclusive Princeton Review account. *(If you already have one, you can just log in.)*

3 Enjoy access to your **FREE** content!

Once you've registered, you can...

- Get our take on any recent or pending updates to the AP Micro or Macro Economics courses

- Take a full-length practice SAT and/or ACT

- Get valuable advice about the college application process, including tips for writing a great essay and where to apply for financial aid

- If you're still choosing between colleges, use our searchable rankings of *The Best 385 Colleges* to find out more information about your dream school.

- Access comprehensive study guides and a variety of printable resources, including: bubble sheets for the practice tests in this book and handy formula sheets

- Check to see if there have been any corrections or updates to this edition

Need to report a potential **content** issue?

Contact **EditorialSupport@review.com** and include:

- full title of the book
- ISBN
- page number

Need to report a **technical** issue?

Contact **TPRStudentTech@review.com** and provide:

- your full name
- email address used to register the book
- full book title and ISBN
- Operating system (Mac/PC) and browser (Firefox, Safari, etc.)

Look For These Icons Throughout The Book

 PROVEN TECHNIQUES

 APPLIED STRATEGIES

 ONLINE ARTICLES

Part I
Using This Book to Improve Your AP Score

- Preview: Your Knowledge, Your Expectations
- Your Guide to Using This Book
- How to Begin

PREVIEW: YOUR KNOWLEDGE, YOUR EXPECTATIONS

Welcome to your *Cracking the AP Economics Micro & Macro Exams, 2020 Edition*. Your route to a high score on the AP Microeconomics or Macroeconomics Exam depends a lot on how you plan to use this book. To help you make that determination, please respond to the following questions.

1. Rate your level of confidence about your knowledge of the content tested by the AP Microeconomics or Macroeconomics Exam:

    A. Very confident—I know it all

    B. I'm pretty confident, but there are topics for which I could use help

    C. Not confident—I need quite a bit of support

    D. I'm not sure

2. Circle your goal score for the exam.

    5   4   3   2   1   I'm not sure yet

3. What do you expect to learn from this book? Circle all that apply to you.

    A. A general overview of the test and what to expect

    B. Strategies for how to approach the test

    C. The content tested by this exam

    D. I'm not sure yet

YOUR GUIDE TO USING THIS BOOK

Cracking the AP Economics Micro & Macro Exams, 2020 Edition is organized to provide as much—or as little—support as you need, so you can use this book in whatever way will be most helpful to improving your score on the AP Microeconomics or Macroeconomics Exam.

- The remainder of **Part I** provides guidance on how to use this book and help you determine your strengths and weaknesses.

- **Part II** of this book provides information on the following topics:
    - the structure, scoring, and content of the Economics Exams
    - making a study plan
    - finding additional resources

- **Part III** of this book explores the following strategies:
    - how to attack multiple-choice questions
    - how to approach free-response questions
    - how to manage your time to maximize the number of points available to you

- **Part IV** of this book covers the content you need for the AP Economics Exams.

- **Part V** contains practice tests, answers and explanations, bubble sheets that you can tear out, and a handy formula sheet for your reference.

You may choose to use some parts of this book over others, or you may work through the entire book. This will depend on your needs and how much time you have. Let's now examine how to make this determination.

Once you register your book online, you can download and print bubble and formula sheets!

HOW TO BEGIN

1. **Measure Your Confidence**
    Before you can decide how to use this book, you need to get a sense for how well you already understand the material. Doing so will give you insight into your strengths and weaknesses, and help you make an effective study plan. If you're feeling anxious about taking your test, remind yourself that this practice is a tool for diagnosing yourself—it's not how well you do that matters, but how you use information gleaned from your performance to guide your preparation.

    Depending on whether you're taking the Micro or Macro Exam, turn to the corresponding Pacing Drills on page 35 and work through each question based on the Economic exam you are taking.

2. **Check Your Answers**
    Using the answer keys, count the number of multiple-choice questions you answered correctly and how many you missed. Don't worry about the explanations for now, and don't worry about why you missed questions. We'll get to that soon.

3. **Reflect on the Diagnostic**
    After checking your answers, respond to the following questions:
    *   How much time did you spend on the multiple-choice questions?
    *   How many multiple-choice questions did you miss?
    *   Which chapters did you feel most and least comfortable solving?
    *   In which chapters did you get the most and least number of questions correct?

4. **Read Part II of this Book and Design Your Study Plan**
    Part II will provide information on how the test is structured and scored. It will also outline areas of content that are tested.

    As you read Part II, re-evaluate your answers to the questions you just answered. At the end of Part II, you will revisit and refine your answers to the previous questions. You will then be able to make a study plan, based on your needs and time available, that will allow you to use this book most effectively.

5. **Engage with Parts III and IV as Needed**

   Notice the word *engage*. You'll get more out of this book if you use it intentionally than if you read it passively, hoping for an improved score through osmosis.

   Strategy chapters will help you think about your approach to the question types on this exam. Part III will open with a reminder to think about how you approach questions now, and then close with a reflection section asking you to think about how/whether you will change your approach in the future.

   Content chapters are designed to provide a review of the content tested on the AP Economics Exams, including the level of detail you need to know and how the content is tested. You will have the opportunity to assess your mastery of the content of each chapter through test-appropriate questions and a reflection section.

6. **Tackle More Practice and Assess Your Performance**

   Once you feel you have developed the strategies you need and gained the knowledge you lacked, you should test that theory by working through some of the free-response questions from previous exams, which are posted on the AP Courses page.

   - Microeconomics:
     apstudent.collegeboard.org/apcourse/ap-microeconomics/exam-practice

   - Macroeconomics:
     apstudent.collegeboard.org/apcourse/ap-macroeconomics/exam-practice

   Assess your confidence in your answers to see which topics you hit and which you missed. Reflect on what areas you still need to work on, and revisit the chapters in this book that address those deficiencies. Through this type of reflection and engagement, you will continue to improve.

7. **Keep Working**

   As discussed before, there are other resources available to you, including a wealth of information on the AP Courses and AP Central websites. You can continue to explore areas in which you can improve and engage in those areas right up to the day of the test.

Part II
About the AP Economics Exams

- The Structure of the AP Economics Exams
- How the AP Economics Exams Are Scored
- Overview of Content Topics
- How AP Exams Are Used
- Other Resources
- Designing Your Study Plan

THE STRUCTURE OF THE AP ECONOMICS EXAMS

Whether you are planning to take the AP Microeconomics or AP Macroeconomics Exam, your exam will include 60 multiple-choice questions and 3 free-response questions.

Let's break that down in handy chart format:

Question Type	Time	Score	More Score Info
60 multiple-choice questions	70 minutes	Section accounts for 66% of AP Exam score	No guessing penalty for any incorrect multiple-choice questions
3 free-response questions (FRQs). 1 long, 2 short	60 minutes: 10 minutes reading/planning time, 50 minutes writing time	Section accounts for 33% of AP Exam score	Within section, long FRQ accounts for 50% of total section score; 2 shorter FRQs each account for 25% total section score.

HOW THE AP ECONOMICS EXAMS ARE SCORED

Each AP exam receives a numerical score of 1 to 5 with each score meaning the following:

> 5 = Extremely Well Qualified
> 4 = Well Qualified
> 3 = Qualified
> 2 = Possibly Qualified
> 1 = No Recommendation

Colleges decide for themselves the minimum score they will accept for college credit and/or advanced placement. The American Council on Education recommends the acceptance of grades of 3 or above, and many colleges adhere to these standards. About 60 percent of students who take the microeconomics or macroeconomics AP exam receive a score of 3 or higher. Check the website of the college(s) of your choice to learn the school's policy on granting credit or advanced placement.

Scoring Your Exam

Each year, the AP Test Development Committee works with experts at ETS (Educational Testing Service) and the College Board to create a formula that converts the raw score on an exam into a composite score, which is then used to determine what grade (from 1 to 5) each test taker receives. As such, we can't tell you how many questions you need to get right in order to get a 5.

What we can tell you is that the 60 multiple-choice questions are worth 66 percent of that raw score, and that the first of the free-response questions is worth twice as much as each of the other two. If you're trying to determine which test (Microeconomics or Macroeconomics) to take, give yourself 1.1 points for each correct multiple-choice question, 18 points for the first free-response question, and 8 points for each of the following two free-response questions.

If you want to get a sense of how frequently each grade is assigned for both the Microeconomics and Macroeconomics Exam, check out the data below. That and your raw score should give you a rough idea of how your score may be converted.

AP Microeconomics – 2018 Score Distributions		
Score	Number of Test Takers	Percentage
5	18,827	21%
4	25,070	27.8%
3	17,238	19.1%
2	13,823	15.4%
1	15,074	16.7%
Total	90,032	100%*

AP Macroeconomics – 2018 Score Distributions		
Score	Number of Test Takers	Percentage
5	28,910	19.7%
4	33,109	22.6%
3	23,790	16.2%
2	24,640	16.8%
1	36,224	24.7%
Total	146,673	100%*

*Data from The College Board, May 2018 AP Exam administrations

OVERVIEW OF CONTENT TOPICS

We'll go into in-depth analysis of AP Economics content in Part IV, but here's a broad overview determined by the College Board of the content topics that you'll need to know for your AP Exam. **NOTE:** The College Board will be modifying the outlines below in a new Course and Exams Description for the 2019-2020 course year. This book will still cover all the material for the exam, but in a potentially different order than your AP Course, one that's designed to help maximize your test-prep.

To stay up-to-date with changes to the AP Economics Micro and Macro courses, please register your book to access your online Student Tools and visit https://apcentral collegeboard.org/courses, ap-microeconomics/course, updates-2019-20

AP Microeconomics	
Content Areas	**Anticipated percentage of questions within multiple-choice section**
Basic Economic Concepts	8–14%
The Nature and Function of Product Markets: Supply and Demand Theory of Consumer Choice Production and Costs Firm Behavior and Market Structure	55–70% (entire section – subsections below) 15–20% 5–10% 10–15% 25–35%
Factor Markets	10–18%
Market Failure and the Role of Government	12–18%

AP Macroeconomics	
Content Areas	**Anticipated percentage of questions within multiple-choice section**
Basic Economic Concepts	8–12%
Measurement of Economic Performance	12–16%
National Income and Price Determination	10–15%
Financial Sector	15–20%
Stabilization Policies	20–30%
Economic Growth	5–10%
Open Economy: International Trade and Finance	10–15%

HOW AP EXAMS ARE USED

Different colleges use AP Exam scores in different ways, so it is important that you go to a particular college's website to determine how it uses AP Exam scores. The three items below represent the main ways in which AP Exam scores can be used.

- **College Credit.** Some colleges will give you college credit if you score well on an AP Exam. These credits count toward your graduation requirements, meaning that you can take fewer courses while in college. Given the cost of college, this could be quite a benefit indeed.

- **Satisfy Requirements.** Some colleges will allow you to "place out" of certain requirements if you do well on an AP Exam, even if they do not give you actual college credits. For example, you might not need to take an introductory-level course, or perhaps you might not need to take a class in a certain discipline at all.

- **Admissions Plus.** Even if your AP Exam will not result in college credit or allow you to place out of certain courses, most colleges will respect your decision to push yourself by taking an AP Course or even an AP Exam outside of a course. A high score on an AP Exam shows mastery of content that is more difficult than what is taught in many high school courses, and colleges may take that into account during the admissions process.

More Great Books

Check out The Princeton Review's college guide books, including *The Best 385 Colleges, The Complete Book of Colleges, Paying for College, 2019 Edition,* and many more!

OTHER RESOURCES

There are many resources available to help you improve your score on the AP Economics Exams, not the least of which are your teachers. If you are taking an AP class, you may be able to get extra attention from your teacher, such as obtaining feedback on your free-response answers. If you are not in an AP course, reach out to a teacher who teaches Economics, and ask if the teacher will review your writing or otherwise help you with content.

Another wonderful resource is **AP Students**, the official site of the AP Exams. The most recent updates of the following items can be found at AP Students:

- course description, which includes detailed information about what content is covered

- sample multiple-choice questions for both AP Microeconomics and AP Macroeconomics

- sample free-response questions for both AP Microeconomics and AP Macroeconomics

- exam practice tips

- information about exam fees and reductions

The AP Students home page address is http://apstudent.collegeboard.org.

New Course and Exam Descriptions for the 2019-2020 AP Economics Micro and Macro!

The College Board is set to release a new course description for both AP Economics exams, so be sure to visit their website to get the latest up-to-date information.

The AP Microeconomics Course home page address is
https://apstudent.collegeboard.org/apcourse/ap-microeconomics.

The AP Macroeconomics Course home page is
https://apstudent.collegeboard.org/apcourse/ap-macroeconomics.

Finally, The Princeton Review offers tutoring for the AP Economics Exams. Our expert instructors can help you refine your strategic approach and add to your content knowledge. For more information, call **1-800-2REVIEW.**

Break up your review into manageable portions. Download our helpful study guide for this book once you register online.

DESIGNING YOUR STUDY PLAN

Review your diagnostic reflection from page 4 and the Overview of Content Topics on page 10 and, next to each one, indicate your rank of the topic as follows: "1" means "I need a lot of work on this," "2" means "I need to beef up my knowledge," and "3" means "I know this topic well." Then answer the following questions.

- How many days/weeks/months away is your AP Economics Exam?

- What time of day is your best, most focused study time?

- How much time per day/week/month will you devote to preparing for your AP Economics Exam?

- When will you do this preparation? (Be as specific as possible: Mondays and Wednesdays from 3:00 to 4:00 p.m., for example)

- Based on the answers above, will you focus on strategy (Part III) or content (Part IV) or both?

- What are your overall goals in using this book?

Based on your answers to these questions, you should now have a better understanding of how to study for the exam. Use your answers to customize a study plan that meets your specific needs based on the amount of time you have until test day. It is important to tailor your study plan to your schedule and topics you need to further review.

Part III
Test-Taking Strategies for the AP Economics Exams

PREVIEW

Review your responses to the questions on page 4 of Part I and then respond to the following questions:

- How many multiple-choice questions did you miss even though you knew the answer?

- On how many multiple-choice questions did you guess blindly?

- How many multiple-choice questions did you miss after eliminating some answers and guessing based on the remaining answers?

- Did you create an outline before you answered each free response question?

- Did you find any of the free-response questions easier/harder than the others—and, if so, why?

HOW TO USE THE CHAPTERS IN THIS PART

Think about what you are doing now before you read the following Strategy chapters. As you read and engage in the directed practice, be sure to consider the ways you can change your approach. At the end of Part III, you will have the opportunity to reflect on how you will change your approach.

Chapter 1
How to Approach Multiple-Choice Questions

CRACKING THE MULTIPLE-CHOICE QUESTIONS

Multiple-choice questions account for two-thirds of your total examination grade. During the multiple-choice section of each exam, you will have 70 minutes to answer 60 questions, or 70 seconds per question. You will encounter several types of multiple-choice questions. One type deals with economic policy, asking for examples of how an expansionary monetary policy is likely to affect interest rates, investment, and aggregate demand. Another question type asks you to interpret a graph. For example, you might be asked which labeled section of a graph represents consumer surplus. A third type of question asks you to distinguish true from false statements. These questions may seem more difficult than a standard true/false question because you will be given three or four statements (labeled with roman numerals) and asked, for example, whether the truth is represented by I, II, III; I and III; or II and IV. You will have an opportunity to practice each of these types of questions in both the practice tests in the book and in the drills that you'll find later in this chapter.

Proven Techniques

Use POE and the Two-Pass System to help boost your score.

Process of Elimination

For questions that stump you, try using a technique we call Process of Elimination, or POE, to help you guess more accurately. Oftentimes it is easier to spot incorrect answer choices than to know the correct answer. To use this technique, first read *all* of the possible responses, even if you think you know the answer right away, just to make sure you aren't missing something. If no answer choice is clearly correct, eliminate as many as you can by actually marking them off in the test booklet. After you have eliminated as many as you can, select an answer from the remaining choices. Every time you get rid of one answer choice, the odds of selecting the correct answer go up significantly.

What is the name for the idea that governments should actively regulate trade in order to maintain a positive balance of trade?

(A)   Free trade
(B)   Mercantilism
(C)   Elasticity
(D)   Monopoly
(E)   Laissez-faire

If you tried to just answer this question from your own knowledge, you'd probably be stumped. Instead, let's use POE!

Well, it can't be free trade or laissez-faire because they were all about removing government restrictions on economic activity, so get rid of (A) and (E). Elasticity refers to the sensitivity of quantities demanded or supplied to changes in prices, which has nothing to do with trade, so get rid of (C). Monopoly refers to one company controlling all of the supply of a good or service, which isn't really about trade, so get rid of (D). This means the answer must be (B)! POE can be a really powerful way to have a fighting chance on even the toughest questions.

Based on personal experience grading non-AP multiple-choice questions (machines check AP multiple-choice questions), we have determined that students who fill in one response and then change to another most often change from the correct answer to an incorrect answer. If you're considering changing an answer and you feel fifty-fifty about which choice is correct, consider the time it will take to erase the first answer and fill in the second. Time is always a factor to consider on the AP exam, so you might be better off just leaving the answer as is. If your test-taking history has proven that your initial response is not as reliable as your second thought, however, go with your gut, sacrifice the time, and make the change.

Use the Two-Pass System

Go through the multiple-choice section twice. The first time, do all the questions that you can get answers to immediately. In other words, first answer questions that require little or no analysis and any questions dealing with economics topics in which you are well-versed.

To put it another way, the first time through, skip the questions in the topics about which you are least confident. Also, you might want to skip the ones that look like number crunchers. (Just because a calculator is not permitted on the exam, that doesn't mean you won't still be expected to crunch a few numbers.) Circle the questions that you skip in your test booklet so you can find them easily during the second pass. Once you've answered all the questions that come easily to you, go back and answer the tough ones that you have the best shot of getting right. And, because you don't lose points for wrong answers on AP Exams, you want to make sure you do not leave any questions blank. When you get to questions that are too time-consuming, or you don't know the answer to (and can't eliminate any options), use what we call your letter of the day (LOTD). Selecting the same answer choice each time you guess will increase your odds of getting a few of those skipped questions right.

That's why the two-pass system is so handy. By using it, you make sure that you see all the questions that you can get right, instead of running out of time because you became bogged down on time-consuming questions.

Which brings us to another important point….

Don't Turn a Question into a Crusade!

Most people don't run out of time on standardized tests because they work too slowly. Instead, they run out of time because they spend half the test wrestling with two or three difficult-seeming questions.

You should never spend more than a minute or two on any question. If a question doesn't involve calculation, then either you know the answer, or you can take an educated guess at the answer, or you don't know the answer. Figure out where you stand on a question, make a decision, and move on.

Any question that requires more than two minutes' worth of calculations probably isn't worth doing. Keep in mind that questions you find easy are worth the same as questions that might stump you. If you're low on time, or just don't know the answer, LOTD and move on!

DRILLS

Below are examples of each of the types of multiple-choice questions already mentioned. In each of these examples, the use of graphs and the Process of Elimination will help you to hone in on the correct answer. Be sure to use these techniques and the two-pass system to maximize your score.

Economic Policy Questions

1. Which of the following policy combinations would most effectively relieve inflationary pressures on the economy?

	Income Taxes	Govt. Spending	Open-Market Operations
(A)	Decrease	Increase	Buy securities
(B)	Increase	Decrease	Buy securities
(C)	Decrease	Decrease	Sell securities
(D)	Increase	Increase	Buy securities
(E)	Increase	Decrease	Sell securities

Apply Strategy

Use POE to crack this question.

Here's How to Crack It

Question 1 asks which policies would most effectively relieve inflationary pressures on the economy. You might begin by drawing an aggregate demand/aggregate supply (AD/AS) graph to help you visualize what needs to happen to decrease the price level.

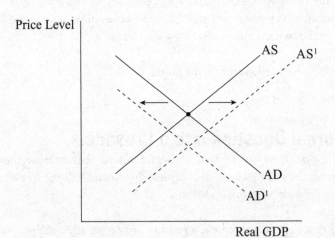

As you look at the AD/AS graph, you should be able to see that the price level will decrease when aggregate demand decreases (shifts left) or aggregate supply increases (shifts right). This information alone allows you to begin the Process of Elimination. Start with government spending. Since government spending is part of aggregate demand (AD), any increase in government spending will increase AD, thus shifting it to the right, which would *increase* prices. Therefore, you can eliminate (A) and (D). Now keep going! If income taxes decrease, then people would have more money in their pockets, which has the same effect as an increase in income, which increases AD. Thus since increasing AD leads to higher prices, you can eliminate (C). Finally, you know that buying securities increases the money supply, lowers the interest rate, increases investment, and thus increases AD and the price level. Therefore, you can rule out (B), and you are left with (E) as the correct answer.

Interpret Graph Questions

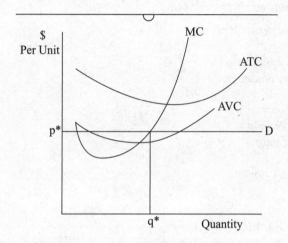

2. A firm is in a perfectly competitive industry. Given the cost and demand schedules depicted in the graph above, what should the firm do in the short run?

    (A) Shut down
    (B) Stay open and produce q*
    (C) Stay open and produce more than q*
    (D) Stay open and produce less than q*
    (E) Stay open but produce zero units

Here's How to Crack It

Question 2 asks you to interpret a graph and determine the optimal behavior for a firm in the short run. Since the price for this firm's product is below its average total cost (ATC), it is losing money. However, if you read carefully, you'll see that the question is asking what the firm should do in the short run, in which the current price exceeds average variable cost (AVC) and covers some of the fixed costs (average fixed costs are the difference between ATC and AVC). The firm should therefore stay open, as it will lose less than if it shuts down. Get rid of (A). In a perfectly competitive industry, marginal revenue (MR) = demand. When the price is less than ATC but greater than AVC, a firm should engage in loss minimization and produce at the level at which marginal cost (MC) = MR. This means that q* is the optimal quantity to produce, making (B) the correct answer. If a firm produces more than q*, then the cost of making each additional unit is more than the revenue the firm would receive.

Eliminate (C). If the firm produces less than q*, then revenue would exceed the cost and the firm would keep producing. Eliminate (D). If a firm produced 0 units, it would not cover its fixed costs, so you can eliminate (E).

Distinguishing True from False Statements Questions

3. Which of the following characterize a non-price-discriminating monopoly?

I. Large barriers to entry
II. MR = P
III. Perfectly elastic demand
IV. A unique product

(A) I and II only
(B) III and IV only
(C) I and IV only
(D) IV only
(E) I, II, and IV only

Here's How to Crack It

Question 3 asks you to identify characteristics of a non-price-discriminating monopoly. Price-discrimination means that a firm charges different prices to different clients. If a firm is non-price-discriminating, it charges the same price to all its clients. By drawing a typical monopoly graph, you immediately see that demand is not perfectly elastic (horizontal) and that price is above marginal revenue. This rules out items II and III and (A), (B), and (E). The distinguishing question between (C) and (D) is whether or not there are large barriers to entry in a monopoly. Because a monopoly by definition has no successful competitors, the barriers to entry must be large and the correct answer must be (C).

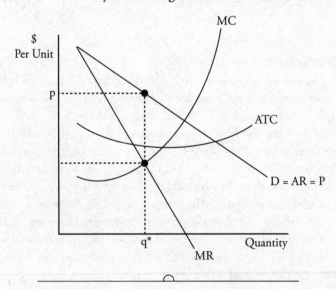

THE EMPHASIS OF MULTIPLE-CHOICE QUESTIONS

The percentages given below are estimates of how the multiple-choice questions on the AP Microeconomics Exam were allocated in previous years among the various economic concepts. As mentioned before, the College Board is planning to reorganize the Micro and Macro course concepts into a 6 unit structure that may be different from the one below. At the time of this book's printing, we are waiting for specifics on this, so please make sure to register your book online and visit your student tools for updated information. The Macroeconomics Concepts breakdown will also be available on your student tools.

AP Microeconomics Concepts

I.   **Basic Economic Concepts (8–14%)**
  A.   Scarcity, choice, and opportunity cost
  B.   Production possibilities curve
  C.   Comparative advantage, absolute advantage, specialization, and trade
  D.   Economic systems
  E.   Property rights and the role of incentives
  F.   Marginal analysis

II.   **The Nature and Functions of Product Markets (55–70%)**
  A.   Supply and demand (15–20%)
    1.   Market equilibrium
    2.   Determinants of supply and demand
    3.   Price and quantity controls
    4.   Elasticity
        -   Price, income, and cross-price elasticities of demand
        -   Price elasticity of supply
    5.   Consumer surplus, producer surplus, and allocative efficiency
    6.   Tax incidence and deadweight loss
  B.   Theory of consumer choice (5–10%)
    1.   Total utility and marginal utility
    2.   Utility maximization: equalizing marginal utility per dollar
    3.   Individual and market demand curves
    4.   Income and substitution effects
  C.   Production and costs (10–15%)
    1.   Production functions: short and long run
    2.   Marginal product and diminishing returns
    3.   Short-run costs
    4.   Long-run costs and economies of scale
    5.   Cost minimizing input combination and productive efficiency
  D.   Firm behavior and market structure (25–35%)
    1.   Profit
        -   Accounting versus economic profits
        -   Normal profit
        -   Profit maximization: MR = MC rule

The College Board is set to release new Course and Exam Descriptions after the publication of this book, so make sure to register your book online and download the most up-to-date outlines for both Micro and Macro Concepts!

2. Perfect competition
   - Profit maximization
   - Short-run supply and shutdown decision
   - Behavior of firms and markets in the short run and in the long run
   - Efficiency and perfect competition
3. Monopoly
   - Sources of market power
   - Profit maximization
   - Inefficiency of monopoly
   - Price discrimination
   - Natural monopoly
4. Oligopoly
   - Interdependence, collusion, and cartels
   - Game theory and strategic behavior
   - Dominant strategy
   - Nash equilibrium
5. Monopolistic competition
   - Product differentiation and role of advertising
   - Profit maximization
   - Short-run and long-run equilibrium
   - Excess capacity and inefficiency

III. **Factor Markets (10–18%)**
   A. Derived factor demand
   B. Marginal revenue product
   C. Hiring decisions in the markets for labor and capital
   D. Market distribution of income

IV. **Market Failure and the Role of Government (12–18%)**
   A. Externalities
      1. Marginal social benefit and marginal social cost
      2. Positive externalities
      3. Negative externalities
      4. Remedies
   B. Public goods
      1. Public versus private goods
      2. Provision of public goods
   C. Public policy to promote competition
      1. Antitrust policy
      2. Regulation
   D. Income distribution
      1. Equity
      2. Sources and measures of income inequality

Chapter 2
How to Approach
Free-Response
Questions

CRACKING THE FREE-RESPONSE QUESTIONS

The free-response questions account for one-third of the total score for each of the exams. There are three free-response questions on each exam. The first is worth about 50 percent of your free-response score. The second and third questions are each worth about 25 percent of your free-response score. The purpose of these questions is to test your analytical and organizational skills, and you will most likely be asked to apply your knowledge of economic graphs and tables. You will be allowed 10 minutes to read over the questions and think about your answers, and then 50 minutes to answer the questions. It is recommended that you allocate 25 minutes to the long question and 12.5 minutes to each of the two short questions. All topics are fair game on the free-response section, so be prepared!

Avoid rambling blindly into inaccuracy. Your first task after reading a free-response question is to determine which of your economic tools to apply to its solution. The use of graphs, equations, and structured reasoning will guide you to correct answers and allow you to check for potentially incorrect statements (if you are unsure of where to start).

Experimenting with possible approaches to the problem is not a bad idea. Apply the graphs, equations, or tables that seem the most relevant; if they don't lead to an answer, try another approach.

How to Approach the Questions—Making Graphs Work for You

President Bill Clinton was elected twice and became the most popular second-term president in half a century—even after being impeached—because of one truth that he understood well: "It's the economy, stupid." The strong economy led directly to more dollars in citizens' pockets. Indirectly, it resolved many more problems involving the deficit, unemployment, and welfare. For you, the secret is this:

It's the graphs, stupid!

Since 1996, students have been required to draw and label their own graphs for some parts of the free-response questions on the AP Microeconomics Exam. Drawing graphs is not only the key to earning points on graph questions, but it is also the secret to solving problems that may not even require a graph. Have you noticed that economists seem compulsive about drawing graphs? It's not that they are repressed artists. Rather, they know this secret: economics may seem very hard to sort out in your head but it can be relatively easy with a few illustrations. Invest the time necessary to learn to draw the graphs. Resist the temptation to interpret the question with words alone. Although the graders often permit a high point allocation for good prose (word-only) responses, the most successful prose responses are typically explanations of graphs that show that the students understood the graphs and visualized them in their minds.

Consider the following question:

4. Suppose there is a drought and a successful advertising campaign for parsley in the same year.

(a) Draw a correctly labeled supply and demand diagram to represent this scenario.

(b) Explain how the shift identified in part (a) will affect the equilibrium and quantity of parsley.

The first part of a free-response question often involves sketching the situation, but even when it doesn't, or if you are dealing with a tricky multiple-choice question, you still want to be able to quickly draw the basic situation. The only difference is that because you're handing in this chart, you'll want to make sure you clearly label everything.

(a)

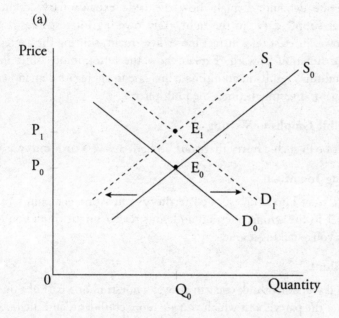

(b) Because a drought decreases supply from S_0 to S_1 and successful advertising increases demand from D_0 to D_1, the new equilibrium price will be higher and the quantity may increase or decrease depending on the size of the supply and demand curve shifts.

Common Mistakes

Don't lose points by making the following common mistakes:

- **Mislabeled or Unlabeled Graphs**

  Labels matter. Just because you drew lines shaped like supply and demand curves when the question clearly is looking for them doesn't mean the graders will assume you knew what you were doing. Label every line and every axis.

- **Skipped Steps in the Story**

  Don't hold back information that is part of the answer even if it seems obvious. The graders want to read about every step between cause and effect. Don't just say, for example, that expansionary monetary policy increases aggregate demand. Explain how the Fed's expansionary action shifts the money supply curve to the right, thus lowering interest rates. Explain how the lower interest rates attract more investment, shifting the aggregate expenditure function upward. Explain how the autonomous shift in aggregate expenditures results in an ultimate increase in aggregate demand equal to the change in investment times the multiplier.

- **Illegible Graphs or Writing**

  Don't be in such a hurry that your brilliant answers turn into wasted ink.

- **Saying Too Much**

  Don't stray into unquestioned territory. You won't get points for the right answer to the wrong question and your reader might think you don't know what you're talking about!

- **The Punt**

  Even if you don't think you can answer a question or a part of a question, first answer the parts about which you are more confident, and then use any spare time to make your best attempt at writing something logical and coherent. Some questions might not be asking for as much complexity as you think. You might pick up a point or two if you show enough signs of intelligent life. Unfortunately, some students give up and write down jokes instead. Not even the best joke will earn any partial credit.

- **Examples without Explanations**

  Too often, questions that seek definitions or conditions are answered merely with examples. If a question asks, for example, "What is distinct about public goods?" explain how they are nonrival and nonexcludable. Don't just say, "National defense is an example of one."

- **Breaking the Golden Rule of Economics: MC = MB**

  One of the primary lessons in economics is that we should do whatever we do until the marginal cost (MC) equals the marginal benefit (MB). Marginal cost is the cost of one more and marginal benefit is the benefit from one more. The answers to many questions have to do with equating marginal cost and marginal benefit, after adapting these terms to the situation. For firms, the marginal "benefit" is generally assumed to be marginal revenue, and every type of firm maximizes profits or minimizes losses by producing where marginal cost equals marginal revenue (if they should operate at all). Likewise, we assume that individuals seek to maximize utility, which is accomplished by consuming goods until the marginal cost to individuals (the price) equals the marginal utility (measured in dollars). We should also continue until MC = MB when renting pizza ovens, searching for a job, studying, eating, shopping, etc.

The reasoning behind this rule is straightforward. Regardless of what we are buying, selling, making, or doing, if one more unit costs less than the benefit it adds, there is a net benefit from proceeding with it. If one more unit costs more than the benefit it adds, we should not proceed with it. So in terms of the AP Economics exam, if you're struggling with a question that has to do with how much of something should happen, try to identify the marginal cost and marginal benefit for the decision maker and suggest that they be equated.

For example, suppose you are asked how a competitive firm should decide how many workers to hire in the short run. The MC of hiring a worker is the worker's wage. The MB is the worker's marginal product (MP)—how many widgets that worker will produce—times the price per widget.

Even if you don't remember the jargon that MC = MB = MP × P, you should earn worthwhile partial credit for explaining that the firm should hire workers until the last worker's wage equals the last worker's contribution to output times the price.

At the same time, the rule that MC = MB applies to you too! If you've been writing for 25 minutes on the long question, even if you feel you have more to say, ask yourself "Does the marginal benefit of writing an extra few sentences on this question equal the marginal cost of maybe not finishing the short questions because I run out of time?" Probably not.

GRAPH DRILL

Now use the advice above to help you answer the following sample of a free-response question.

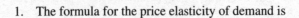

1. The formula for the price elasticity of demand is

$$\frac{\dfrac{\text{change in } Q_d}{Q_d}}{\dfrac{\text{change in } P}{P}}$$

(i) Explain why price elasticity of demand values is typically negative.

(ii) Explain the relationship between the price elasticity of demand and the slope of a demand curve.

(iii) Explain why a monopoly should never operate on the inelastic portion of its demand curve.

Here's How to Crack It

Although the question does not ask for a graph, the use of graphs will lead you to the correct answer and help convey that answer to the graders.

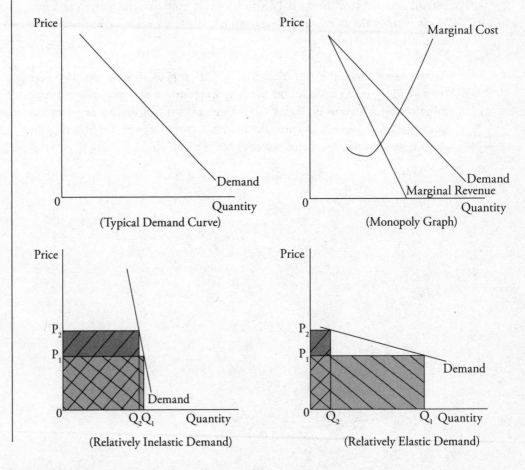

(Typical Demand Curve)

(Monopoly Graph)

(Relatively Inelastic Demand)

(Relatively Elastic Demand)

For part (i), draw a typical demand curve graph and remember the law of demand: when the price goes up, the quantity demanded goes down, and vice versa. In the elasticity formula, price (P) and quantity (Q) will always be positive. According to the law of demand, if the change in the price demanded is positive, the change in quantity demanded will be negative. If the change in the price demanded is negative, the change in quantity demanded will be positive. Either way, there will be a single negative value on the top or bottom of the formula, resulting in a negative elasticity value. After drawing the graph, you can explain this answer to the grader just as it is explained above.

For part (ii), you should gather your thoughts on the two items in question before venturing into a comparison. You probably remember that slope is "rise" over "run." Draw a complete demand curve graph including the axes. You will note that the vertical change, or "rise," in the demand curve represents a change in the price and the horizontal change, or "run," is a change in quantity. Thus,

$$\frac{\text{rise}}{\text{run}} = \frac{\text{change in P}}{\text{change in Q}}$$

A comparison of this formula with the elasticity formula clearly shows that slope and elasticity are not the same. Slope is the inverse of the elasticity formula without the P and Q. Thus, as slope increases, elasticity decreases (and vice versa), but elasticity also changes when P and Q change regardless of the slope. Use of the graph, the slope equation, and this explanation of the nature of the inverse relationship should yield a high score.

Part (iii) might seem difficult until you construct some visual cues. Because the question is about a monopoly, draw a complete monopoly graph including D, MR, and MC. Perhaps you remember the relationship between demand elasticity and MR: demand is elastic where MR is positive, is elastic where MR is zero, and is inelastic where MR is negative. Putting this information together with what is on the graph will tell you the answer. Because MC is always positive and firms operate where MR = MC (if at all), the firm must operate where MR is positive. Producing on the inelastic portion of the demand curve is equivalent to producing where MR is *negative,* meaning that total revenue would increase by producing less.

If you don't remember the relationship between MR and elasticity, there is still hope. Because the question asks about elasticity, draw a very inelastic (steep) and very elastic (almost flat) demand curve to exaggerate the characteristics of these two types of demand. On the relatively inelastic demand curve, if the monopoly raises prices and correspondingly lowers production, total revenue (the rectangle on the graph representing price times quantity of output) increases. With revenues increasing and output (and therefore costs) decreasing at the same time, profits must be rising. Thus, the monopoly should keep increasing prices as long as it is operating on the inelastic portion of the demand curve. It is clear from the elasticity formula that as price increases and quantity decreases, demand becomes more and more elastic. On the exaggerated elastic demand curve, since price increases result in lower revenues, before a monopolist raises prices, he or she should determine whether the loss in revenues is less than the decrease in costs. If we lower P to sell one more unit, Q_d will change by a smaller percent so that P × Q = TR will fall.

Chapter 3
Using Time
Effectively
to Maximize
Points

Very few students stop to think about how to improve their test-taking skills. Most assume that if they study hard, they will test well, and if they do not study, they will do poorly. Most students continue to believe this even after experience teaches them otherwise. Have you ever studied really hard for an exam and then blown it on test day? Have you ever aced an exam for which you thought you weren't well prepared? Most students have had one, if not both, of these experiences. The lesson should be clear: factors other than your level of preparation influence your final test score. This chapter will provide you with some insights that will help you perform better on the AP Economics Exams and on other exams as well.

PACING AND TIMING

A big part of scoring well on an exam is working at a consistent pace. The worst mistake made by inexperienced or unsavvy test takers is that they come to a question that stumps them, and, rather than just skip it, they panic and stall. Time stands still when you're working on a question you cannot answer, and it is not unusual for students to waste five minutes on a single question (especially a question involving a graph or the word EXCEPT) because they are too stubborn to cut their losses. It is important to be aware of how much time you have spent on a given question and on the section you are working on. There are several ways to improve your pacing and timing for the test.

- **Know your average pace.** While you prepare for your test, try to gauge how long you take on 5, 10, or 20 questions. Knowing how long you spend on average per question will help you identify how many questions you can answer effectively and how best to pace yourself for the test.

- **Have a watch or clock nearby.** You are permitted to have a watch or clock nearby to help you keep track of time. It is important to remember, however, that constantly checking the clock is in itself a waste of time and can be distracting. Devise a plan. Try checking the clock after every 15 or 30 questions to see if you are keeping the correct pace or need to speed up. This will ensure that you are cognizant of the time but will not permit you to fall into the trap of dwelling on it.

- **Know when to move on.** Since all multiple-choice questions are scored equally, investing appreciable amounts of time on a single question is inefficient and can potentially deprive you of the chance to answer easier questions later on. If you are able to eliminate answer choices, do so, but don't worry about picking a random answer and moving on if you cannot find the correct answer. Remember, tests are like marathons; you do best when you work through them at a steady pace. You can always come back to a question you don't know. When you do, very often you will find that your previous mental block is gone, and you will wonder why the question perplexed you the first time around (as you gleefully move on to the next question). Even if you still don't know the answer, you will not have wasted valuable time you could have spent on easier questions.

- **Be selective.** You don't have to do any of the questions in a given section in order. If you are stumped by a free-response or multiple-choice question, skip it or choose a different one. In the section below, you will see that you may not have to answer every question correctly to achieve your desired score. Select the questions or FRQs that you can answer and work on them first. This will make you more efficient and give you the greatest chance of getting the most questions correct.

- **Use Process of Elimination on multiple-choice questions.** Many times, one or more answer choices can be eliminated. Every answer choice that can be eliminated increases the odds that you will answer the question correctly. Review the section on this strategy in Chapter 1 to find these incorrect answer choices and increase your odds of getting the question correct.

Remember, because all the multiple-choice questions on this test are of equal value, no one question is that important. Your overall goal for pacing is to get the most questions correct. Finally, you should set a realistic goal for your final score. In the next section, we will break down how to achieve your desired score and provide ways of pacing yourself to do so.

GETTING THE SCORE YOU WANT

Depending on the score you need, it may be in your best interest *not* to try to work through every multiple-choice question. If you're aiming for credit hours and need to score a 5, it's best to find out as early in your preparation as possible. On the other hand, if you're simply aiming for placement and you find out your first choice of college sets the cut-off point at a score of 3, some of the pressure is off and you can prepare without feeling crushed by anxiety.

It's important to remember that AP exams in all subjects no longer include a "guessing penalty" for incorrect answers. Instead, students are assessed only on their total number of correct answers. A lot of AP materials, even those you receive in your AP class, may not include this information. So, if you find yourself running out of time, you should fill in all the bubbles before the time for the multiple-choice section is up. Even if you don't plan to spend a lot of time on every question and even if you have no idea what the correct answer is, it's to your advantage to fill something in.

The Lord of the Ding
Remember your Letter of the Day (LOTD); when it's down to the buzzer, just fill it in for any remaining choices to maximize your chances for more points.

TEST ANXIETY

Everybody experiences anxiety before and during an exam. To a certain extent, test anxiety can be helpful. Some people find that they perform more quickly and efficiently under stress. If you have ever pulled an all-nighter to write a paper and ended up doing good work, you know the feeling.

However, too much stress is definitely a bad thing. Hyperventilating during the test, for example, almost always leads to a lower score. If you find that you stress out during exams, here are a few preemptive actions you can take.

- **Take a reality check.** Evaluate your situation before the test begins. If you have studied hard, remind yourself that you are well prepared. Remember that many others taking the test are not as well prepared, and (in your classes, at least) you are being graded against them, so you have an advantage. If you didn't study, accept the fact that you will probably not ace the test. Make sure you get to every question you know something about. Don't stress out or fixate on how much you don't know. Your job is to score as high as you can by maximizing the benefits of what you do know. In either scenario, it is best to think of a test as if it were a game. How can you get the most points in the time allotted to you? Always answer questions you can answer easily and quickly before you answer those that will take more time.

- **Try to relax.** Slow, deep breathing works for almost everyone. Close your eyes, take a few slow, deep breaths, and concentrate on nothing but your inhalation and exhalation for a few seconds. This is a basic form of meditation, and it should help you to clear your mind of stress and, as a result, concentrate better on the test. If you have ever taken yoga classes, you probably know some other good relaxation techniques. Use them when you can (obviously, anything that requires leaving your seat and, say, assuming a handstand position won't be allowed by any but the most free-spirited proctors).

- **Eliminate as many surprises as you can.** Make sure you know where the test will be given, when it starts, what type of questions are going to be asked, and how long the test will take. You don't want to be worrying about any of these things on test day or, even worse, after the test has already begun.

The best way to avoid stress is to study both the test material and the test itself. Congratulations! By buying and reading this book, you are taking a major step toward a stress-free AP Economics Exam.

Chapter 4
Pacing Drills

Use the following multiple-choice drills to practice the pacing techniques and strategies you've learned. Then check your answers at the end of the chapter.

MICROECONOMICS DRILL

1. Suppose that there are only two goods: x and y. Which of the following is NOT correct?

   (A) One can have comparative advantage in producing both goods.
   (B) One can have both an absolute advantage and a comparative advantage in producing x.
   (C) One can have absolute advantage and no comparative advantage in producing x.
   (D) One can have comparative advantage and no absolute advantage in producing x.
   (E) All the statements above are true.

2. A change in which of the following will NOT cause a shift in the demand curve for hamburgers?

   (A) The price of hot dogs
   (B) The price of hamburgers
   (C) The price of hamburger buns
   (D) Income levels of hamburger consumers
   (E) The price of ketchup

3. The ability for firms to enter and exit a market over time means that

   (A) the marginal cost is zero
   (B) the marginal revenue is zero
   (C) the long run supply curve is more elastic
   (D) the long run supply curve is more inelastic
   (E) the firms make positive economic profit

4. When a good is taxed, the tax burden falls mainly on the consumer if

   (A) the demand is inelastic and the supply is inelastic
   (B) the demand is inelastic and the supply is elastic
   (C) the demand is elastic and the supply is inelastic
   (D) the demand is elastic and the supply is elastic
   (E) the tax is levied on the consumers

5. Elsa values her time at $50 per hour, and tutors David for two hours. David is willing to pay $175 for two hours of tutoring, but they negotiate a price of $125 for the entire two hours. Which of the following statements is true about the transaction above?

   (A) Consumer surplus is greater than producer surplus by between $50 and $75.
   (B) Producer surplus is greater than consumer surplus by between $50 and $75.
   (C) Consumer surplus is greater than producer surplus by more than $75.
   (D) Producer surplus is greater than consumer surplus by more than $75.
   (E) The difference between consumer and producer surplus is $25.

6. An externality

   (A) causes the equilibrium price to be artificially high
   (B) causes the equilibrium price to be artificially low
   (C) exists when markets cannot reach equilibrium
   (D) results in an equilibrium that does not maximize the total benefit to society
   (E) is an action taken by the government to bring the equilibrium price to a more equitable level

MICROECONOMICS FREE-RESPONSE QUESTION

1. The graph below shows the rental market for
    1-bedroom apartments in Beach City. The city
    government is considering intervening in this rental
    market.

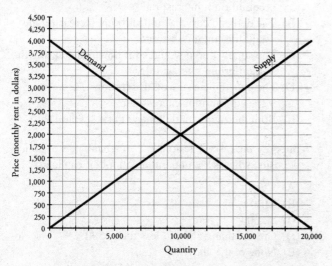

(a) Calculate the total consumer surplus at the market
     equilibrium price and quantity. Show your work.

(b) If the city imposes rent control—that is, sets a
     maximum price that landlords can charge for
     rent—at $1,500 per month, is there a housing
     shortage, a surplus, or neither? Explain.

(c) If instead the city sets a price floor of $2,400 per
     month, is there a housing shortage, a surplus, or
     neither? Explain.

(d) If instead the city tries to limit overcrowding by
     restricting the number of 1-bedroom apartments
     that can be put up for rent to 6,000 apartments,
     calculate the deadweight loss. Show your work.

MACROECONOMICS DRILL

1. An American buys an entertainment system that was manufactured in China. How do the U.S. national income accounts treat this transaction?

   (A) Net exports and GDP both rise.
   (B) Net exports and GDP both fall.
   (C) Net exports and GDP go in opposite directions.
   (D) Net exports fall, and there is no change in GDP.
   (E) There is no change in net exports, and GDP falls.

2. Which of the following would be included in U.S. GDP calculations?

   (A) An auto mechanic fixing his dentist's car for a filling
   (B) A stay-at-home dad providing childcare for his children
   (C) A worker donating $200 to the Red Cross
   (D) High school students spending their Saturdays building homes for the homeless
   (E) A college student paying another student $50 in cash for a used laptop

3. Suppose a country produces only crude oil. Which of the following statements is true based on the production and price data below?

	Production (millions of barrels)	Price (per barrel)
2014	300	$25.00
2015	250	$30.00

   (A) Real GDP decreased and nominal GDP increased.
   (B) Both real and nominal GDP increased.
   (C) Both real and nominal GDP decreased.
   (D) Real GDP decreased and nominal GDP remained unchanged.
   (E) Real GDP remained unchanged and nominal GDP increased.

4. A financial planner on a popular TV show convinces more Americans to save for retirement. What is the result on the supply and demand for loanable funds?

   (A) The supply curve would shift up, increasing the equilibrium interest rate.
   (B) The demand curve would shift up, increasing the equilibrium interest rate.
   (C) The supply curve would shift down, decreasing the equilibrium interest rate.
   (D) The demand curve would shift down, decreasing the equilibrium interest rate.
   (E) Both the supply and demand curves would shift.

5. Suppose the reserve ratio is 0.1. If a bank gets $200 in deposits, what is the maximum amount it can lend?

   (A) $20
   (B) $180
   (C) $2,000
   (D) Greater than $200 but less than $500
   (E) None of the above

MACROECONOMICS FREE-RESPONSE QUESTION

1. The following is a simplified balance sheet for Java
    Bank in the United States.

Assets	Liabilities
Required Reserves $5,000	Demand Deposits $50,000
Excess Reserves $3,000	
Government Bonds $7,000	
Loans $35,000	

(a) What is the reserve requirement?
(b) Assume that Kingston deposits $10,000 in his
     checking account.
     (i) By how much will Java Bank's required
          reserves change based on Kingston's deposit?
     (ii) As a result of the deposit, what is the new
          value of excess reserves based on the reserve
          requirement?
(c) Suppose that the Federal Reserve Bank purchases
     $6,000 worth of bonds from Java Bank. What
     will be the immediate change in dollar value of
     each of the following after the purchase?
     (i) excess reserves
     (ii) the M1 measure of the money supply

MICROECONOMICS DRILL: ANSWERS AND EXPLANATIONS

1. **A** Application-of-definition questions can be very tricky. The best approach is to see if the answer choice "fits" the definition or not. Given past classical examples, (B), (C), and (D) can be quickly eliminated. (See the Specialization and Comparative Advantage section in Chapter 5 for more discussion on this.) This question has one more wrinkle in (E), forcing test takers to think about the possibility of having a comparative advantage in producing both goods (which cannot be possible). It is possible to have absolute advantage in producing both goods, but not have comparative advantage in producing both goods (as one can only have a comparative advantage in only one good). Therefore the answer is (A).

2. **B** A shift in the demand curve comes about due to changes in the price of substitutes, changes in price of complimentary goods, or changes in income (this last point is sometimes forgotten on the AP Exam). Shifts in the demand curve are caused by price changes in substitutes and complimentary goods. This helps eliminate (A) and (C). Choice (E) is tricky, as the price of ketchup would cause a shift in the demand curves for both hot dogs and hamburgers. As our focus is only hamburgers, (E) can be eliminated. Changes in income level will cause the demand curve for hamburgers to shift, so (D) can be eliminated. As the price of hamburgers changes, the demand curve does not shift, but there is a movement along the (existing) demand curve. Therefore the answer is (B).

3. **C** As companies can enter and exit the market over time, only those suppliers who can efficiently supply will choose to remain in the market. This would make the long run supply curve more elastic, so the answer is (C).

4. **B** The tax burden falls primarily on those who have the greatest relative inelasticity. As the question is asking for conditions for which the consumer bears most of the tax burden, eliminate (C) and (D). For the consumers to bear most of the burden, the supply needs to be elastic; therefore, eliminate (A). Choice (E) is tricky. Because consumers are charged the tax, suppliers may bear the tax burden through the shift in demand curve. Eliminate (E), and you're left with (B) as the answer.

5. **E** The best way to approach numerical questions that give answer choices in ranges is to do the math. In this case, Elsa is willing to provide her services for $100, but she received $125. Therefore the producer surplus is $25. David is willing to pay $175 for the services he receives, but he pays $125 for them. Therefore consumer surplus is $50. The difference between consumer and producer surplus is $25, so the answer is (E).

6. **D** For "straight" definition questions, the best approach is to write the definition in your own words and eliminate answer choices that do not match the definition. In this case, externalities are incidental costs that are not accounted for by the buyer or seller. Externalities can be positive (vaccinations) or negative (pollution). Therefore the answer is (D).

MICROECONOMICS FREE-RESPONSE ANSWERS AND EXPLANATIONS

1.

(a)

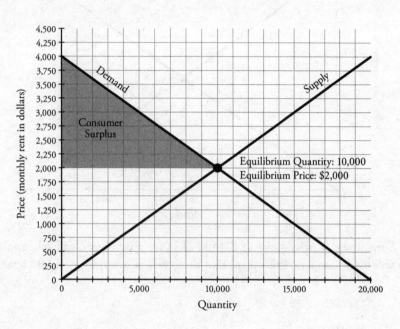

At equilibrium, the quantity of 1-bedroom apartments is 10,000 and the price is $2,000. Therefore, the total consumer surplus is (1/2 × 10,000 × $2,000) = $10,000,000.

(b)

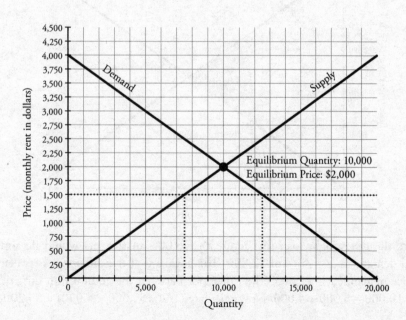

If the government sets a price ceiling of $1,500, 12,500 apartments will be demanded, but only 7,500 apartments will be supplied. This means that there will be a shortage of 5,000 apartments.

(c)

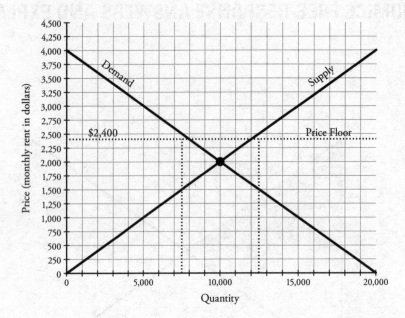

If the government sets a price floor of $2,400, 12,000 apartments will be supplied, but only 8,000 apartments will be demanded. This means that there will be a surplus of 4,000 apartments.

(d)

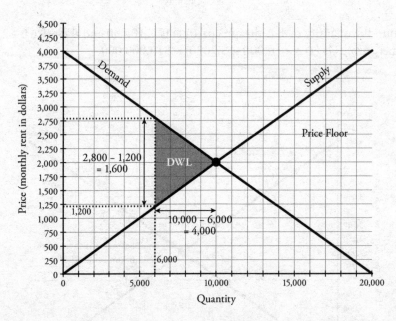

To calculate the deadweight loss, first figure that 6,000 apartments would be supplied at a price of $1,200 and demanded at a price of $2,800. This means that the difference between the price supplied and the price demanded is $1,600. The difference between the equilibrium quantity and the imposed quantity is 10,000 − 6,000 = 4,000. Now calculate (1/2 × $1,600 × 4,000) = $3,200,000.

MACROECONOMICS DRILL: ANSWERS AND EXPLANATIONS

1. **B** GDP is the sum of consumption, investment, government spending, and net exports (in equation form: GDP = C + I + G + X). In this case, as the American is buying something made in China, net exports would fall, causing GDP to fall. The answer is (B).

2. **C** For a transaction to be captured in GDP calculations, it needs to be recorded and reported to the government. The answer is (C) because all other transactions are not reported to the government. On a side note, other countries (United Kingdom and Germany) are looking at ways to include parallel market transactions as part of their GDP.

3. **D** Real GDP is a measure of a country's actual production. In this case, the production fell, so eliminate (B) and (E). Nominal GDP is the price of total production. In this case, the price for 2014 is 300 × $25 = $7,500 and the price for 2015 is 250 × $30 = $7,500. Therefore the answer is (D).

4. **C** As there is more money available to invest, the supply curve would shift down (from S to S′ in the figure below). This would decrease the equilibrium interest rate (from I to I′). The answer is (C).

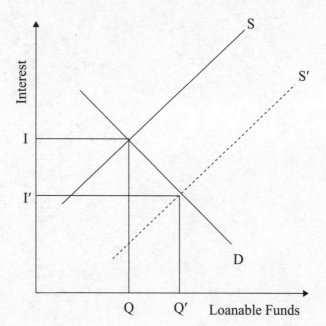

5. **C** The reserve ratio is defined as follows: *Reserve Ratio* = $\frac{Bank\ Reserves}{Total\ Deposits}$. If the bank holds the $200 in reserve, it can lend $\frac{\$200}{0.1}$ = $2,000. Therefore the answer is (C).

MACROECONOMICS FREE-RESPONSE ANSWERS AND EXPLANATIONS

1. **(a)** Since the required reserves are $5,000 and demand deposits are $50,000, the reserve requirement is $5,000 divided by $50,000, or 10 percent.

    (b) (i) If Kingston deposits $10,000, then the demand deposits will now equal $60,000 and required reserves will now have to increase to $6,000.

    (ii) Since required reserves increased to $6,000, then $1,000 of Kingston's deposit will go to required reserves. The remaining $9,000 will go to excess reserves, increasing it to $12,000.

    (c) (i) If the Federal Reserve Bank purchases $6,000 worth of bonds, then the excess reserves increase by $6,000. Since the excess reserves were at $12,000, they are now at $18,000.

    (ii) This is a bit of a trick. The M1 money supply does not immediately change at all. While the bank is now able to loan out more money based on the increase in its excess reserves, which would increase the money supply, until it makes the loan, M1 remains the same.

REFLECT

Think about what you've learned in Part III, and respond to the following questions:

- How long will you spend on multiple-choice questions?

- How will you change your approach to multiple-choice questions?

- What is your multiple-choice guessing strategy?

- What will you do before you begin answering a free-response question?

- How will you change your approach to the free-response questions?

- Will you seek further help, outside of this book (such as a teacher, tutor, or AP Students), on how to approach multiple-choice questions, the free-response questions, or a pacing strategy?

Part IV
Content Review for the AP Economics Exams

Review of
Microeconomics
Concepts

Chapter 5
Basic
Microeconomics
Concepts

The Economics "Cheer"

Perhaps the easiest and most concise review of economic concepts is the economics cheer. The cheer is a series of body positions accompanied by the chanting of economic concepts to help you learn the essentials. It might not help you understand the meaning behind the graphs, but it will remind you what they look like. Properly drawn graphs are valuable both as a signal to the grader of intelligent life, and as a springboard to the correct answers that you can often bring to light by visualizing the graphs. The cheer is easy to learn and is performed by making the shapes of different curves with your body. In each case, make the curve so that it looks correct from your own perspective, not that of someone looking at you. Now, follow along (but you might want to do this in private).

"Supply"—Use your left arm to make a line sloping upward to the right.

"Demand"—Use your right arm to make a line sloping downward to the right.

"Equilibrium"—Touch your nose to the point where the demand curve (your right arm) intersects the supply curve (your left arm).

"Elastic"—Represent a perfectly elastic (horizontal) demand curve by placing horizontal arms side by side.

"Inelastic"—Represent a perfectly inelastic (vertical) demand curve by placing arms vertically on either side of your body.

"Substitutes"—Pump one hand up into the air twice, showing that the demand for one item goes up when the price of a *substitute* goes up.

"Complements"—Pump one hand up and then down, showing that when the price of one item goes up, the demand for a *complement* goes down.

"Production Possibilities"—Move your left hand back and forth from a twelve o'clock position to a three o'clock position, mapping out the shape of a production possibilities frontier.

"The Floor's Up High"—Place your arm, with your hand horizontal, above your head to represent an effective price floor (which must be *above* the equilibrium price).

"The Ceiling's Down Low"—Place your arm, with your hand horizontal, below your torso to represent an effective price ceiling (which must be below the equilibrium price).

"And That's the Way the Econ Cheer goes!"—If all onlookers are giggling, you did it right.

SCARCITY: THE NATURE OF ECONOMIC SYSTEMS

Economics is the study of how societies allocate scarce resources among competing ends. Although some think economics is only about business and money, in truth, the field is as broad as the list of scarce resources, and deals with everything from air to concert tickets. Few things have an infinite supply or zero demand, meaning that the need to make choices in response to scarcity—economics—can apply to almost everything and everyone. Even the world's 1,800-plus billionaires must struggle with constraints in time and resources. That brings us to reason number 493 why economics is great: almost any topic is within its domain. Economists are currently studying war, crime, endangered species, marriage, systems of government, child care, legal rules, death, birth . . . the sky's the limit.

Economists view the world in terms of positive economics and normative economics. **Positive economics** *describes* the way things are, whereas **normative economics** addresses the way things *should* be. For example, "The unemployment rate hit a three-year high" is a positive statement, while "The Fed should lower the federal funds rate" is a normative statement.

Scarcity occurs because our unlimited desire for goods and services exceeds our limited ability to produce them due to constraints on time and resources. The **resources** used in the production process are sometimes called **inputs**, or **factors of production**. They include:

- **capital**—manufactured goods that can be used in the production process, including tools, equipment, buildings, and machinery (this is often referred to as **physical capital**)

- **labor**—the physical and mental effort of people, including **human capital**, the knowledge and skill acquired through training and experience

- **entrepreneurship**—the ability to identify opportunities and organize production, and the willingness to accept risk in the pursuit of rewards

- **natural resources/land**—either term can refer to any productive resource existing in nature, including wild plants, mineral deposits, wind, and water

Energy and technology are also important contributors to the production process, but they can be treated as by-products of the four factors of production listed above. Because economists like to work with two-dimensional graphs, the production model is often simplified to include just two inputs: labor and capital.

Consider the factors of production needed for a bagel shop. The shop building, mixers, and ovens are examples of capital. Natural resources, including land and rain, will help provide the wheat for the dough. Labor will form the dough into bagels, place them into the ovens, and sell them. The bagel chef uses her skill and experience—human capital—to make the bagels smooth on the outside and soft on the inside. How did this shop come about? An entrepreneur risked a large amount of money and poured his ideas and organizational talents into the success of the shop. Thus, our bagel shop requires all four factors of production. In contrast, a soda-pop vending machine is an example of a capital-intensive business that requires little beyond canned drinks and the machine itself to produce soft drink sales.

Fierce Actors of Production

Memorable initialisms can be a good way to keep track of concepts. Here's one for the factors of production:

Crazy—Capital
Leopards—Labor
Envy—Entrepreneurship
Narwhals—Natural resources/land

Opportunity Costs and the Production-Possibilities Frontier

Because economics is the study of the distribution of scarce goods, economists are always looking for ways to analyze human choices. For example, the fact that you are reading this book right now means that you cannot simultaneously be doing a number of other things, like reading the newspaper, swimming, or horseback riding. If the best alternative to reading this book is swimming, then the opportunity cost of reading this book is not being able to go swimming. **Opportunity cost** is the value of the best alternative sacrificed as compared to what actually takes place. The opportunity cost of going to the prom with Pat may be that you can't go with Chris. The opportunity cost of going to college may be that you can't spend the same time working at McDonald's.

When we use resources to produce one good or service, the opportunity cost is that we cannot produce another good or service. When we make birdcages, we cannot use the same resources to make chairs. The choices an economy faces and the opportunity cost of making one good rather than another can be illustrated with a **production-possibilities frontier** (PPF). Figure 1 illustrates a production-possibilities frontier for a simplified economy that can use its resources to produce either birdcages or chairs.

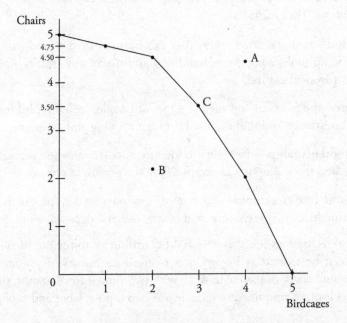

Figure 1: Production-Possibilities Frontier

The curve or "frontier" itself represents all of the combinations of the two goods that could be produced using all of the available resources and technology. For example, the economy could produce 5 birdcages and 0 chairs, or 5 chairs and 0 birdcages, or 3 birdcages and 3.5 chairs, and so on.

Birdcage-chair combinations outside the frontier, like point A on the figure, require more resources than the economy has, and are therefore unobtainable. Points inside the frontier are obtainable, but inefficient. **Efficiency** in this context means that the economy is using all of its resources productively, as is true at every point on the PPF. Producing a birdcage-chair combination that lies inside the PPF, such as point B, results in some resources going to waste. Rather than producing at B, more of both products could be produced by moving to a point such as C on the frontier. Only those points on the frontier itself correspond with the use of all of the available resources.

Resources are often specialized for making one thing rather than another. For example, wood may be ideal for producing chairs, but troublesome as a source of birdcage walls because drilling or carving is necessary to make the birds visible. On the other hand, metal may be simple to weave into a wire birdcage but less than ideal for chairs, because a solid-feeling chair becomes heavy and expensive when made of metal.

When the economy is producing only one good, say chairs, all of the available resources are devoted to that good, including resources that are not especially useful for chair production. Starting from the production of chairs only, the opportunity cost of birdcages—the number of chairs that must be given up to make another birdcage—is initially small because the resources used will be those specialized for making birdcages (metal, plastic, wire-bending machines) and not so useful for making chairs.

Notice that opportunity costs can be read directly off the PPF in Figure 1. Start from the point at which 5 chairs and 0 birdcages are made and stay on the PPF. Making 1 birdcage necessitates a decrease in chair production of 0.25 (from 5 to 4.75). That is, the opportunity cost of the first birdcage is a quarter of a chair. Likewise, the opportunity costs of the second through fifth birdcages are 0.25, 1, 1.5, and 2 chairs respectively. Why does the opportunity cost of making birdcages increase? Because as more birdcages are produced, the resources that must be used to make birdcages are those less and less specialized for birdcage production and more and more specialized for chair production. The economy must therefore give up an increasing number of chairs for each additional birdcage.

The **slope** of a line between two points is "the rise over the run," meaning the vertical change divided by the horizontal change between the two points. The **absolute value**, the value after removing the negative sign, of the slope of the PPF between two points also indicates the average opportunity cost of the horizontal axis good (birdcages) between those two points. This is because the movement from left to right along the horizontal axis, the "run," indicates an increase in birdcages, while the movement along the vertical axis, "the rise," indicates the corresponding decrease in the number of chairs. To summarize, the decrease in chairs per increase in birdcages defines both the opportunity cost of birdcages and the slope of the PPF. The slope of the PPF increases in absolute value from left to right, reflecting the increasing opportunity cost of birdcages.

In the special case in which an economy must allocate its resources between two goods that involve no specialization of resources, the PPF will be a straight line. Consider an economy that allocates its resources between radishes and carrots. It may be that the skills, tools, fertilizer, and other resources needed to produce the two goods are virtually identical, and thus the opportunity cost of each good and the PPF slope would not change at different production levels, as in Figure 2.

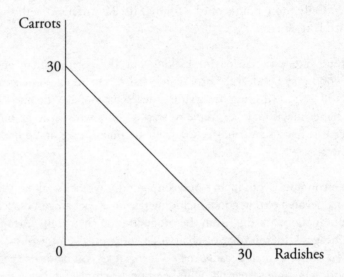

Figure 2

The production-possibilities frontier apparatus is also useful for analyzing production decisions between consumer goods and capital goods. **Consumer goods** are products that are for sale in any typical retail or consumer market and used directly by consumers. Anything purchased in a supermarket or shopping mall would be a consumer good. **Capital goods** are things purchased to produce other goods. If a baker decides to invest in an industrial mixer, that mixer would be a capital good. We could use all available resources to produce food, clothing, and other items to be consumed in the present, but that would contribute nothing to our ability to produce goods in the future. Alternatively, we could forgo some current consumption to produce tractors, looms, and other capital goods that add to the ability to produce both capital and consumer goods later on.

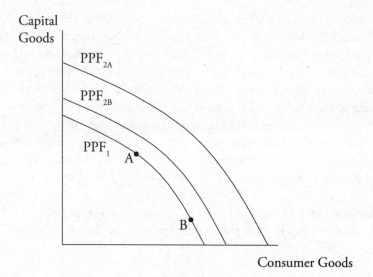

Figure 3

Let PPF$_1$ in Figure 3 represent the production possibilities in Period 1. Point A represents a combination of capital and consumer goods that includes a relatively large investment in capital. The substantial investment in capital comes at the expense of current consumption but allows for considerable growth in future production possibilities as represented by the Period 2 production possibilities frontier labeled PPF$_{2A}$. Point B represents a production combination that caters to current consumers at the expense of future production. The relatively low level of investment in capital goods results in limited growth in Period 2 as represented by PPF$_{2B}$. If no capital goods were produced at all, the inability to replace worn-out capital would decrease production possibilities and lead to a Period 2 PPF that fell below the current PPF$_1$. In summary, current investment in capital leads to future growth, so there are important **trade-offs** between consumption and growth that can be captured with the PPF diagram.

SPECIALIZATION AND COMPARATIVE ADVANTAGE

When people have different abilities, having them specialize in what they are relatively good at enhances productivity. **Specialization** is more efficient than having each person contribute equally to every task. It is better for LeBron James to be a full-time basketball player and Brad Pitt to be a full-time actor than to have them both divide their time equally between the court and the stage. Even if every person were identical, efficiency would be improved by a division of necessary tasks among those carrying out the tasks. This is because such a **division of labor** permits people to develop expertise in the task(s) that they concentrate on—practice improves performance. If different members of your family specialize in shopping, car repair, cooking, or child care, your family exhibits a division of labor not unlike what occurs in businesses and governmental agencies.

Just as individuals benefit from specialization, so too do larger groups. There are two types of advantages that economists focus on when comparing countries (or other groups of individuals). A country is said to have an **absolute advantage** in the production of a good when it can produce that good using fewer resources per unit of output than another country. A country is said to have a **comparative advantage** in the production of a good when it can produce that good at a lower opportunity cost (a smaller loss in terms of the production of another good) than another country. The opportunity for two countries to benefit from specialization and trade rests only on the existence of a *comparative* advantage in production between the two countries.

Consider Brazil and Mexico and the production of coffee and broccoli. Figure 4 illustrates fictional production-possibilities frontiers for the two countries, simplified to be straight lines.

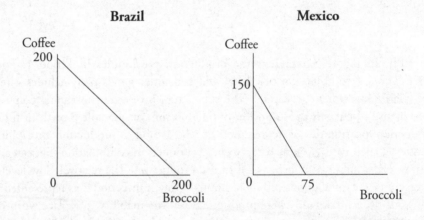

Figure 4

If we assume that the two countries have identical resources, the PPFs indicate that Brazil has an absolute advantage in both coffee and broccoli, because it can produce more of each good with the same resources. In order to examine comparative advantages, we need to look at the opportunity costs facing each country. When Brazil goes from producing 200 units of broccoli to producing 200 units of coffee, it gives up one unit of broccoli for each unit of coffee, so the opportunity cost of coffee in terms of broccoli is 1. (Because the PPF is a straight line, the opportunity cost is the same for each increment of production.) When Mexico goes from producing 75 units of broccoli to producing 150 units of coffee, it gives up one-half as much broccoli as it increases in coffee, so the opportunity cost of coffee in terms of broccoli is 0.5. Mexico has a comparative advantage in the production of coffee because each unit of coffee costs Mexico 0.5 unit of broccoli, which is less than the opportunity cost of 1 in Brazil. Likewise, Brazil has a comparative advantage in the production of broccoli because each unit of broccoli costs Brazil 1 unit of coffee, which is less than the opportunity cost of 2 units of coffee per unit of broccoli in Mexico.

Because relative production costs differ, these two countries can each benefit from trade. Suppose that in the absence of trade, each country divides its resources equally between the two goods—Brazil produces and consumes 100 units of each, and Mexico produces and consumes 75 units of coffee and 37.5 units of broccoli. A beneficial trade agreement will have each country specialize in the good for which it has a comparative advantage. Mexico should satisfy the two countries' needs for coffee up to the first 150 units, and Brazil should satisfy the countries' needs for broccoli up to the first 200 units. As an example of a mutually beneficial trade situation, Mexico could produce 150 units of coffee, and Brazil could produce 150 units of broccoli and 50 units of coffee. Mexico could then trade 60 units of coffee for 40 units of broccoli—representing an exchange price of 1.5 units of coffee per unit of broccoli. Because Brazil and Mexico have opportunity costs for broccoli of 1 and 2 respectively, any exchange price for broccoli between 1 and 2 will give Brazil more than its production cost and allow Mexico to purchase at less than its private production cost. After the trade, Brazil can consume 110 units of broccoli and 110 units of coffee, while Mexico can consume 40 units of broccoli and 90 units of coffee. In the end, *each* country can enjoy more of *each* good than if it did not trade because, remember, we supposed that in the *absence* of trade Brazil produced and consumed 100 units of each, and Mexico produced and consumed 75 units of coffee and 37.5 units of broccoli. In other words, with trade, each country enjoys a **consumption possibilities frontier** that exceeds its production possibilities frontier. The slope of the consumption possibilities frontier is determined by the **terms of trade**.

THE NATURE AND FUNCTIONS OF PRODUCT MARKETS

Supply and Demand

Price and Quantity Determination

The **demand curve** displays the relationship between price and the quantity demanded of a good within a given period. For example, Figure 5 indicates that Davon would purchase 6 avocados at a price of 25 cents each and 3 avocados at a price of 95 cents each.

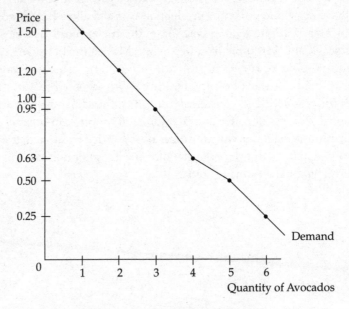

Figure 5: The Demand Curve

An individual's demand curve for a good reflects the additional benefit or "marginal utility" (measured in dollars) received from each incremental unit of the good. Davon values the first avocado at $1.50, the second at $1.20, the third at $0.95, and so on. A line through the points on this graph makes a demand curve. The same information is represented in Table 1, which is known as a **demand schedule.**

Price (dollars per avocado)	Quantity of avocados demanded
1.50	1
1.20	2
0.95	3
0.63	4
0.50	5
0.25	6

Table 1

Notice that Davon receives less and less additional benefit—his marginal utility decreases—as he gets more and more avocados. That first avocado will go toward his greatest need, perhaps extreme hunger. However, as he consumes more avocados, he becomes less hungry, and his avocados are used to satisfy less and less important needs (e.g., feeding the cat, batting practice). The decreasing satisfaction gained from additional units of a good consumed in a given period is called the **law of diminishing marginal utility**.

The law of diminishing marginal utility corresponds with the **law of demand**, which states that as the price of a good rises, the quantity of that good demanded by consumers falls. Similarly, as the price of a good falls, the quantity demanded of that good rises. Davon would buy three avocados at a price of 75 cents because each of the first three is worth more than 75 cents to him, but the fourth and subsequent units are worth less than 75 cents to him, so he wouldn't buy them. If the price fell to 35 cents, the quantity he demanded would increase, because then the fourth and fifth avocados (in addition to the first, second, and third as before) would be worth more to him than the price. This explains the inverse relationship between prices and the quantity demanded suggested by the law of demand.

The market demand curve is found by simply adding up the demands of all the individual demanders in the market. For simplicity, assume that Davon and Mary are the only two purchasers of avocados (perhaps they share a tropical island). Figure 6 exhibits the individual demand curves for Davon and Mary and the associated market demand curve.

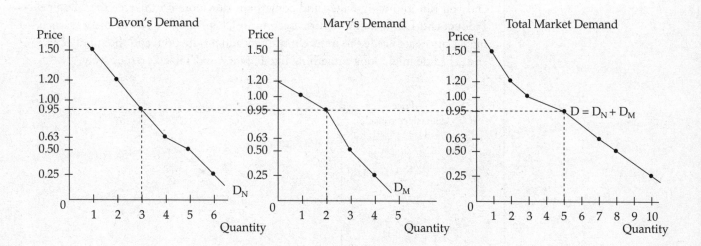

Figure 6

At each price, the market demand curve combines the demand curves of the two consumers. At $1.50 Davon purchases one and Mary purchases zero so the market demand is one. At $0.95, Davon purchases three and Mary purchases two, so the market demand is five, and so on.

The standard supply and demand model is built upon the assumption of a perfectly competitive market, meaning that many small firms sell the same product and can enter or leave the market without cost.

The **supply curve** (Figure 7) for a perfectly competitive firm and the corresponding **supply schedule** (Table 2) show the relationship between price and quantity supplied by that firm within a given period.

The **law of supply** says that as the price increases, the quantity of a good supplied in a given period will increase, other things being equal. Think about how many avocados you would be willing to supply at different prices. At a price of $0.25 you probably wouldn't be very enthused about the prospects, but perhaps you would be willing to give up some of your least valuable time—the time you spend watching *The Simpsons* reruns—to grow 100 avocados as a hobby. With such a low return, you might not want to give up your second-least-favorite pastime of picking on your sibling. However, if the price rose to $0.50 per avocado, forget picking on your sibling; you might be willing to spend more time and invest more money into growing 200 avocados.

Although efficiencies may come about in the beginning, eventually the additional cost of producing another unit—the **marginal cost**—will increase for several reasons. The opportunity cost of your time will increase as you have to give up more and more valuable alternatives in order to grow more avocados. You will start by hiring the best and cheapest inputs (avocado pickers, tractors, land) and then resort to inferior inputs as necessary. You might get less and less out of each additional unit of an input as opportunities for efficient specialization are exploited and you run into redundancy and congestion (for more on this, see the Marginal Product and Diminishing Returns section in Chapter 7). For all of these reasons, higher prices are needed to induce more avocado production, and the supply curve and schedule might look something like Figure 7 and Table 2, respectively.

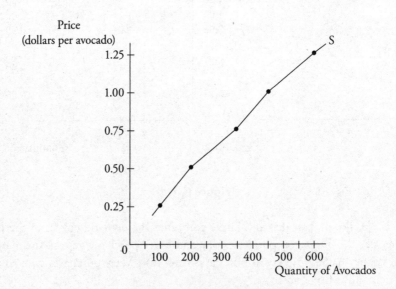

Figure 7: The Supply Curve

Price (dollars per avocado)	Quantity of avocados supplied
1.25	600
1.00	450
0.75	350
0.50	200
0.25	100

Table 2

The **market supply curve** indicates the total quantities of a good that suppliers are willing and able to provide at various prices during a given period of time. It is the horizontal summation of all of the firm supply curves. Figure 8 illustrates how the supply curves of two firms are added to find the market supply.

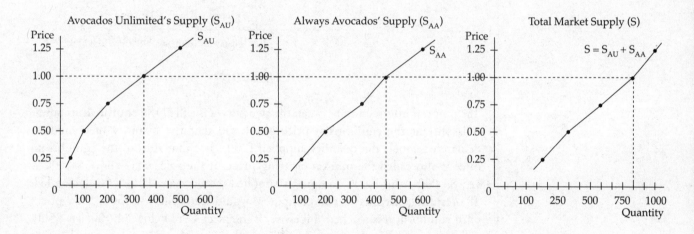

Figure 8

For example, if Avocados Unlimited is willing to produce 350 avocados for $1 each, and Always Avocados is willing to produce 450 at $1 each, and these are the only two producers in the market, then the market supply is 350 + 450 = 800 at a price of $1. The market supply curve reflects the marginal cost (MC) of producing various quantities of a good and the size and number of firms in the market (see Chapter 7 for a discussion of when a firm will shut down and supply zero).

The demand curve and the supply curve for a particular good live on the same graph with price on the vertical axis and quantity on the horizontal axis. Because the consumer's marginal utility (additional benefit) from the first few units of a good is often relatively high and the supplier's marginal (additional) cost of producing the first few units is often relatively low, the demand curve begins above the supply curve as in Figure 9.

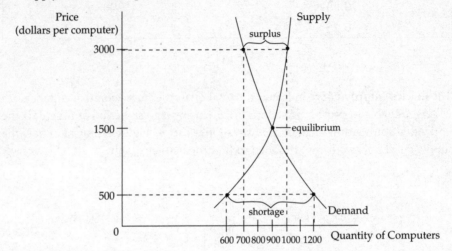

Figure 9

The point of intersection between the two curves is called the **equilibrium** point. It is only at the equilibrium price of $1,500 that the quantity of computers demanded equals the quantity supplied (900). For that reason, the equilibrium price is also called the **market clearing price**. If the price were above $1,500—say, $3,000—the 1,000 computers supplied would exceed the 700 demanded. The resulting **surplus** of 300 computers would lead sellers to lower their prices until equilibrium is reached. Likewise, if the price were below $1,500, say $500, a **shortage** of 600 computers would exist because the 1,200 demanded would exceed the 600 supplied. With lines out their doors for computers, the computer sellers would raise their prices until equilibrium was reached. Economic theory predicts that in the long run the market price and quantity will equal the equilibrium price and quantity.

KEY TERMS

Basic Concepts

economics
scarcity
positive economics
normative economics
resources
inputs
factors of production
labor
human capital
physical capital
entrepreneurship
natural resources
land
opportunity cost
trade-offs
production-possibilities frontier
efficiency
slope
absolute value

Specialization and Comparative Advantage

specialization
productivity
division of labor
absolute advantage
comparative advantage
consumption-possibilities frontier
terms of trade

Product Markets

demand
demand curve
demand schedule
law of demand
law of diminishing marginal utility
supply
supply curve
supply schedule
market supply curve
law of supply
marginal cost
equilibrium
market clearing price
surplus
shortage

CHAPTER 5 REVIEW QUESTIONS

See Chapter 9 for answers and explanations.

1. A demand curve slopes downward for an individual as the result of

   (A) diminishing marginal utility
   (B) diminishing marginal returns
   (C) the Fisher effect
   (D) diminishing returns to scale
   (E) increasing marginal cost

2. The supply curve for lawn-mowing services is likely to slope upward because of

   (A) decreasing marginal costs
   (B) increasing opportunity cost of time
   (C) diminishing marginal utility
   (D) increasing returns to scale
   (E) economies of scope

3. If both supply and demand increase, the result is

   (A) a definite increase in price and an indeterminate change in quantity
   (B) a definite increase in quantity and an indeterminate change in price
   (C) a definite decrease in quantity and an indeterminate change in price
   (D) a definite decrease in price and a definite increase in quantity
   (E) a definite increase in price and a definite increase in quantity

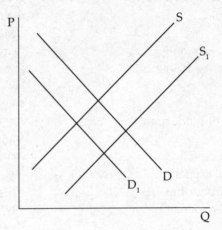

4. For the market supply and demand graph above, when the demand curve shifts from D to D_1 and the supply curve shifts from S to S_1, then

   (A) the equilibrium price falls and the equilibrium quantity is undetermined
   (B) the equilibrium price falls and the equilibrium quantity is unchanged
   (C) the equilibrium price is unchanged and the equilibrium quantity rises
   (D) the equilibrium price is undetermined and the equilibrium quantity falls
   (E) None of the above

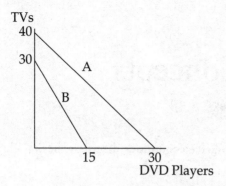

5. The above diagram represents the production possibilities of Country A and Country B, with the use of the same resources. Which of the following would be true for both Country A and Country B?

    (A) Countries A and B cannot benefit from trade with each other.
    (B) Country A has a comparative advantage in TVs and Country B has a comparative advantage in DVD players.
    (C) Country A has a comparative advantage in DVD players and Country B has a comparative advantage in TVs.
    (D) Country A has an opportunity cost of 1 ¼ DVD players when they produce 1 TV.
    (E) Country B has an opportunity cost of ½ TV when they produce one DVD player.

6. Which of the following would NOT be considered a factor of production for a car company?

    (A) the cost of the car designer's studio
    (B) the car designer's time
    (C) the car designer's creativity
    (D) the car designer's preference for designing homes instead of cars.
    (E) the steel and rubber used in car production.

Chapter 5 Summary: Basic Microeconomics Concepts

Basic Concepts

o **Positive economics** describes the way things are; **normative economics** describes the way things should be.

o **Economics** is the study of how to allocate scarce resources among competing ends.

o The **resources** used in the production process are called **inputs**, or **factors** of **production**. They include the following factors:
   - capital
   - labor (human capital)
   - entrepreneurship
   - natural resources/land

Opportunity Cost and Production Possibilities

o **Opportunity cost** is the value of the best alternative sacrificed as compared to what actually takes place.

o A **production-possibilities frontier** is a curve that represents all of the combinations of the two goods that could be produced using all of the available resources and technology.

o **Efficiency** in this context means that the economy is using all of its resources productively, as is true at every point on the PPF.

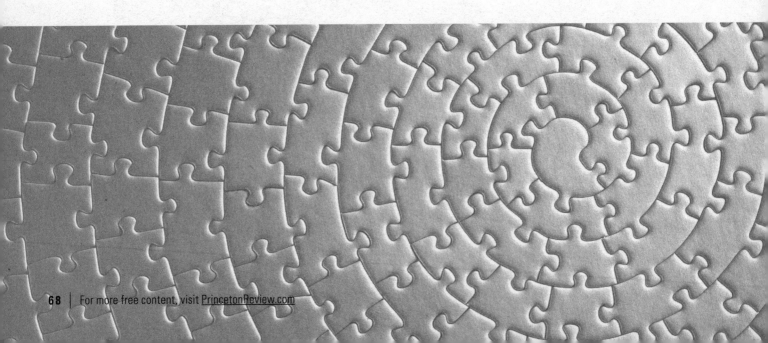

Specialization and Comparative Advantage

o   The **division of labor** permits people to develop expertise in the task(s) that they concentrate on.

o   A country is said to have an **absolute advantage** in the production of a good when it can produce that good using fewer resources per unit of output than another country.

o   A country is said to have a **comparative advantage** in the production of a good when it can produce that good at a lower opportunity cost than another country.

The Nature and Function of Product Markets

o   The **demand curve** illustrates the **law of demand** that describes the inverse relationship between price and the quantity demanded of a good within a given period.

o   The **law of diminishing marginal utility** states that consumers will experience decreasing satisfaction from additional units of a good consumed.

o   The **supply curve** illustrates the **law of supply** that says that as the price increases, the quantity of a good supplied in a given period will increase, other things being equal.

o   The **marginal cost** is the additional cost a supplier faces when producing one more unit of a good.

o   The **market supply curve** indicates the total quantities of a good that suppliers are willing and able to provide at various prices during a given period of time.

o   The **equilibrium point** is the price at which the quantity demanded of a good equals the quantity supplied of a good.

o   A **surplus** occurs when too many of a good are provided; a **shortage** occurs when too few of a good are provided.

Chapter 6
Supply, Price Determination, and Firm Behavior

UNDERSTANDING AND MANIPULATING SUPPLY

Remember that the law of supply says that as the price increases, the quantity of a good supplied in a given period will increase, other things being held equal. In this section, you will study how supply changes with different economic factors.

It is important to distinguish between a **change in quantity supplied** and a **change in supply**. A movement of the equilibrium along a stationary supply curve represents a change in the quantity supplied. In other words, there has been a change in price, and sellers adjust the quantity they are willing to sell accordingly. Because the supply curve shows the relationship between quantity supplied and price, changes in price simply bring us to different points on the same supply curve, thereby causing changes in the quantity supplied.

In contrast, a shift in the supply curve represents a change in the overall supply, meaning that at each price point along the curve, there is an increase in the quantity supplied. In other words, sellers are willing to sell more of a good at any given price than they were previously.

An increase in supply (a rightward shift in the supply curve) can result from anything that leads to more units of the good being produced at any given price, as illustrated in Figure 1.

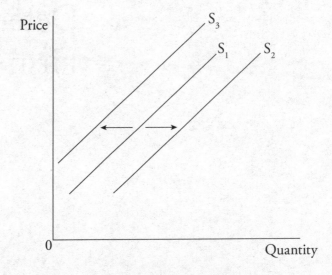

Figure 1: Shifts in Supply

Specifically, an increase in supply is expected to follow these events:

- **A decrease in input costs**. If wages, rents, or other costs associated with the provision of the good go down, more will be provided for a given price.

- **An improvement in technology**. For example, the advent of the airplane increased the supply of cross-country package delivery.

- **Expectations of lower prices in the future**. Think of ticket scalpers at a ballgame. As the game approaches, they know they will soon be unable to charge much, if anything, for their tickets, so they become increasingly willing to sell at lower prices.

- **An increase in the number of sellers**. More sellers mean more supply curves have to be added horizontally to find the market supply curve.

- **A decrease in the price of a substitute in production**. Paper and lumber are substitutes in production, as are milk and cheese. If the price of cheese goes down, then more milk will be supplied because less will be used for the production of cheese, because the producer stands to make more money selling it alone. Imagine you're a farmer with 100 gallons of milk. You sell some of it as milk and make the rest into cheese. If the price you can fetch for cheese falls, what are you going to do? Sell more as milk. Similarly, as the price of lumber goes up, more dead trees are devoted to lumber rather than paper.

- **An increase in the price of a joint product**. Lumber and wood mulch are **joint products,** as are leather and beef—the production of one makes the other available. If the price of leather increases, more cows will be slaughtered and the supply of beef will increase.

- **Lower taxes or higher subsidies**. For example, the government subsidizes the creation of roads into the national forests. This decreases the cost of cutting down trees and increases the supply of lumber.

- **Less restrictive regulations**. For example, if the government allowed companies to pollute more, the cost of toxic waste disposal would go down and the supply of the associated goods would increase.

The opposite of each of these changes would result in a **decrease** in supply (a leftward shift in the supply curve).

You can remember the primary reasons for a **shift in supply** with the acronym ROTTEN.

R – Resource costs

O – Other goods' prices (substitutes in production and joint products)

T – Taxes and subsidies

T – Technology changes

E – Expectations of suppliers

N – Number of suppliers

THE FUNCTIONS OF AN ECONOMIC SYSTEM—WHAT, HOW, AND FOR WHOM TO PRODUCE

Every economy must make three important decisions: what goods and services will be produced, how much of each input will be used in the production of each good, and who will receive the final products. How these questions are answered determines a society's economic structure and standard of living and involves various types of efficiency.

What Goods and Services Will Be Produced?

When an economy asks what to produce, it is seeking **allocative efficiency** or **efficiency in output**. Allocative efficiency requires that national output reflect the needs and wants of consumers. More precisely, resources are allocated efficiently if each good is produced until the **marginal cost** (the cost of producing one more unit) equals the **marginal value** (the value of one more unit). Because the equilibrium price represents the marginal value of output (equilibrium is discussed in the section on supply and demand later in this chapter), the condition for allocative efficiency is that price equals marginal cost (**P = MC**) for each type of output.

How Much of Each Input Will Be Used in the Production of Each Good?

When an automaker makes a car, it could do so using many different combinations of labor and machinery (capital). The manufacturer could assemble the car using mostly hand assemblers, robots, or a balance of these two inputs. When an economy asks how much of each input to use in the production process, it is seeking **efficiency in production** or **technical efficiency**.

Imagine a simplified firm in which labor and capital are the only two inputs needed to produce a particular good. The price of labor is the **wage**, and the price of capital is called the **rental rate**. The cost-minimizing production condition requires that the wage (w) divided by the rental rate (r) of capital equal the **marginal product of labor** (MP_L) (the additional output produced by one more unit of labor) divided by the **marginal product of capital** (MP_K) (the additional output produced by one more unit of capital). Note that the marginal product of an input is sometimes referred to as the **marginal physical product**. The equation looks like this:

$$\frac{\text{labor cost}}{\text{capital cost}} = \frac{\text{wage}}{\text{rental rate}} = \frac{w}{r} = \frac{MP_L}{MP_K}$$

If you simply multiply both sides of the first equation by MP_K and divide both sides by w, you get this equivalent:

$$\frac{MP_K}{r} = \frac{MP_L}{w}$$

The second equation makes more sense intuitively, indicating that cost minimization means equating the additional output gained for each dollar of input cost—the "bang per buck." If the marginal product of labor per dollar of wages (the right side of the second equation) is larger than the marginal product of capital per dollar of rental costs (the left side), the firm should hire more labor and less capital because labor is a better value (and vice versa). As more labor is hired, its marginal product will decrease; and as less capital is used, its marginal product will increase. Thus, as the firm alters its input mix to favor the input with the largest "bang per buck," the two sides of the efficiency equation will come closer and closer to equality. When they are equal, the firm has achieved efficiency in production.

Whom Will Receive the Final Products?

When an economy asks whom will receive the final products, it is seeking **distributive efficiency** or **efficiency in exchange**. This type of efficiency requires that those who place the highest relative value on goods receive them. Auctions, for example, distribute goods to those who value them the most, while lotteries do not. Suppose Pat loves chocolate and has a mild interest in football, while Chris loves football and dislikes chocolate. If Chris receives chocolate for Valentine's Day and Pat receives football tickets through a lottery, distributive efficiency would not be achieved. An exchange of Chris's chocolates for Pat's tickets would benefit both parties.

An economy achieves distributive efficiency when consumers make purchases that maximize their satisfaction, or **utility**, given their budgetary constraints. Just as firms achieve productive efficiency by maximizing their "bang for the buck" in terms of inputs, consumers should do the same for their purchases. Consumers get the most utility for a given budget by equating the **marginal utility** or **MU** (the additional utility from the last unit) per dollar in the **price** (P) of each good they purchase. That is, if consumers purchase food (F) and clothing (C), utility is maximized when

> An efficient allocation of inputs requires that the output of one good cannot be increased without decreasing the output of another good. This is true when firms satisfy the cost-minimizing production condition, which says that the ratio of input prices equals the ratio of marginal products (MP) of the inputs. (The proof of this is beyond the scope of introductory economics, but previous AP exams have tested for an understanding of this condition, so we will explain it and provide a bit of insight.)

$$\frac{MU_F}{P_F} = \frac{MU_C}{P_C}$$

By multiplying both sides by P_C and dividing both sides by MU_F, this equation becomes

$$\frac{P_C}{P_F} = \frac{MU_C}{MU_F}$$

The ratio of marginal utilities on the right-hand side of this equation is called the **marginal rate of substitution** (MRS). The formal condition for distributive efficiency is that the marginal rate of substitution be equal for every consumer; for example, $MRS_{PAT} = MRS_{CHRIS}$. With consumers facing the same prices, $\dfrac{P_C}{P_F}$ will be the same for every consumer; if all consumers maximize utility by equating their MRS to $\dfrac{P_C}{P_F}$, then everyone will have the same MRS and distributive efficiency will be achieved.

A long-run competitive equilibrium implies that P = MC. With firms minimizing their costs and consumers maximizing their profits, economic theory holds that all three types of efficiency are achieved when a perfectly competitive market is in long-run equilibrium.

ANALYZING COSTS OF PRODUCTION

In order to efficiently produce goods, business owners compare the quantity of goods produced—output—to the amount of investment required in production—input. **Marginal product** is the additional output produced per period when one more unit of an input is added, *holding the quantities of other inputs constant*. If we are producing bagels, the marginal product of labor is the additional number of bagels produced per hour when one more worker is hired. Using   to represent change, TP to represent total product, and L to represent the number of units of labor hired per hour, the formula for the marginal product of labor is

$$MP_L = \frac{\Delta TP}{\Delta L}$$

This is sometimes called the marginal *physical* product of labor (MPP_L) to clarify the fact that dollars are not involved—it is simply a measure of physical output. The marginal products of other inputs are found the same way, substituting the appropriate letter (K for capital, etc.) for L.

Figure 2 illustrates a **marginal product curve** for labor and the corresponding average and total product curves.

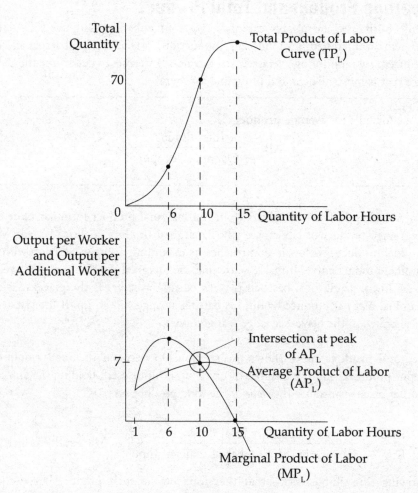

Figure 2

Marginal product often increases with the first few workers because they are able to take advantage of specialization. When operating a bagel shop with only one worker, that worker must do everything—work the ovens, mix the dough, service customers, answer the phone, and so on. As additional workers are hired, each can become better at a particular task than the smaller number of less specialized workers were, so for a while each additional worker will contribute more to total output than the one before her. This is why the marginal product curve increases for the first few workers.

The **law of diminishing marginal returns** states that as the amount of one input is increased, *holding the amounts of all other inputs constant*, the incremental gains in output ("marginal returns") will eventually decrease. In the bagel example, after so many workers have been hired, opportunities to take advantage of specialization will dwindle. Remember that we are increasing only the number of workers; the amounts of the other inputs remain the same. Additional workers will become redundant—they may not have enough ovens, counter space, or phones to work with, and congestion will eventually take a toll. Added workers who become bored might even start distracting the original workers or create a party atmosphere. When additional workers contribute less to total output than the workers before them, **diminishing marginal returns** have set in and the marginal product curve starts falling. In Figure 2, that occurs after six workers are hired.

Average Product and Total Product

While businesses are always exploring ways to enhance marginal production, they remain interested in monitoring production costs as averaged across all units produced. By monitoring average costs, businesses are able to determine the selling price that is most efficient and profitable for them.

> The formula for **average product** is
> $$AP = \frac{\text{Total Product}}{\text{Quantity of Input}}$$

Can you identify how this differs from the marginal product formula? Note that the average product of labor rises when marginal product is above it, falls when marginal product is below it, and reaches its maximum at its intersection with the marginal product curve. It makes sense that the marginal product pulls the average up or down. Think of a baseball player's batting average. If the player's last (or "marginal") at-bat produced a hit, his batting average will go up. If the last at-bat was a strikeout, the player's average will go down.

The **total product curve** shows the relationship between the total amount of output produced and the number of units of an input used, holding the amounts of other inputs constant. The *slope* of the total product curve is

$$\frac{\text{Rise}}{\text{Run}} = \frac{\text{Change in Total Product}}{\text{Change in the Number of Units of Input}} = \text{Marginal Product}$$

Knowing this simple trick—that the slope of the total product curve equals marginal product—makes it easier to tell what the total product curve looks like when you have a marginal product curve, and vice versa. When marginal product is positive, the total product curve has a positive slope (it rises from left to right). When the marginal product is increasing or decreasing, the slope of the total product curve is increasing or decreasing respectively. And when the marginal product is zero, the slope of the total product curve has zero slope (it is flat). In Figure 2, we see the marginal product and the slope of the total product increase, decrease, go to zero, and then become negative.

There is a similar trick for relating the average product curve and the total product curve. The average product for a given quantity of an input is the slope of a line from the origin—the lower left corner with coordinates (0, 0)—to the point on the total product curve corresponding to that quantity of the input. For example, in Figure 2 the average product when 10 workers are employed is the slope of the dotted line from the origin to the total product curve where 10 workers are employed. The line has a rise of 70 and a run of 10, so the slope and average product are $\frac{70}{10} = 7$. Using these tricks, if you remember or are given what a total product curve looks like, you can draw the corresponding marginal and average product curves or vice versa.

Average and Marginal Costs and Revenues

When economists talk about costs, they mean all costs including opportunity costs. Even if the bagel maker owns her ovens, she could sell or rent them to someone else if she were not using them, so there is a clear opportunity cost of their use. Similarly, if the bagel maker spends time in the shop that could be spent earning money elsewhere, the value of that time is included in the cost, whether she explicitly pays herself for it or not. Thus, the costs discussed below are not necessarily actual expenditures by the firm as accountants would measure them. Instead, these costs tell a more complete story and permit more appropriate decision making.

Production costs are divided into two types, fixed and variable, which are added together to find total costs. **Fixed costs** *do not change* when more output is produced. In a bagel shop, these might include rent and payments for ovens, mixers, display cases, and the like. Whether the shop makes one bagel or 1,000, it has to pay the rent and purchase a minimal amount of equipment. **Variable costs** are those that *do change* as more output is produced. For example, as more bagels are made, the shop will hire more workers and purchase more ingredients. When you put all the costs together, you have total costs.

> Total Costs = Total Fixed Costs + Total Variable Costs
> or
> TC = TFC + TVC

An example of this calculation is provided in Table 1, where for each level of output, the fixed cost of 10 plus the variable cost in the third column equals the total cost in the fourth column.

Number of Bagels	Fixed Cost	Total Variable Cost	Total Cost	Marginal Cost	Average Fixed Cost	Average Variable Cost	Average Total Cost
0	10	0	10	—	—	—	—
1	10	5	15	5	10	5	15
2	10	8	18	3	5	4	9
3	10	9	19	1	3.3	3	6.3
4	10	11	21	2	2.5	2.75	5.25
5	10	15	25	4	2	3	5

Table 1

An exam question might provide a table with total cost levels for each quantity of output and ask you to determine the fixed cost, among other things. You can identify the fixed cost as the total cost when quantity is zero, because when no output is produced, there is no variable cost and the total cost equals the fixed cost.

Figure 3 illustrates typical TC, TFC, and TVC curves.

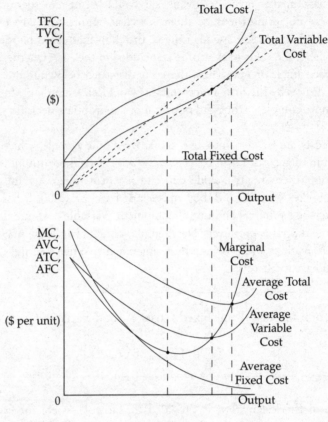

Figure 3

The total fixed cost curve is horizontal because, by definition, fixed costs do not change as output increases. The slope of the total cost (TC) and total variable cost (TVC) curves—the amount by which costs increase when one more unit of output is produced—is called the **marginal cost** (MC). Because the only part of total cost that changes is variable cost, total cost and total variable cost change by the same amount when output is increased, and they have the same slope at any given level of output:

$$MC = \frac{\Delta TC}{\Delta Q} = \frac{\Delta TVC}{\Delta Q}$$

Marginal cost and equivalently the slope of TC and TVC decrease in the beginning because the first few units of *input* produce more additional output than the units before them (refer back to the discussion on marginal product to review). Getting more output from each additional worker translates into lower costs for each additional unit of output. The law of diminishing marginal returns indicates that additional units of an input will eventually yield less and less additional output. This causes the marginal cost and equivalently the slope of the total and variable cost curves to increase.

The fifth column of Table 1 illustrates the calculation of marginal cost. For example, going from an output of zero bagels to an output of one bagel, the variable cost increases by five. Five is thus the marginal cost of the first bagel. Likewise, the marginal cost of the fourth bagel is four because total and variable cost each increase by four when output increases from three to four bagels. A typical marginal cost curve is illustrated in the lower half of Figure 3. Note that it decreases and then increases, just as the slope of the total and variable cost curves decreases and then increases.

Average total costs, **average variable costs**, and **average fixed costs** are found by simply dividing the total cost values by the quantity of output.

$$\text{Average Total Cost (ATC)} = \frac{\text{Total Cost (TC)}}{\text{Quantity of Output (Q)}}$$

$$\text{Average Variable Cost (AVC)} = \frac{\text{Total Variable Cost (TVC)}}{\text{Quantity of Output (Q)}}$$

$$\text{Average Fixed Cost (AFC)} = \frac{\text{Total Fixed Cost (TFC)}}{\text{Quantity of Output (Q)}}$$

Look at Table 1 for examples of the average cost values and look at Figure 3 for typical average cost curves. Note that the average total and average variable cost curves rise when marginal cost is above them, fall when marginal cost is below them, and intersect marginal cost at their minimum points. Average fixed cost continually falls as quantity increases because the same fixed cost is divided by a larger and larger quantity. *Do not just look at these graphs—practice drawing them yourself!*

The tricks described in the previous section for finding average and marginal product from the total product curve also work for finding average and marginal cost from the total cost curve. That is, the AFC, AVC, and ATC values when a particular quantity is produced are equal to the slopes of the lines from the origin to the corresponding points on the TFC, TVC, and TC curves respectively. And as mentioned, the marginal cost when a given quantity is produced is the slope of the total cost curve (and equivalently the slope of the total variable cost curve).

Long-Run Costs and Economies of Scale

There are two primary distinctions between the **long run** and the **short run.** One is that in the short run, the amount of at least one input (also known as a "factor of production") cannot change. In a simple model with only capital and labor as inputs, it is usually assumed that in the short run, the amount of labor can change but the amount of capital is fixed. For example, in the short run you can't get out of your lease, and you don't have time to build, so you are stuck with your present building. The other distinction is that for similar reasons, firms can neither enter nor leave an industry in the short run.

The ability to change the amount of capital and other inputs in the long run has repercussions on the long-run and short-run cost curves. Because everything is variable in the long run, there are no fixed costs. Total, average, and marginal costs will be higher in the short run than in the long run if the fixed amount of capital held in the short run is more or less than the cost-minimizing amount for producing the desired quantity of output.

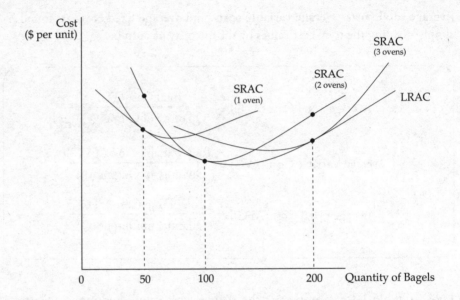

Figure 4: Long-Run and Short-Run Average Cost

Figure 4 illustrates a **long-run average cost (LRAC)** curve and the **short-run average cost (SRAC)** curve supposing that the number of bagel ovens (capital) held in the short run is the cost-minimizing number for producing 100 bagels. To produce 200 bagels in the short run, only the amount of labor and not the number of ovens can be increased. This permits an expansion of output, but the average cost per bagel will be higher than if both the ovens and labor could be increased by the proportions that minimize costs. Likewise if the shop wishes to produce 50 bagels, it cannot decrease the number of ovens in the short run; it can release only workers, so the average cost will again be higher than in the long run when it can adjust the amount of capital to its ideal level.

If the current amount of capital were the cost-minimizing amount for producing 150 or 250 bagels, the short-run average cost curve would share a point with the long-run average cost curve where quantity equals 150 or 250. A different short-run average cost curve could be drawn corresponding to every possible amount of capital, touching the long-run average cost curve at the quantity for which that amount of capital is the cost-minimizing amount.

Important Distinctions Between Similar Terms

> There is often confusion over a set of similar terms that describe the relationship between costs and output. AP exam questions often test students' understanding of the distinctions among these terms. Read on!

The relationships between costs and output are defined in close proximity below, so that you can compare and contrast their meanings.

Economies of scale are enjoyed over the range of output where the long-run average cost curve slopes downward (has a negative slope), meaning that the cost per unit is falling. This can result from increasing returns to scale as described below. It can also result from the use of equipment, such as combines, robots, and assembly lines, that becomes economically efficient only when handling large volumes of output. And it can result from the cost of inputs like copyrights to a book that need not increase whenever output increases and thus are spread over larger and larger output levels. (This is a long-run phenomenon.)

Diseconomies of scale exist over the range of output when LRAC is increasing.

Increasing returns (to scale) exist when output increases (proportionately) more than increases in *all* inputs—for example, when doubling all of the inputs would result in more than double the amount of output. This is frequently confused with increasing *marginal* returns, which involve an increase in only one input, holding all of the other inputs constant. An example of increasing returns to scale is the following: suppose a storage container consists of a box with six $1' \times 1'$ cardboard sides. Thus 6 square feet of cardboard (the input) creates 1 cubic foot of storage space (the output). If instead the storage company uses six $2' \times 2'$ sides, the input increases to $6' \times 2' \times 2' = 24$ square feet of cardboard and the output increases to $2' \times 2' \times 2' = 8$ cubic feet of storage space. Because the input increased fourfold (from 6 to 24 sq. ft.) and the output increased eightfold (from 1 to 8 cu. ft.), increasing returns to scale are in place. (This is a long-run phenomenon.)

Decreasing returns (to scale) exist when output increases (proportionately) less than increases in all inputs. For example, doubling all of the inputs would result in less than double the amount of output.

Constant returns (to scale) exist when output increases in proportion to increases in all inputs. For example, doubling all inputs would result in double the amount of output.

Diminishing (marginal) returns exist when an additional unit of an input increases total output by less than the previous unit of the input, *holding all other inputs constant*. (This is a short-run phenomenon.)

An **increasing cost firm** is a firm facing decreasing returns to scale, meaning that output increases less than in proportion to all inputs.

A **decreasing cost firm** is a firm facing increasing returns to scale, meaning that output increases more than in proportion to all inputs.

An **increasing cost industry** experiences increases in average production costs as industry output increases, perhaps because input prices are bid upward by increasing demand. This is more likely to occur in large industries such as automobile production that use a large proportion of an input such as steel. The result is a positively sloped, long-run supply curve.

A **constant cost industry** is one that does not experience increased production costs as output grows. This might be the case for industries that use a small proportion of the inputs they employ. For example, an expansion in the marble industry would probably not bid up the price of glass, because marble manufacturers make up a small fraction of the world demand for glass. The result is a horizontal long-run supply curve.

A **decreasing cost industry** experiences decreasing average production costs as industry output increases, perhaps because mass production of inputs becomes feasible with increased input demand. This might be the case for solar panels and electric cars. The result is a negatively sloped long-run supply curve.

Figure 5 illustrates the decreasing cost scenario. Short-run industry supply and demand, S_1 and D_1, intersect at quantity Q_1 and determine the market price P_1. The representative firm produces q_1 and receives zero economic profits. With an increase in demand from D_1 to D_2, price will initially rise to P_2, leading the existing firms to produce q_2 and raising the quantity supplied by the market to Q_2. Notice that with a price of P_2, the representative firm is earning economic profits, because its price (which is also its average revenue and marginal revenue) is above its average cost. The availability of profits in this market will attract new firms, causing the market supply curve to shift to the right. As a decreasing cost industry expands, the average and marginal costs paid by each firm decrease. When market supply has increased far enough to bring the market price back down to P_1, firms will still receive economic profits because their costs will be lower than in the beginning when a price of P_1 corresponded with zero economic profits. Thus, the supply curve will continue to increase, until falling prices catch up to falling average and marginal costs, and zero economic profits are earned by the firms. This occurs at the intersection of S_2 and D_2 with a market price of P_3 and a market quantity of Q_3. At this price, the representative firm will select the quantity q_3 at which marginal revenue (the price) equals marginal cost on the new, lower MC_2. The elimination of economic profits will discourage any additional firms from entering, and the market will have arrived at a new point on its long-run supply curve at Q_3, P_3.

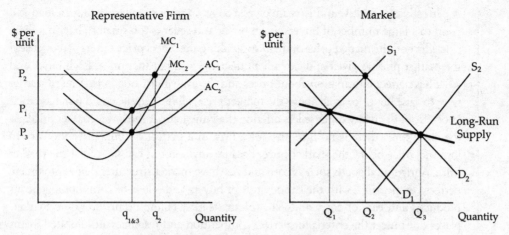

Figure 5: Decreasing Cost Industry

Productive efficiency occurs when a firm produces at the lowest unit cost, where MC = AC.

Economies of scope exist when a firm's average production costs decrease because multiple products are being produced. This occurs when the production of two or more products—such as juice and fruit, or pork and pigskin—is complementary. It also occurs when several products can share research and development costs or distribution networks.

MARKET AND INDIVIDUAL FIRM PRODUCT PRICING AND OUTPUTS

Perfect Competition (also called Pure Competition)

Perfect competition describes a theoretical market structure in which supply and demand determine the market price and quantity of a good sold. Though perfect competition is extremely rare in reality, considering perfect competition provides economists with a benchmark to assess the efficiency and efficacy of any given marketplace.

These are the characteristics of perfect competition:

- many sellers, each seller representing a small market share

- identical products

- firms are "price takers"

- sellers and buyers can freely enter and exit the market

- buyers have complete and perfect information about the product

A perfectly competitive industry involves a large number of sellers selling an identical good to a large number of buyers. Each buyer and seller is too small to have a noticeable effect on the market price or quantity, making the sellers **price takers**—they accept the market price as given and can sell all that they want at that price. Each buyer and seller has perfect information about prices and the availability of goods. Thus, if a seller were to raise her price at all above the market price, all the buyers would purchase their goods from the many other sellers offering the same item at the lower market price. At the same time, there is no incentive for a firm in a perfectly competitive industry to lower its price below the market price, because any amount can be sold at the market price. Agricultural goods such as corn and rice have market structures that approximate perfect competition, with their thousands of buyers and sellers of corn, homogeneous products, and ease of entry and exit. (Note: Market failure occurs any time marketplaces don't meet the criteria for perfect competition and resources are allocated inefficiently. See Chapter 8 for further discussion of market failure.)

In a perfectly competitive industry there are no barriers to entry or exit. Anyone can become a seller in this market at relatively little expense. It follows that there are zero economic profits in the long run, because firms will enter the market and compete away any existing profits, and firms will leave until output prices and input costs adjust to eliminate any losses. Do not think that earning zero economic profits is a bad thing. **Economic profits** are total revenues minus total costs, with opportunity costs included among the costs. If the entrepreneur could be making $100,000 per year doing something else, that opportunity cost is included in the total cost. Thus, making zero economic profit means you couldn't make any more doing anything different.

Entrepreneurs earning zero economic profits are often described as earning **normal profits**, or **breaking even**, because they are earning a return equivalent to the opportunity cost of their time. The calculation of **accounting profits** yields more attractive-sounding results. Accountants determine profits by subtracting from revenues only the explicit (monetary) cost of production, not such implicit costs as the opportunity cost of entrepreneurs' time. If a coffee shop owner took in revenues of $250,000, paid $150,000 in expenses, and could be earning $100,000 per year as a computer programmer, her accounting profit is $250,000 − $150,000 = $100,000, while her economic profit is $250,000 − $150,000 − $100,000 = 0. In economics books such as this one, the term *profit* refers to economic profit.

Figure 6 illustrates the relationship between the firm and market.

Note that the price for any given good produced by the representative firm is set by the industry market, meaning that anything affecting the equilibrium price in the industry market will also affect the factor market. When it comes to demand, that relationship is direct. Anything that increases demand for a product will also increase demand for the factors of production for that product.

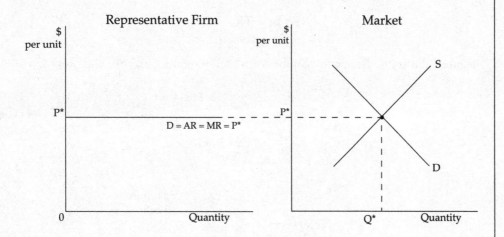

Figure 6

The graph in Figure 6 shows the industry demand and supply curves found by adding all the individual demand curves and firm supply curves horizontally as described earlier in this review. The market price (P*) is established by the equilibrium between the industry supply and demand curves. This price is dictated to the individual firms, which face a horizontal demand curve as illustrated for a representative firm on the left graph. The vertical axis on each graph measures the price per unit of output. The horizontal axis on the left measures the output of an individual firm and that on the right measures the total industry output.

To examine decisions about firm production levels, we must first consider revenue and the associated curves. **Total revenue** (TR) is the amount of money taken in from the sale of a good, calculated by multiplying price (P) by the quantity of output sold (Q): TR = P Q. As you might expect, **marginal revenue** (MR) is the addition to revenue gained when one more unit is sold, and **average revenue** (AR) is the total revenue divided by quantity.

$$MR = \frac{\Delta TR}{\Delta Q}$$

$$AR = \frac{TR}{Q}$$

Because a competitive firm can sell as much as it wants at the market price, that price is both the additional amount gained from selling one more unit and the average amount gained per unit sold. That is, for a competitive firm, price equals marginal revenue and average revenue.

$$P = MR = AR$$

Profit is the difference between total revenue and total cost.

$$\text{Profit} = \text{TR} - \text{TC}$$

Figure 7 illustrates the relationship between total revenue, total cost, and profit.

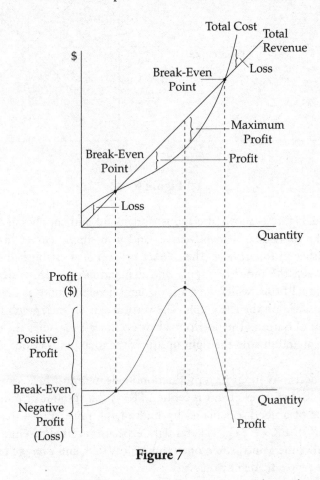

Figure 7

The points on the upper graph where total revenue equals total cost are called **break-even points**. When total revenue exceeds total cost, the vertical distance between the two curves represents profits. When total revenue is less than total cost, the vertical distance between the two represents losses. The lower graph illustrates the profits or losses resulting from each level of output in the upper graph. You can use a graph like this one to determine the point of profit maximization, also known as loss minimization.

A profit-maximizing firm wants to produce where TR > TC and where the distance between the total revenue curve and the total cost curve is as large as possible. In the range where positive profits are being made, if the slope of the total revenue curve is larger than the slope of the total cost curve, the gap between them is widening, and it pays to produce more. If the slope of the total revenue curve is less than that of the total cost curve, then the two curves are coming together, and the gap would be wider at a lower quantity. It is at the point where the two slopes are equal where the gap between them is the widest and profits are maximized. Because marginal revenue is the slope of the total revenue curve and marginal cost is the slope of the total cost curve, equating the slopes of these two lines is equivalent to following the golden rule of economics and setting marginal revenue equal to marginal cost. Thus, the firm will maximize profits by producing where MR = MC (read on for a discussion of when a firm should not operate at all).

Figure 8 illustrates the profit-maximizing point for the representative firm. Note that some teachers and books refer to the AC curve as the ATC for Average Total Cost.

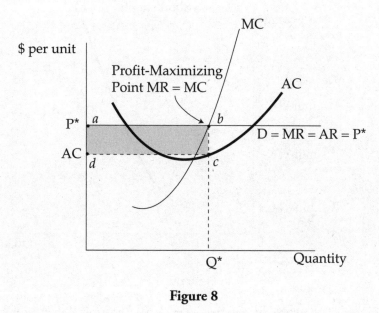

Figure 8

> The individual firm graph is often used in practice and on AP exams to illustrate the profit or loss story.

Unlike the graph with total cost and total revenue, the firm graph measures dollars per unit of output rather than total dollars. To find profit, note that the **average profit** is the difference between average revenue and average cost. Average profit is positive if AR > AC and negative if AR < AC. Given that

$$\text{Average Profit} = \frac{\text{Total Profit}}{\text{Quantity}}$$

it follows, by multiplying both sides by the quantity of output, that

$$\text{Average Profit} \times \text{Quantity} = \text{Total Profit}$$

In Figure 8, the area of the rectangle *abcd* represents total profit—its length *ab* is quantity, its width *bc* is average profit, and its area is length times width, which is average profit times quantity, or total profit. Remember that if the price (which is average revenue) is less than average cost, the analogous rectangle represents total losses.

The **shutdown decision** for a firm in a perfectly competitive industry hinges on whether or not the price covers average variable cost. Consider the three price ranges in Figure 9, keeping in mind that purely competitive firms maximize profits by producing the quantity that equates marginal revenue (the price per unit for a competitive firm) and marginal cost. If price is *above* minimum average total cost, the average revenue (price) exceeds the average total cost at the profit maximizing quantity.

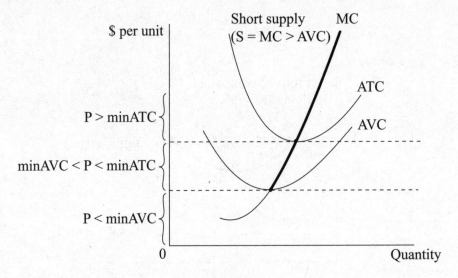

Figure 9

Use your pencil to represent the perfectly elastic (horizontal) demand for the purely competitive firm at a price level above ATC on Figure 9. Because P = MR = AR at the demand price for a purely competitive firm, the point at which your pencil intersects the MC curve is where MR = MC, and the profit maximizing quantity is shown on the Quantity axis directly below this point. Note that AR (again represented by the height of your pencil) exceeds ATC at this quantity. The firm is making more than enough to cover all of its costs, and economic profits are positive. This is an enviable situation that will lead other firms to enter the market and compete for some of these economic profits in the long run.

For the range of prices between minimum average total cost and minimum average variable cost (minAVC < P < minATC), losses are being incurred. However, it is important to examine the two choices the firm faces in the short run.

1. The firm can shut down and not incur any variable costs, but not obtain any revenues to help pay for fixed costs.

2. The firm can remain open, cover all of its variable costs (because P > AVC), and pay off some of its fixed costs with the difference between price and average variable cost.

The lesser of these two evils is to stay open and recover some of the fixed costs in addition to paying all of the variable costs.

As an example, suppose that at the market price of $0.25 per bagel the bagel shop minimizes its losses by producing 500 bagels per day (it is at this quantity that MR = MC). The fixed cost per day for shop and equipment rental, utilities, and insurance is $50, meaning an average fixed cost of $\frac{\$50}{500}$ = $0.10. The total variable cost for labor and ingredients is $100 when 500 bagels are produced, giving an average variable cost per bagel of $\frac{\$100}{500}$ = $0.20. By producing the 500 bagels for $0.25 each, the shop covers its variable cost of $0.20 per bagel and collects an additional $0.05 per bagel—a total of $25 per day—to pay half of the fixed costs. The alternative is to shut down and lose the entire $50 per day of fixed costs. In the long run, however, when the shop owner has a choice of canceling or renewing her rental, utility, and insurance contracts, these costs will no longer be fixed, and it would be wise to shut down if losses are still being incurred.

If the price is below average variable cost, the firm is spending more on the average for each unit sold than it costs to supply the labor and ingredients for those units. It would lose less by shutting down immediately than it would by staying open. To continue the bagel shop example, suppose the market price is $0.20 per unit and that MR = $0.20 = MC at a quantity of 300. The average fixed cost for this quantity will be $\frac{\$50}{300}$ ≈ $0.17. Suppose that the total variable cost is $66, meaning an average variable cost of $0.22 per bagel. If the shop stays open and produces 300 at $0.20, it will lose the entire fixed cost, plus an average of $0.22 − $0.20 = $0.02 per unit on variable costs, for a grand total of $56. (It would lose even more by producing any other nonzero quantity.) Its best strategy is to shut down immediately and limit losses to only $50.

Major Market Structures

Table 2 summarizes the characteristics of the major market structures.

	Perfect Competition	Monopolistic Competition	Oligopoly	Monopoly
Firms	very many	many	few	one
Barriers	none	low	high	prohibitive
Market Power	none	some	substantial	complete
Product	homogenous	differentiated	homogenous or differentiated	unique
Long Run Economic Profit	zero	zero	positive or zero	positive or zero

Table 2

Monopoly

A **monopoly** is the sole provider of a unique product. Local monopolies are common. For example, many towns have only one movie theater or supermarket. Utility companies often have a regional monopoly. At the national and international level, absolute monopolies are rare, although individual companies often control large shares of markets, as does De Beers with diamonds and Microsoft with operating systems. Barriers to the entry of competitors allow successful monopoly firms to sustain economic profits even in the long run. These barriers include

- patents (for example, on new drugs)

- control of resources (for example, diamond mines or the mind of Bill Gates)

- economies of scale and other cost advantages (for example, small towns could not support a second movie theater)

- exclusive licenses (for example, intellectual property rights granted by the patent office to an inventor for his or her invention)

- network externalities (for example, social media networks are more valuable as more people join one specific site and old sites die off)

The demand curve for a monopoly is the entire downward-sloping market demand curve. Unless the monopoly can price discriminate by charging different prices to different customers (as discussed further below), a lower price must be charged for all units to sell more. This means that the additional revenue from selling one more unit of output, the **marginal revenue**, is not simply the price as it is for a perfectly competitive firm that can sell as much as it wants at the market price. Rather, the marginal revenue for a firm facing a downward-sloping demand curve is the price minus the decrease in revenues resulting from the lower prices on all the units previously sold at a higher price. For example, suppose that Monopoly Ale Company sells 10 bottles a day for $1.00 per bottle and that in order to increase sales to 11 bottles per day, it must decrease its price to $0.95 per bottle. The marginal revenue from the eleventh bottle sold is the $0.95 price, minus the decrease in revenue from the 10 bottles previously sold for $1.00: $0.95 – (10 $0.05) = $0.45. Another way to find the marginal revenue from the eleventh bottle is to subtract the total revenue from selling 10 bottles at $1.00 each from the total revenue from selling 11 bottles at $0.95 each: $10.45 – $10.00 = $0.45. Similarly, any firm that charges every customer the same price and faces a downward-sloping demand curve will earn a marginal revenue that is below its price.

A typical monopoly graph appears in Figure 10.

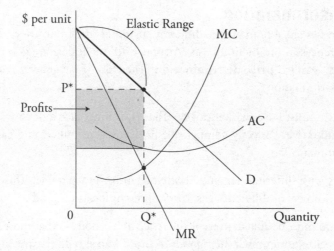

Figure 10: The Monopoly Graph

As a rule, if the downward-sloping demand curve is a straight line, the marginal revenue curve is a straight line with twice the slope of the demand curve and located halfway between the demand curve and the vertical axis. The relationship between elasticity and revenue described in the section on elasticity above provides a useful way of determining the elasticity of demand at various points along the demand curve. The elasticity of demand is 1 at the quantity where marginal revenue equals 0, demand is elastic (greater than 1 in absolute value) at quantities where marginal revenue is positive, and demand is inelastic (less than 1 in absolute value) at quantities where marginal revenue is negative. Like a competitive firm, the monopoly maximizes profits by producing the quantity that equates marginal cost and marginal revenue. Because marginal cost is positive, it must equal marginal revenue where marginal revenue is positive, meaning that demand is elastic. Thus, when maximizing profits, a monopoly always operates on the elastic portion of its demand curve. We repeat,

> When maximizing profits, a monopoly always operates on the elastic portion of its demand curve.

Having found the profit-maximizing quantity where MR = MC, the monopolist will go straight up from that quantity to the demand curve, and then over to the price axis to determine the most that consumers will pay for that quantity. It is a common misconception that monopolies can charge whatever price they want and remain in business. Of course, they would love to be able to charge an infinite amount, but nobody would buy their product if the price level were higher than the demand curve. In order to sell Q* in Figure 10, the monopoly can't charge more than P*. As with a competitive firm, profits are represented by the area of a box from average cost to the demand curve (above Q*) in height and from 0 to Q* in width. If average cost is above price at the quantity where marginal revenue equals marginal cost, the firm experiences losses rather than profits.

Price Discrimination

Some businesses are able to charge different customers different prices that do not reflect differences in production costs. Airlines and car dealers are good examples. This practice is called **price discrimination**. There are three general requirements for price discrimination.

1. The firm must have market power. That is, it must face a downward-sloping demand curve. Perfectly competitive firms are price takers and cannot price discriminate.

2. Buyers with differing demand elasticities must be separable. This is the case for consumers of different ages, from different locations, and so on.

3. The firm must be able to prevent the resale of its goods so that those paying the lower price cannot resell their goods to those who should pay the higher price.

The ideal for the firm is to charge every customer the most he or she will pay, thus capturing his or her consumer surplus and avoiding the need to lower prices on more than one unit in order to sell one more. This practice is called **perfect price discrimination**, and it results in a marginal revenue curve that coincides with the demand curve.

Remember This!

You can remember the three general requirements for price discrimination with the following initialism:

Many—Market power

Sneaky—Separable buyers

Prices—Prevent resale

If it helps, know that MSP also refers to the Manufacturer's Sales Price, which reflects the differing cost charged by a manufacturer to wholesalers, retailers, and direct consumers.

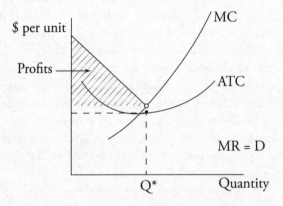

Figure 11: Perfect Price Discrimination

As illustrated in Figure 11, because marginal revenue equals demand, a perfectly discriminating monopolist will maximize profits by producing the quantity that equates marginal cost and demand. This results in the allocatively efficient output level at which P = MC. The downside for consumers is that the monopoly receives among its profits everything that consumers would have received as consumer surplus if the market were perfectly competitive.

Another possibility is that the firm can charge different prices to different groups, as airlines do for business and leisure travelers by charging more for those not staying over a Saturday night. Figure 12 illustrates the case of a firm selling to two separate markets with differing demand elasticities.

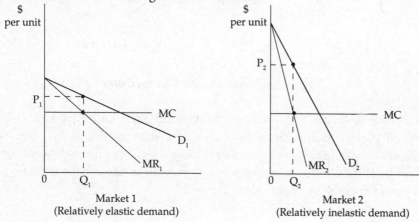

Figure 12: Price Discrimination

For simplicity, the marginal cost is assumed to be constant. In each market, the firm equates marginal revenue and marginal cost to find its profit-maximizing quantity and then goes up to the demand curve to find the most it can charge for that quantity. As one would expect, the market segment on the right with the relatively inelastic demand (meaning that it is less sensitive to price increases) pays a higher price than the segment with the relatively elastic demand.

Monopolistic Competition

A monopolistically competitive firm faces more competition than an oligopoly or monopoly but maintains some market power due to product differentiation. Examples include restaurants, gas stations, radio stations, and clothing stores. Like any type of firm, monopolistically competitive firms can enjoy economic profits in the short run. As with perfectly competitive firms, due to low barriers to entry, new firms will enter in the long run until economic profits are reduced to zero.

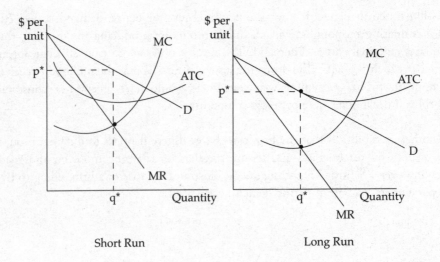

Figure 13: Monopolistic Competition

The left side of Figure 13 illustrates a monopolistically competitive firm making short-run profits. As new firms enter seeking a share of the profits, they take customers away from existing firms, thus shifting the existing firms' demand curves to the left. This process continues until every firm earns zero economic profits and their graphs resemble the right side of Figure 13.

Oligopoly

An **oligopoly** is an industry with a small number of firms selling a standardized or differentiated product. Barriers to entry are high, and **market power** (the ability of an individual firm to influence price) is substantial. Examples include the airline, automobile, cereal, and soft drink industries. Unlike perfectly competitive firms that are so small that they have no significant effect on one another and monopolies that face an entire market, oligopolistic firms must consider the reactions of their rivals to marketing decisions. The mutual interdependence among oligopolistic firms complicates decisions regarding price, quantity, advertising, and product offerings. Nonetheless, economists have developed tools that address the uncertainties of strategic behavior, as you will see in the section on game theory below.

Don't let the various types of market structures intimidate you. In each type of market that doesn't involve price discrimination, firms follow these steps to maximize profits.

1. Locate where marginal revenue equals marginal cost.

2. Draw a line straight down to the quantity axis to determine the optimal quantity to produce, q^*.

3. Draw a line straight up from that quantity to the firm demand curve to determine the highest price that can be charged for that quantity, p^*.

4. If that price is below average variable cost, they shut down. Otherwise they produce q* and sell it for p*.

5. p* – average total cost = profit (if positive) or loss (if negative) per unit sold. The total profit or loss is (p* – ATC) q*.

Practice that process on graphs for each type of firm and you'll get the hang of it.

GAME THEORY

When studying single firm behavior, perfect competition, and monopoly, graphs serve to illustrate relevant economic theory. In oligopoly, firms must engage in strategic decision-making. **Strategic decision-making** occurs anytime one individual must make a choice, but the consequences of that choice depend on factors unknown to the decision maker. Meaning, one firm's profits are affected by the unpredictable choices of other firms. For example, if Sally's Sportsware is across the street from Samantha's Sportsware, Sally needs to consider her factors of production, consumer demand, and the prices at Samantha's Sportsware when trying to maximize her profits. Sally cannot necessarily predict when Samantha will put her sportsware on sale, so Sally needs to make strategic decisions about when to put her sportsware on sale to maximize profits. Because oligopoly forces firms into strategic decision-making, economists use game theory to illustrate theoretical relationships therein.

Game theory considers the strategic decisions of "players" (including interdependent oligopolistic firms, and consumers) in anticipation of their rivals' reactions. Figure 14 illustrates what is called a **payoff matrix** for a simple game between car dealerships.

		Seda	
		High	Low
Bob	High	B: 400 S: 300	B: –800 S: 500
	Low	B: 600 S: –800	B: –500 S: –500

Figure 14

The players, Bob and Seda, each must decide whether to follow a strategy of high prices or low prices. Suppose that each must submit an advertisement to the newspaper a week in advance for the upcoming Labor Day sales. They must commit to a strategy before knowing the other side's strategy. The profits for Bob and Seda under each possible set of strategies appear in the boxes corresponding to the sets of strategies. Bob's profits are listed first, followed by Seda's. For example, if Bob sets his prices high and Seda sets her prices low, Seda will attract the lion's share of the customers; Bob will lose $800 and Seda will gain $500. If they both set high prices, Bob will make $400 and Seda will make $300.

To analyze the likely outcome, isolate one strategy and one player at a time and circle the best choice for the other player. The order does not matter; let's start with Seda choosing the high price strategy. Looking at the payoffs in the left column that represents Seda going high, we see that Bob will make $400 going high and $600 going low, so Bob would prefer to go low in that situation (Figure 15).

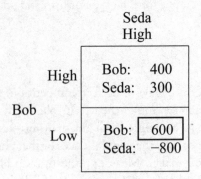

Figure 15

If Seda goes low, Bob will lose $800 going high and $500 going low, so he prefers to go low (Figure 16).

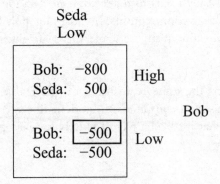

Figure 16

Now consider Seda's outlook depending on Bob's strategy. If Bob goes high, Seda will make $300 going high and $500 going low, so she prefers to go low (Figure 17).

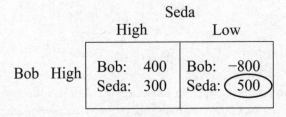

Figure 17

If Bob goes low, Seda will lose $800 going high and $500 going low, so she prefers to go low (Figure 18).

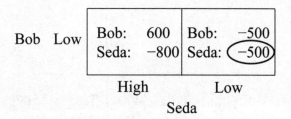

Figure 18

As you can see in Figure 19, because both of Bob's boxes are in the "low" row, we can conclude that Bob has a **dominant strategy** of going low, meaning that he prefers to go low regardless of what Seda does. Seda also has a dominant strategy of going low, indicated by the two circles in her "low" column.

		Seda	
		High	Low
Bob	High	Bob: 400 Seda: 300	Bob: −800 Seda: (500)
	Low	Bob: [600] Seda: −800	Bob: [−500] Seda: (−500)

Figure 19

It is generally assumed that when each player has a dominant strategy, those strategies will be followed, and the resulting collection of actions (Bob low, Seda low) is called a **dominant strategy equilibrium**. A **Nash equilibrium** occurs whenever two circles appear in the same square. When this happens, neither party has an incentive to deviate from his or her strategy given the strategy of the other side. When a player's outcomes are the same regardless of which course of action they take, they are said to be indifferent. Every dominant strategy equilibrium is a Nash equilibrium, but not every Nash equilibrium is a dominant strategy equilibrium.

Take a look at the game in Figure 20.

Alice

	High	Low
High	Ted: 400 Alice: 500	Ted: 50 Alice: 500
Low	Ted: 600 Alice: 150	Ted: 100 Alice: 200

Ted (row label)

Figure 20

As you can see in Figure 21, this is an example of a game that has a Nash equilibrium that is not a dominant strategy equilibrium (Alice does not have a dominant strategy—she prefers high when Ted is high and low when Ted is low).

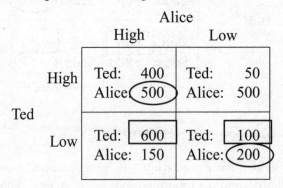

Figure 21

The irony of the first game is that both sides would be better off if they switched to the alternative strategy.

The classic version of this game is played by two people accused of collaborating on a crime. In separate rooms, they must choose to confess or deny, and as illustrated in Figure 22, the "payoffs," the length of their prison terms, might be such that they both confess even though they would be better off if they both denied committing the crime.

X

	Confess	Deny
Confess	X: 5 Y: 5	X: 1 Y: 10
Deny	X: 10 Y: 1	X: 2 Y: 2

Y is labeled on the left side between Confess and Deny rows.

Figure 22

This type of game is called a **prisoner's dilemma**. Prisoner's dilemmas help to explain arms races (purchasing arms is a dominant strategy even though both sides are better with peace), the failure of cartels (cheating on the cartel is a dominant strategy), and excessive spending on advertising expenditures, among other interesting applications in economics and the social sciences.

KEY TERMS

Understanding and Manipulating Supply
change in quantity supplied
change in supply
shift in supply (ROTTEN)

The Functions of an Economic System
functions of an economic system
allocative efficiency P = MC
productive efficiency P = min ATC
efficiency in output
marginal cost
marginal value
efficiency in production
technical efficiency
wage
rent
rental rate
marginal product of labor
marginal product of capital
marginal physical product
distributive efficiency
efficiency in exchange
utility
marginal utility
price
marginal rate of substitution

Marginal Product and Diminishing Returns
marginal product
marginal product curve
law of diminishing marginal returns
diminishing marginal returns
average product
total product
fixed cost
variable cost
marginal cost

average total cost
average variable cost
average fixed cost
long run
short run
long-run average (total) cost
short-run average (total) cost
economies of scale
diseconomies of scale
increasing returns to scale
decreasing returns to scale
constant returns to scale
increasing cost firm
decreasing cost firm
increasing cost industry
constant cost industry
decreasing cost industry
productive efficiency
economies of scope

Product Pricing and Outputs
price takers
economic profits
normal profits/breaking even
accounting profits
total revenue
marginal revenue
average revenue
profit
profit maximization/loss minimization
average profits
shutdown decision
break-even point
perfect competition
price takers
monopoly
price discrimination
perfect price discrimination
monopolistic competition
oligopoly
market power

Game Theory

strategic decision making
game theory
payoff matrix
dominant strategy
dominant strategy equilibrium
Nash equilibrium
prisoner's dilemma

CHAPTER 6 REVIEW QUESTIONS

See Chapter 9 for answers and explanations.

1. The long-run average cost curve

   (A) is always below the short-run average cost curve
   (B) is always above the short-run average cost curve
   (C) always intersects the short-run average cost curve at the minimum of short-run average cost
   (D) is above the short-run average cost except at one point
   (E) is below the short-run average cost except at one point

2. A monopoly with a straight, downward-sloping demand curve has a marginal revenue curve that is

   (A) upward sloping
   (B) halfway between the demand curve and the vertical axis
   (C) initially downward sloping and then upward sloping
   (D) parallel to the demand curve
   (E) parallel to the vertical axis

3. Marginal cost always intersects average variable cost at

   (A) the profit-maximizing quantity
   (B) the minimum of marginal cost
   (C) the maximum of average variable cost
   (D) the minimum of average variable cost
   (E) the maximum of marginal cost

4. In an oligopoly market, firms

   (A) cannot earn economic profits
   (B) are interdependent
   (C) are not subject to antitrust legislation
   (D) are large in number
   (E) have no market power

5. Relative to a competitive product market with the same costs, a monopoly can be expected to involve

   (A) more deadweight loss
   (B) lower prices
   (C) higher production levels
   (D) more firms
   (E) higher-quality products

Company A

		Expand	Don't Expand
Company B	Expand	200 \ 300	100 \ 800
	Don't Expand	800 \ 100	200 \ 200

6. Company A and Company B are competing firms that are deciding whether or not to expand their operations. The payoff matrix provided shows the profit to be earned (expressed in thousands) from any decision that is made. Based on the data provided

   (A) Company A has a dominant strategy and Company B does not.
   (B) Company B has a dominant strategy and Company A does not.
   (C) Neither company has a dominant strategy and a Nash equilibrium exists.
   (D) Both companies have a dominant strategy and a Nash equilibrium exists.
   (E) Company A and Company B should expand their operations.

7. Consider a profit-maximizing firm in a perfectly competitive market with several sellers and several buyers (i.e., the firm is a "price taker" of the goods it sells and a "price taker" of the hourly wages it pays its workers). If a technological innovation made by someone in this firm were to significantly raise the firm's marginal physical product (but not that of any other firm's), then this innovation would

   (A) reduce the firm's employment level, because fewer workers are now needed
   (B) raise the workers' hourly wage as they now contribute more marginal revenue
   (C) lead the firm to hire more workers but not to raise their wages
   (D) lead the firm to hire more workers and to pay them higher wages
   (E) None of the above

8. A competitive firm's demand for labor is determined directly by

   (A) profits
   (B) the opportunity cost of workers' time
   (C) the wage and the average (physical) product of labor
   (D) the marginal (physical) product of labor and the output price
   (E) marginal utility and marginal cost

9. Assume a firm hires labor for $15 each and sells its products for $3 each. If the MP of the third worker is 10, which of the following statements would be the most true?

(A) The firm should hire more labor so that the MRP_L will increase.
(B) The firm should hire more labor so that the MRP_L will decrease.
(C) The firm should hire less labor so that the MRP_L will increase.
(D) The firm should hire less labor so that the MRP_L will decrease.
(E) The firm should do nothing because it is currently maximizing profit.

10. Marginal revenue equals marginal cost at the point where

(A) total revenue is greater than total cost at its greatest distance
(B) total revenue is equal to total cost
(C) marginal product is at its highest point
(D) total product is at its highest point
(E) average total cost is at its minimum

11. A price discriminating monopoly differs from a non-discriminating monopoly because a discriminating monopoly

(A) has a demand curve that is more elastic than a non-discriminating monopoly
(B) earns less revenue than a non-discriminating monopoly
(C) earns more revenue than a non-discriminating monopoly
(D) will produce less than a non-discriminating monopoly
(E) has a marginal revenue curve that is less than a non-discriminating monopoly

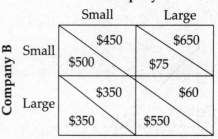

Company A

12. Company A and Company B above operate in a non-collusive oligopolistic market. Each needs to decide whether to have a large or small advertising strategy. According to the data, the dominant strategy for Company A and Company B would be

(A) Company A small, Company B small
(B) Company A small, Company B large
(C) Company A large, Company B small
(D) Company A large, Company B large
(E) There is no dominant strategy for A or B.

13. A monopoly is less efficient than a perfect competitor because

(A) a monopoly produces more output and sells for a higher price
(B) a monopoly produces less output and sells for a higher price
(C) a monopoly can make profit in the short run but not in the long run
(D) a perfect competitor breaks even in the short run and the monopoly does not
(E) a monopoly is allocatively efficient whereas the perfect competitor is productively efficient

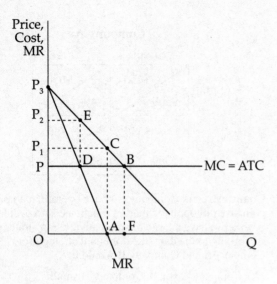

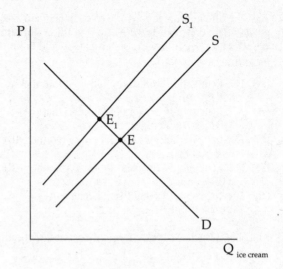

14. For this monopolist, profit is the area represented by

    (A) P_1OAC
    (B) triangle P_3PD
    (C) triangle DBE
    (D) POFB
    (E) $PDEP_2$

15. In the graph above, the shift in the supply curve from S to S_1 for ice cream could occur because

    (A) consumer incomes declined and ice cream is an inferior good
    (B) the price of ice cream rose
    (C) chocolate sauce production increased
    (D) the cost of milk, which is used in the production of ice cream, fell
    (E) the cost of milk, which is used in the production of ice cream, rose

Chapter 6 Summary

Understanding and Manipulating Supply

○ The supply curve shifts with
  - **R**esource costs
  - **O**ther goods' prices
  - **T**axes and subsidies
  - **T**echnology changes
  - **E**xpectations of suppliers
  - **N**umber of suppliers

The Functions of an Economic System

○ An economy reaches **allocative efficiency**, or **efficiency in output**, when the **marginal cost** (the cost of producing one more unit) equals the **marginal value** (the value of one more unit).
  - Allocative efficiency is reached when **P = MC**.

○ An economy reaches **efficiency in production**, or **technical efficiency**, when factors of supply are used to maximize production.

  - The cost-minimizing production condition requires that the **wage** (w), divided by the **rental rate** (r) equal the **marginal product of labor** (MP_L) divided by the **marginal product of capital** (MP_K), the additional output produced by one more unit of capital.

  - Efficiency of production is calculated by the following formula: $\dfrac{MP_K}{r} = \dfrac{MP_L}{w}$

○ An economy reaches **distributive efficiency**, or **efficiency in exchange**, when those who place the highest relative value on goods receive them; distributive efficiency is when the **marginal rate of substitution** (the ratio of marginal utility for two given goods) is equal for every consumer.

Analyzing Costs of Production

o **Marginal product** is the additional output produced per period when one more unit of an input is added, holding the quantities of other inputs constant.

o Using Δ to represent change, TP to represent total product, and L to represent the number of units of labor hired per hour, the marginal product of labor is calculated as follows:

$$MP_L = \frac{\Delta TP}{\Delta L}$$

o The **law of diminishing marginal returns** states that as the amount of one input is increased, holding the amounts of all other inputs constant, the incremental gains in output ("marginal returns") will eventually decrease.

o **Average product** is calculated as follows:

$$AP = \frac{\text{Total Product}}{\text{Quantity of Input}}$$

o The **total product curve** shows the relationship between the total amount of output produced and the number of units of an input used, holding the amounts of other inputs constant.

o **Fixed costs** do not change when more output is produced; **variable costs** are those that do change as more output is produced.

o **Total Costs** (TC) = Total Fixed Costs (TFC) + Total Variable Costs (TVC)

o The **marginal cost** is the amount by which costs increase when one more unit of output is produced.

o The **short run** is a time frame of analysis in which at least one factor of production is held constant and firms can neither enter nor exit the market; in the **long-run** view, all factors of production are variable and there are no fixed costs.

o **Economies of scale** exist over the range of output where the long-run average cost curve slopes downward, meaning that the cost per unit is falling.

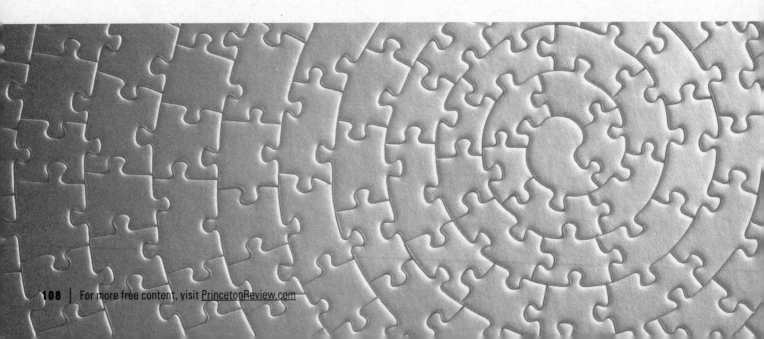

o **Diseconomies of scale** exist over the range of output where LRAC is increasing.

o **Increasing returns (to scale)** exist when output increases proportionately more than increases in all inputs, as compared to **decreasing returns** and **constant returns**.

o **Diminishing (marginal) returns** exist when an additional unit of an input increases total output by less than the previous unit of input.

o An **increasing cost firm** faces decreasing returns to scale; a **decreasing cost firm** faces increasing returns to scale.

o An **increasing cost industry** experiences increases in average production costs as industry output increases; a **constant cost industry** is one that does not experience increased production costs as output grows; a **decreasing cost industry** experiences decreasing average production costs as industry output increases.

o **Productive efficiency** occurs when a firm produces at the lowest unit cost, where MC = AC.

o **Economies of scope** exist when a firm's average production costs decrease because multiple products are being produced.

Market and Individual Firm Product Pricing and Outputs

o Perfect competition is characterized by
   * many sellers
   * standardized products
   * firms that are **price takers**, they accept the market price
   * firms that can enter and exit the market freely

o **Economic profits** are total revenues minus total costs (as opposed to **normal profits** or **accounting profits**).

o Firm production levels are a product of **total revenue**, the amount of money taken in for the sale of a good; **marginal revenue**, the addition to revenue gained when one more unit is sold; and **average revenue**, total revenue divided by quantity.

$$MR = \frac{\Delta TR}{\Delta Q} \qquad\qquad AR = \frac{TR}{Q}$$

o **Profit** is the difference between total revenue and total cost.

o A **monopoly** is the sole provider of a unique good.

o **Price discrimination** occurs when a seller can provide the same good to different buyers at different prices; **perfect price discrimination** occurs when a seller can charge each buyer the most they are willing to pay.

o An **oligopoly** is an industry in which a few firms sell a standardized or differentiated product.

o **Market power** is the ability of an individual firm to influence price.

Game Theory

o **Strategic decision making** occurs anytime one individual must make a choice, but the consequences of that choice depend on factors unknown to the decision maker.

o **Game theory** considers strategic decisions individuals in a game (or in a market place) will make in anticipation of their rivals' actions.

o The **prisoner's dilemma** identifies a situation in which distrust leads two individual actors to choose a less than optimal result.

Chapter 7
Demand, Elasticity, and the Factors of Production

UNDERSTANDING AND MANIPULATING DEMAND

Remember that the law of demand says that as the price of a good decreases, the quantity of demanded will also decrease, all other things being held equal. In this chapter, you will study how and why the law of demand holds true. You will also study how and why demand changes.

It is important to distinguish between a **change in the quantity demanded** and a **change in demand**. A movement of the equilibrium *along* a stationary demand curve represents a change in the quantity demanded.

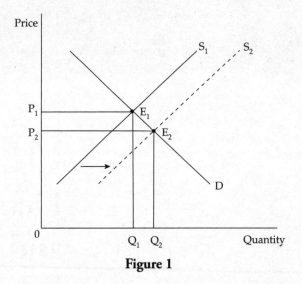

Figure 1

For example, when the supply increases from S_1 to S_2 in Figure 1, the equilibrium moves from E_1 to E_2, and the equilibrium price moves from P_1 to P_2. This results in a change in the quantity demanded from Q_1 to Q_2. Because the demand curve shows the relationship between quantity demanded and price, changes in price simply bring us to different points on the same demand curve, thereby causing changes in the quantity demanded. In contrast, a *shift* in the demand curve represents a change in demand. Keep in mind that the demand curve maps out the value of each additional unit of a good to consumers. A shift in demand would result from any change that affects the value of that good to consumers or the number of consumers in the market.

Anything other than a lower price that induces increased consumption of a good causes a shift to the right of the demand curve as in Figure 2.

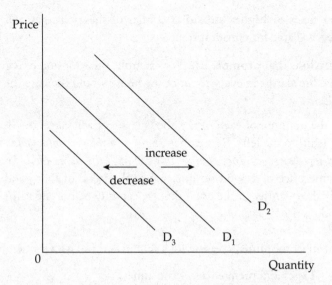

Figure 2: Shifts in Demand

Specifically, an increase (shift to the right) in demand can result from the following:

- **A positive change in tastes or preferences**. Such a change could result from a successful advertising campaign or a research report finding the good to have positive effects on health.

- **An increase in the price of substitute goods**. For example, if the price of Pepsi goes up, the demand for Coke will increase.

- **A decrease in the price of complements**. For example, if the price of gasoline goes down, the demand for large cars will increase.

- **An increase in income for normal goods.** (By definition, a **normal good** is one that the consumer buys more of when income increases.) For example, a higher income might lead to a higher demand for steak.

- **A decrease in income for inferior goods.** (By definition, an **inferior good** is one that the consumer buys more of when income decreases.) For example, a lower income might lead to a higher demand for hot dogs if people start substituting them for steak.

- **An increase in the number of buyers**. With more buyers, more individual demand curves are added to find the market demand curve.

- **Expectations of higher future income**. If you pass your board exam and realize you're going to make big money, you will probably start spending more now. This is called **consumption smoothing**.

- **Expectations of higher future prices**. This is a good reason to buy more now rather than later.

- **Expectations of future shortages**. For example, when a severe storm is predicted, people often stock up on canned goods and bottled water beforehand.

- **Lower taxes or higher subsidies**. Either of these changes will make more money available for consumption.

- **Regulations that promote use**. For example, the adoption of regulations that require fire alarms in every room of the house would increase the demand for fire alarms.

Of course, the opposite of each of the above changes will cause the demand curve to decrease (shift to the left). Remember, *changes in the price of a good do not change the demand for that good. They change only the quantity demanded.* This is because changes in the price of a good do not change the value of that good to us. They change only the quantity of the good that we can buy before the value of the good falls below the price.

You can remember the primary reasons for a shift in demand with the acronym TRIBE.

T – **T**astes and preferences of consumers

R – the prices of **R**elated goods (substitutes and complements)

I – the **I**ncome of buyers

B – the number of **B**uyers

E – **E**xpectations for the future

Concurrent Shifts in Demand and Supply

Let's explore how shifts in both supply and demand affect each other. It can be confusing to sort out in one's head but easy to determine by simply drawing the graph.

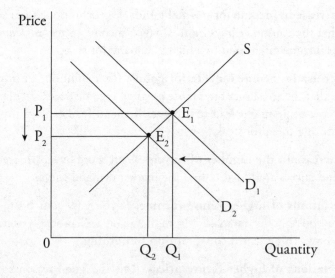

Figure 3

If demand decreases (for example, as the result of a decrease in income), a comparison of the old and new equilibrium price and quantity in a quick sketch like Figure 3 will immediately indicate that both price and quantity decrease.

It is a common mistake on AP exams to shift both supply and demand when only one of the two should be shifted. Think carefully about whether the influence described in an exam question will affect production costs and therefore the supply curve, or consumers' willingness and ability to pay and therefore the demand curve.

It is always possible that two influences will occur at once. Suppose there is a massive beetle infestation in the farm belt and at the same time a study finds that carrots prevent heart disease. The beetles will increase the cost of producing carrots and thus decrease their supply. The study will increase consumers' willingness to pay for carrots and thus increase the demand. Figure 4 illustrates the new equilibrium.

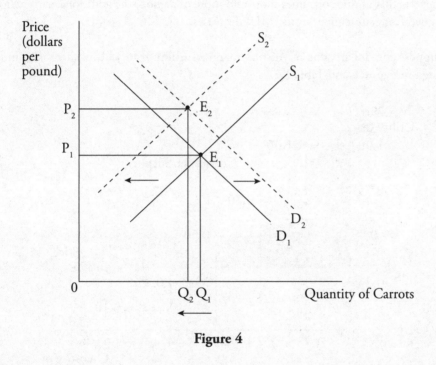

Figure 4

Whenever both supply and demand shift at the same time, the effect on equilibrium price OR quantity will be certain, and the effect on the other will depend on the relative size of the shifts in supply and demand. In Figure 4 it is clear that the equilibrium price increases, because both a decrease in supply and an increase in demand result in a higher price. However, because a decrease in supply decreases the equilibrium quantity and an increase in demand increases the equilibrium quantity, the net effect on quantity depends on the relative sizes of the shifts. As it is drawn here, the supply shift dominates the demand shift and there is a net decrease in quantity. Don't let supply and demand-shifting questions intimidate you; simply draw the graph and describe the evident outcomes. It may help to label clearly the original equilibrium and the new equilibrium so that you don't get confused about the four points of intersection while you are interpreting the graph. When both supply and demand shift and you do not know the relative size of the shifts, it is appropriate to state that the change in the variable (price or quantity) that is pulled in both directions is "indeterminant" (cannot be determined).

A tip on shifting curves: It can be confusing that a decrease in supply shifts the supply curve up, while a decrease in demand shifts the demand curve down. To clear things up, remember that for both curves, **Left** is **Less** and **Right** is **Rising**!

MEASURING CONSUMER PREFERENCE

Remember that utility is a measure of individuals' satisfaction. **Marginal utility** (MU) is the additional utility gained from consuming one more unit of a good and is often quantified in terms of the amount of money an individual would be willing to spend on that good. The principle of diminishing marginal utility suggests that as one consumes more and more of a good, the additional satisfaction gained from subsequent units (MU) decreases.

Suppose the dollar value of Austin's marginal utility from cheese slices is as indicated in Figure 5 and Table 1.

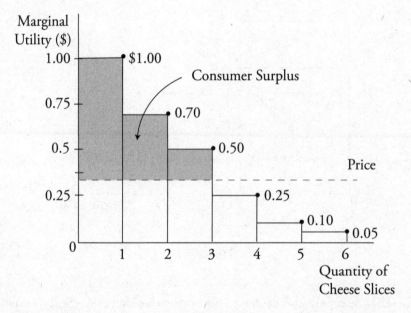

Figure 5

Quantity of Cheese Slices	Marginal Utility (in dollars)	Total Utility (in dollars)
1	1.00	1.00
2	0.70	1.70
3	0.50	2.20
4	0.25	2.45
5	0.10	2.55
6	0.05	2.60

Table 1

The first slice is worth $1.00 to him, the second is worth 70 cents, and so forth. He will choose to consume until one more slice would be worth less to him than the price. If the price were $0.35, he would consume the first three, which are worth $1.00, $0.70, and $0.50 to him. He would not pay $0.35 for the fourth slice, which is worth only $0.25 to him. The points drawn on this graph outline Austin's demand curve, and tell us everything we need to know to calculate his total utility and consumer surplus (explained below).

Total utility is found by adding the marginal utility values gained from each of the units consumed. Because Austin consumes three slices of cheese, his total utility is $1.00 + $0.70 + $0.50 = $2.20. More generally, the relationship between marginal utility and total utility is as illustrated in Figure 6 on the next page. As more and more of a typical good is consumed, the total utility received from that good increases at a decreasing rate, reaches a peak, and then decreases at an increasing rate. This is because marginal utility—the contribution to total utility from the last unit consumed—diminishes as more of the good is consumed. Total utility reaches a maximum at the quantity for which marginal utility is zero, after which point each additional unit provides a negative marginal utility and therefore detracts from total utility.

Take note of the graphical relationship between the curves representing total and marginal utility: the marginal utility at any particular quantity is the slope of the total utility curve at that quantity. Thus, when marginal utility is positive, total utility is rising with a positive slope. When marginal utility is zero, total utility is at a peak with a zero slope. When marginal utility is negative, total utility is declining with a negative slope.

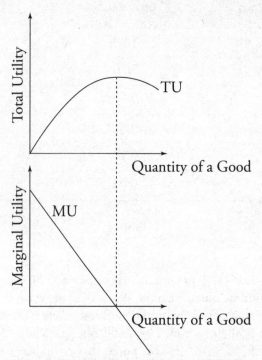

Figure 6: Total Utility and Marginal Utility

Consumer surplus is the value a buyer receives from the purchase of a good *in excess of what is paid for it*. With a price of $0.35 for the first, second, and third slices, Austin receives consumer surpluses of $1.00 − $0.35 = $0.65, $0.70 − $0.35 = $0.35, and $0.50 − $0.35 = $0.15, respectively. To be more general, consumer surplus is the area below the demand curve and above the price line up to the quantity that is consumed. **Producer surplus** is the difference between the price a seller receives for a good and the minimum price for which she would be willing to supply a quantity of the good. Producer surplus is thus the area below the price line and above the supply curve. Figure 7 illustrates consumer surplus and producer surplus in a general case.

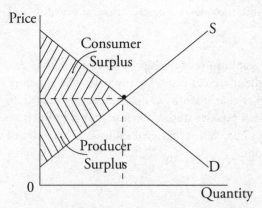

Figure 7: Consumer and Producer Surplus

The distinction between total and marginal utility helps to sort out a paradox that dates back to Plato. It may seem strange that we pay very little money for some goods, such as water, which are essential to life, while we pay much more money for some goods that are inessential, such as diamonds. Although the value of water is very high, this value is reflected in the total utility gained from it, not in the marginal utility. Because water is plentiful, we consume it until the marginal utility is very small. In contrast, diamonds are scarce, so although the initial units are worth less to us than the life-sustaining first units of water, supply restricts our consumption of diamonds to a point where the marginal utility is still very high.

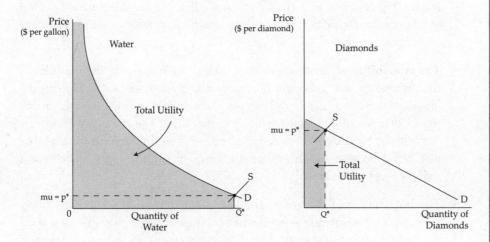

Figure 8: The Water–Diamond Paradox

In Figure 8, notice that the total utility from water is much larger than that for diamonds, but the marginal utility is much smaller for water than for diamonds. Thankfully, price corresponds with the marginal utility rather than the total utility.

ELASTICITY

Elasticity indicates how responsive consumer behavior is to changes in the product or service they want. In this section we will discuss changes in the product or service they want.

Price Elasticity of Demand

Suppliers often consider how changes in the price of a good or service will affect demand for that good or service. If the price of gum increased by 50 percent from 4 cents to 6 cents, by what percent would the quantity demanded decrease? How many fewer people would buy a ticket for a vacation cruise if the cost increased by 50 percent from $1,000 to $1,500? The **price elasticity of demand** indicates how responsive the quantity demanded of a good is to price changes. In other words, when economists think about the price elasticity of demand, they're thinking about how sensitive consumer behavior is to changes in the price of a good. Generally speaking, when consumer behavior is affected by price, the good is elastic; When consumer behavior is unaffected by changes in price, the good is inelastic. The elasticity (responsiveness to price changes) of a good's demand tends to relate to the following factors:

How Flexible Is Your Money?

You can remember the determinants of demand elasticity with the acronym PAID.

P–Proportion

A–Availability

I–Importance

D–Delay

- **The proportion of income spent on the good**. If a good represents a high proportion of a consumer's income, the demand for the good will likely be elastic. Consider the gum and cruise price-change scenarios mentioned above. The quantity of cruises purchased will probably be more affected by a 50 percent price increase than the quantity of gum, because an extra 2 cents is not a big deal, but an extra $500 is more likely to be prohibitive. In other words, consumers are more sensitive to a particular percent change in price at higher price levels.

- **The availability of close substitutes**. If there are many substitutes available, the demand for the good will likely be elastic. For example, if there are 10 brands of bicycles available and the price of one of them increases, the quantity of that brand demanded is likely to fall a lot. On the other hand, the demand for bicycles as a whole is less elastic than the demand for a particular brand because the substitutes for bikes in general—cars, skateboards, walking—are not as close.

- **The importance of the good**. The less essential a good is, the more likely consumers are to forego the good when it becomes more expensive. If a good is very important to the consumer, the consumer will continue to purchase it even if the price changes, and demand for that good will be inelastic.

- **The ability to delay the purchase of the good**. When time is short, it is more difficult to change purchasing patterns in response to price changes; therefore, when less time is available, demand for a given good is less elastic. The more time consumers have to adapt, the more they are able to find substitutes or learn to do without goods whose prices have increased.

When thinking about elasticity, economists divide goods into three groups: elastic, unit elastic, and inelastic. If the percentage change in quantity demanded exceeds the percentage change in price for a particular good—meaning, for example, that a 50 percent price increase results in more than a 50 percent decrease in quantity demanded—the demand for that good is on the more price-sensitive side and is labeled **elastic**. Goods with an elastic demand are categorized as **luxuries**. If the percentage change in quantity demanded equals the percentage change in price, demand for the good is labeled **unit elastic**. If the percentage change in quantity demanded is less than the percentage change in price, the demand is labeled **inelastic** and the good is categorized as a **necessity**.

Allowing Δ to represent change and Q_d to represent the quantity demanded, the formula for price elasticity is the percentage change in quantity demanded divided by the percentage change in price:

$$\frac{\%\Delta Q_d}{\%\Delta P} = \frac{\dfrac{\Delta Q_d}{Q}}{\dfrac{\Delta P}{P}} = \frac{\dfrac{Q_{new} - Q_{old}}{Q_{old}}}{\dfrac{P_{new} - P_{old}}{P_{old}}}$$

The above formula uses the initial price and quantity as the basis for calculating the percentage change. Although this is the simplest way to do it, the following formula is more precise, especially when the changes in price or quantity are large:

$$\frac{\dfrac{\text{Change in quantity}}{\text{Average quantity}}}{\dfrac{\text{Change in price}}{\text{Average price}}} = \frac{\dfrac{Q_{new} - Q_{old}}{\left(\dfrac{Q_{new} + Q_{old}}{2}\right)}}{\dfrac{P_{new} - P_{old}}{\left(\dfrac{P_{new} + P_{old}}{2}\right)}}$$

This is more precise because a percent increase in price or quantity is different from a percent decrease in price or quantity over the same range. Here's an example: a percent increase from $4 to $5 = 25 percent, whereas a percent decrease from $5 to $4 = 20 percent.

Conveniently, the second formula produces the same elasticity measure between two points on a demand curve, regardless of which point you consider the "old" point and which you consider the "new" point. Finding the elasticity measure is simply a matter of plugging in the new and old price and quantity.

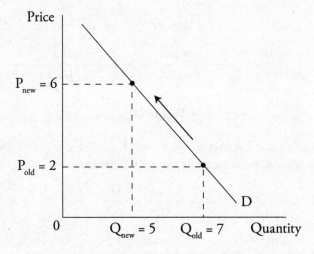

Figure 9

For example, the price elasticity of demand in the range shown in Figure 9 is

$$\frac{\dfrac{5-7}{\left(\dfrac{5+7}{2}\right)}}{\dfrac{6-2}{\dfrac{6+2}{2}}} = \frac{\dfrac{-2}{6}}{\dfrac{4}{4}} = \frac{-1}{3} = -.3\overline{3}$$

Because the elasticity quotient is less than one, the demand is inelastic. In this equation, 1 is the critical number in determining elasticity. If the quotient is less than 1, as is the case here, then the denominator ($\%\Delta P$) is greater than the numerator ($\%\Delta Q_d$), and the good is therefore inelastic. If the numerator and the denominator are equal, the result is 1, and the good is unit elastic. If the result is greater than 1, then the numerator is greater than the denominator, and the good is elastic.

Keep in mind that the results for the equation to determine elasticity will always be negative given the law of demand. As the law of demand says, an increase in price should result in a decrease in the quantity demanded, and a decrease in price should result in an increase in the quantity demanded. Because price and quantity demanded are always going in opposite directions, either the top or the bottom of the elasticity formula will always be negative and the other half will be positive. Either way, the elasticity of demand will come out negative. This being the case, it is conventional to drop the negative sign (take the *absolute value*) and refer to price elasticities in positive terms. The above elasticity would thus be $\frac{1}{3}$.

Elasticity Quotient of Demand

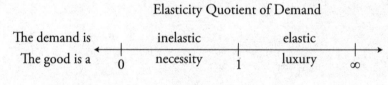

Figure 10

The elasticity of demand relates to the slope of the demand curve, but it *does not equal the slope of the demand curve*. Note the difference:

$$\text{slope} = \frac{\text{rise}}{\text{run}} = \frac{\Delta P}{\Delta Q_d}$$

$$\text{elasticity} = \frac{\dfrac{\Delta Q_d}{Q_d}}{\dfrac{\Delta P}{P}} = \frac{\Delta Q_d}{\Delta P}\left(\frac{P}{Q_d}\right)$$

Looking at the last part of each equation, you can see that elasticity is the inverse of the slope multiplied by price over quantity. The relationship between slope and elasticity is such that for a given P and Q, a steeper demand curve (one with a greater slope) is less elastic than a flatter demand curve (one with a smaller slope). A vertical demand curve as in Figure 11 is called **perfectly inelastic** because price has no influence on the quantity demanded and the elasticity value is 0.

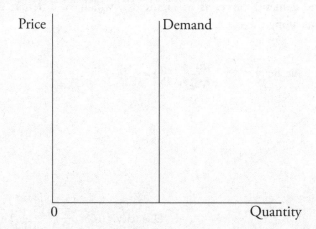

Figure 11: Perfectly Inelastic Demand

This approximates the demand for a lifesaving operation, insulin for a diabetic person, or a drug to which the user is addicted.

A horizontal demand curve, as in Figure 12, is called **perfectly elastic** because any increase in price will result in a quantity demanded of zero and the elasticity value is infinite.

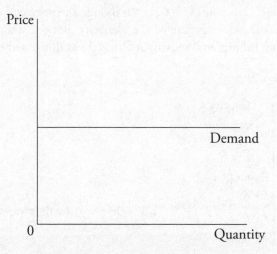

Figure 12: Perfectly Elastic Demand

This approximates the demand curve facing a corn farmer. As one of thousands of sellers of an identical product, she can sell all she wants at the price set by the market, but if she raises her price even one cent, no one will buy from her, because there are thousands of others selling the same product for the lower price. Because of price regulations, she is unable to lower her price.

A straight line demand curve, as in Figure 13, will have different elasticities at different points along the curve.

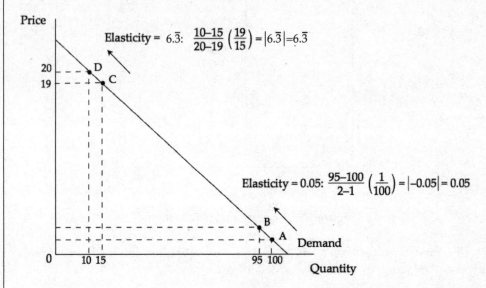

Figure 13

Note that the elasticity moving from point A to point B is 0.05 while the elasticity moving from point C to point D is 6.3 even though the price and quantity changes are of the same size. More generally, the elasticity along a straight line demand curve will go from infinity to 0 moving left to right as illustrated in Figure 14.

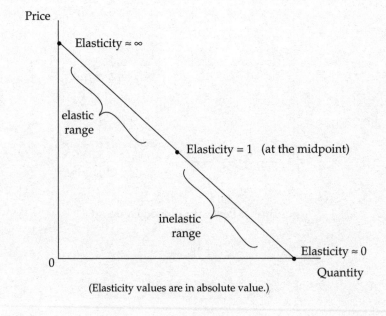

(Elasticity values are in absolute value.)

Figure 14

Why should a business care about the elasticity of demand? One reason is that the elasticity determines what happens to revenue when price changes. Note that total revenue (TR) equals price times quantity, which can be graphically related to the area of a rectangle that has a length equal to the price and a width equal to the quantity (length × width equals the area of a rectangle). Figure 15 illustrates three demand curves: one relatively inelastic, one unit elastic, and one relatively elastic.

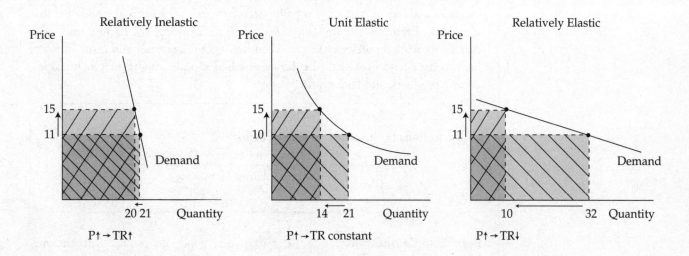

The price in each case has risen by the same amount. Nonetheless, it is clear that revenue (the area of the rectangle) has increased in the inelastic case, stayed the same in the unit elastic case, and decreased in the elastic case. Thus, businesses should remember this rule: when facing an inelastic demand, the best way to bring in more revenue (while selling fewer units) is to raise the price of the good. Use Figure 16 to help you remember all that.

Price and Total Revenue

Elastic	Price ↑	TR ↓
	Price ↓	TR ↑
Inelastic	Price ↑	TR ↑
	Price ↓	TR ↓

Figure 16

Income Elasticity of Demand

Because income is a large factor in an individual's purchasing patterns, changes in income typically result in shifts in the demand curves for particular goods, thus changing the quantities of those goods demanded at any given price. The **income elasticity of demand** measures the responsiveness of the quantity demanded to changes in income. Goods that an individual purchases more of when her income increases and less of when her income decreases are called **normal goods** for that individual. Examples might include steak, designer clothing, and diamonds. Goods that an individual purchases less of when her income increases and more of when her income decreases are called **inferior goods**. Examples might include hot dogs, generic products, and fake pearls.

> The formula for income elasticity of demand is
> $$\frac{\text{Percentage Change in Quantity Demanded}}{\text{Percentage Change in Income}}$$

Because the quantity demanded of a particular good can change with income, income elasticity can be either positive or negative. The sign (positive/negative) on income elasticity can be used to determine whether a good is normal or inferior. Figure 17 summarizes the relationship between income elasticity and product type.

Income Elasticity and Product Type

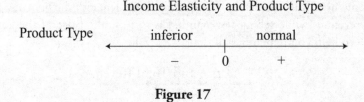

Figure 17

If the quantity demanded changes in the same direction as income—increasing as income increases and vice versa—the income elasticity of the good is positive and the good is normal. If quantity demanded changes in the opposite direction as income, the income elasticity of the good is negative and the good is inferior.

Cross-Price Elasticity of Demand

Elasticity is also used to describe the relationships between associated goods. The **cross-price elasticity of demand** measures the responsiveness of the quantity demanded of one good to the price of another good. For example, as the entrance fee for ski resorts drops, more vacationers go to these resorts, increasing the demand for rental skis. This *inverse* relationship between the price of entry and the demand for rental skis makes them **complements**. Other examples are coffee and cream, peanut butter and jelly, and gasoline and large cars. On the other hand, if the price of burgers goes up, then people will probably buy more hot dogs. If the price of one good and the quantity demanded of another good move in the *same* direction, they are called **substitutes**.

The formula for cross-price elasticity of demand is

$$\frac{\text{Percentage Change in Quantity Demanded of Good X}}{\text{Percentage Change in Price of Good Y}}$$

The elasticity value will be positive for substitutes and negative for complements. This relationship is summarized in Figure 18.

Cross-Price Elasticity and Product Relationship

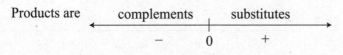

Figure 18

Elasticity of Supply

The **elasticity of supply** measures the responsiveness of the quantity supplied to price changes. The law of supply tells us that higher prices lead to larger quantities being supplied (supply curves slope upward), so the elasticity of supply should be positive. The formula for this elasticity is identical to that for demand elasticity, except that "quantity demanded" is replaced with "quantity supplied."

$$\frac{\text{Percentage Change in Quantity Supplied}}{\text{Percentage Change in Price}}$$

As with demand elasticity, when supply elasticity is greater than 1, supply is elastic, and if it is less than 1, supply is inelastic. In many cases the elasticity of supply will increase over time as producers are able to adjust their production processes to respond to changes in prices. If the price of radishes increases, there may be little that can be done to increase supply within a few weeks, but within a few months farmland that was used to produce carrots can be replanted with radishes and the supply will become more responsive to price. The supply curve for particular entertainers like Taylor Swift is perfectly inelastic (vertical), because there is only one Taylor Swift to supply, regardless of the price.

A Case Study in Elasticity

Let's consider how the concepts of supply, demand, elasticity, and surplus work together in real life. Imagine a product with relatively elastic demand, such as over-the-counter painkillers. There are many substitute brands producing them, and they aren't absolutely necessary (minor aches and pains usually fade with time). As a result, demand for over-the-counter painkillers is relatively elastic, as illustrated by Figure 19.

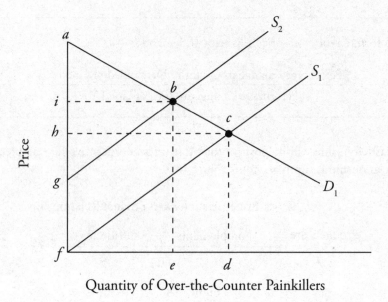

Figure 19

The initial supply and demand for over-the-counter painkillers are illustrated by S_1 and D_1. Suppose there is an environmental catastrophe, and one of the ingredients for over-the-counter pain killers becomes more expensive, causing the supply curve to shift inward. This shift is illustrated by S_2. As a result, the equilibrium price increases from h to i, and the quantity demanded decreases from d to e. The change in total revenue is reflected by the difference between areas *HCDF* and *IBEF*. Consumer surplus shifts from areas *ACH* to *ABI*. Producer surplus shifts from areas *HCF to IBG*. Note that the changes in both consumer and producer surplus are relatively proportionate to the change in supply.

Now consider a product with relatively inelastic demand, such as opioid painkillers. There are few substitutes, and opioids are highly addictive, causing people to feel as though they are life dependent. As a result, the demand curve for opioids is relatively inelastic, as illustrated by Figure 20.

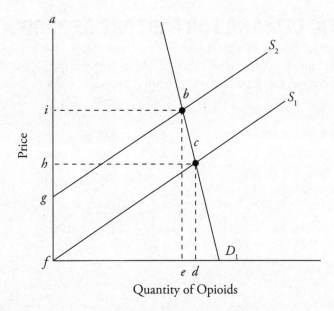

Quantity of Opioids

Figure 20

The initial supply and demand for opioids are illustrated by S_1 and D_1. Suppose another environmental catastrophe strikes, this time limiting opioid production. As a result, the supply curve shifts inward to S_2. Notice the change in price, from h to i, and the adjusted total revenue *IBEF*.

Due to the inelasticity of the demand curve, the change in supply affects opioids differently than over-the-counter painkillers. For opioids, the reduction in quantity, from d to e, is less than over-the-counter painkillers, and the increase in price, from h to i, is greater than for over-the-counter painkillers. Due to the inelasticity of the demand curve, there is a greater change in price and total revenue for opioids per percent change in supply than for over-the-counter painkillers.

The effect of elasticity can also be seen in consumer surplus. While consumer surplus is illustrated by area *ABI* in Figure 19, the corresponding point *A* for opioids can't be captured within the confines of Figure 20 because the demand curve is so steep. While consumer surplus is restricted in Figure 19, one can imagine that in a situation of perfect inelasticity, consumer surplus approaches infinity because the demand curve never intersects with the *y*-axis. In this way, both elasticity and consumer surplus model consumer behavior. The slope of the demand curve models consumer sensitivity to price, and consumer surplus models the utility buyers experience beyond the cost they paid for the good.

DERIVING DEMAND FOR FACTORS OF PRODUCTION

The demand for factors of production such as land, labor, and capital is derived from the demand for the products they produce. For example, if the demand for ice cream increases, the demand for ice cream ingredients will also increase.

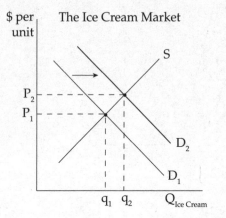
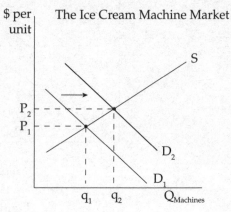

Figure 21

If the demand for ice cream increases as illustrated on the left side of Figure 21, the price of ice cream—the value of the output of ice cream machines—will increase. Thus, the demand for such machines (a form of capital) will increase as illustrated on the right side of Figure 1.

The most that firms would be willing to pay for additional factors of production is determined by the value of each factor's contribution to the production process. If a fourth bagel baker in a price-taking bagel shop would increase bagel production by 10 bagels per hour and bagels sell for $0.50 each, the most the bagel shop would pay for another baker is 10 × $0.50 = $5.00 per hour. In the language of economics, the marginal product of labor here is 10, the marginal revenue is $0.50, and the **marginal revenue product of labor** (MRP_L) is $5.00. More generally

$$MRP_L = MP_L \times P_{output}$$

The fourth baker will be hired if the wage is less than $5.00 per hour. (If the wage is exactly $5.00 per hour, the shop is indifferent toward hiring the worker or not.)

Firms with market power face downward-sloping demand curves and are not price takers. In order to sell the additional output produced by additional units of an input, firms with downward-sloping demand curves must lower their prices on all units sold (assuming they cannot price-discriminate). Thus, the marginal revenue from each additional unit of output is not the price, but the price minus the losses on units previously sold at a higher price. The most such a firm would be willing to pay for another worker in the short run is again the MRP_L.

The "L" for labor in the MRP_L equation could be replaced with any other factor of production to establish the marginal revenue product formula for that factor. The MRP_L curve represents the demand curve for either type of firm when only one factor of production is variable. In the long run when capital (for example) is variable in addition to labor, changes in the amounts of capital among other factors of production can affect the MP_L and thus the MRP_L and result in a labor demand curve that differs from the MRP_L curve.

The MRP_L curve slopes downward due to diminishing marginal returns, as explained above.

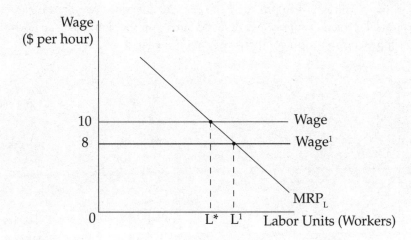

Figure 22

If the wage is $10 per hour as illustrated in Figure 22, the optimal quantity of labor to hire (L^*) is found on the labor axis directly below the intersection, between the wage line and the MRP_L line. If fewer than L^* workers are hired, there is an opportunity to hire more workers and pay them less than the value of their contribution to revenues. If more than L^* workers are hired, those in excess of L^* are paid more than the value of their contribution to revenues and the firm would increase profits or decrease losses by cutting labor back to L^*.

If the wage fell to $8, it would then be beneficial to hire those workers with marginal revenue products between $8 and $10; a total of L^1 workers should be hired. If MRP_L increased, as it would if the price of output increased or the marginal product of workers increased (for example, due to better training or technology), the demand for labor would shift to the right and more workers would be hired at any given wage. Decreases in MRP_L would similarly shift the labor demand to the left.

DETERMINING WAGES AND OTHER FACTOR PRICES

As in the previous section, labor will be used here as an example in the explanation of factor markets. The determination of other factor prices is analogous.

In a perfectly competitive labor market, each firm is a **wage taker**, just as firms are price takers in a perfectly competitive output market. The market demand for labor is the sum of the firm demand curves. Market demand will thus increase or decrease in response to changes in the number of firms or the MRP_L in the individual firms. The market supply of labor is the sum of all of the individual labor supply curves, and thus depends on the number of workers in the market and each worker's willingness to provide labor services at various wage rates. Figure 23 illustrates labor market supply and demand curves on the right, and the horizontal labor supply confronting a competitive firm on the left.

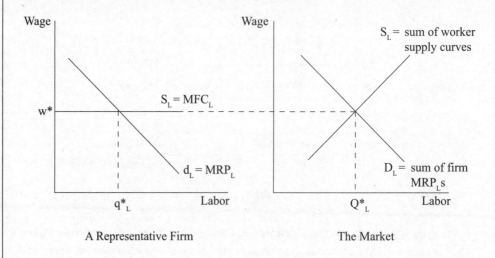

Figure 23: A Perfectly Competitive Labor Market

The intersection of the labor market demand and supply curves establishes the equilibrium wage. At this wage, everyone who would like to work has the opportunity to do so, meaning that there is no unemployment in this market. As described above, legislation that sets a minimum wage above the market equilibrium can act as a price floor for labor and cause unemployment. We will discuss unemployment further in the review of macroeconomic concepts.

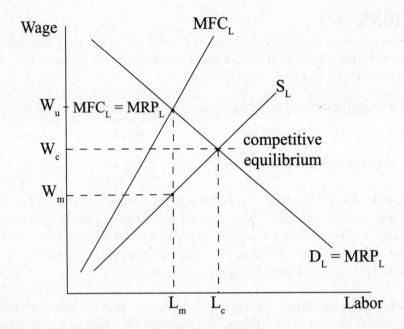

Figure 24: Monopsony

When one firm is the sole purchaser of labor services in a market, as a mining company might be in a small mining town, this firm is called a **monopsony**. Recall that marginal revenue is below price for a monopoly because it faces a downward-sloping market demand curve and must lower its price on *all* units sold in order to sell more. Similarly, a monopsony faces the entire upward-sloping labor supply curve as in Figure 24 and must raise wages to hire more workers. This results in a **marginal factor cost** or **MFC** (the additional cost of hiring one more worker) that is above the wage. For example, suppose a firm employing three workers for $10 per hour must pay $12 per hour to attract a fourth worker. The marginal factor cost of the fourth worker per hour is $12 *plus* the additional $2 per hour it must pay each of the first three workers to bring their wages from $10 to $12. The MFC is thus $12 + $2 + $2 + $2 = $18. Firms in a competitive labor market are wage takers, and their marginal factor cost equals the wage because they can hire all the workers they want at the same market wage.

A monopsony chooses the employment level at which $MRP_L = MFC_L$, indicated by L_m in Figure 24. The lowest wage the firm can pay to attract L_m workers, W_m, is determined by the labor supply curve directly above L_m. Notice that relative to the competitive labor market wage (W_c) and quantity of workers (L_c), the monopsony hires fewer workers and pays them less.

UNIONS

Workers in many industries increase their collective bargaining and lobbying strengths by forming labor unions. Unions use three general methods to increase the wages for their members. They attempt to

- increase the demand for labor

- decrease the supply of labor

- negotiate higher wages

Because the demand for labor is derived from the demand for the products labor produces, one way to increase labor demand is to increase product demand. This is accomplished with calls for consumers to "look for the union label," to lobby for favorable regulations and government expenditures, and to support protective tariffs and quotas that impede foreign competition.

Featherbedding agreements require employers to hire union members for particular tasks whether they are needed or not. Although the Taft-Hartley Act attempted to outlaw featherbedding and similar "make-work" agreements, the Supreme Court has permitted payments for nonproductive work. Examples include unnecessarily large minimum crew sizes on trains, and agreements that theaters will pay union musicians for performances even when orchestras from out of town are brought in to play.

Using an approach called exclusive unionism, some craft unions such as plumbers and electricians attempt to increase wages by restricting the supply of workers with their skills. When employers agree to hire only union workers, restricting the labor supply is as simple as restricting union membership. In other situations, unions can reduce the labor supply by lobbying for child labor laws, immigration restrictions, compulsory retirement, and occupational licensing.

For unskilled and semiskilled workers, it makes less sense to form an exclusive union because there are many available workers who could provide the same services. Instead, these groups tend to form inclusive or industrial unions that encourage as many workers as possible to join. Industrial unions try to use their size to their advantage when negotiating wage floors and compensation packages. On average, union members earn about 18 percent more than nonunionized workers in similar positions.

BILATERAL MONOPOLY

A monopoly exists when there is only one seller and a monopsony exists when there is only one buyer. A situation in which there is just one seller and one buyer in the same market, is called a **bilateral monopoly**. Because a union acts as a single seller of labor, and there are many industries dominated by a small number of employers that hire labor, situations resembling bilateral monopolies are not uncommon.

According to Figure 24, the monopsony desires to hire L_m workers and pay them W_m. The union will seek a wage of W_u, which is the marginal revenue product of the last worker hired (the MRP is what the last worker is worth to the employer, and the employer will most likely not pay workers more than what they are worth). Unlike the simple monopoly and monopsony situations, theory cannot predict the final wage in a bilateral monopoly. This will depend on the relative bargaining skills and strengths of the union and employer involved.

KEY TERMS

Understanding and Manipulating Demand

change in quantity demanded
change in demand
determinants of demand (TRIBE)
tastes and preferences
substitutes
complements
normal goods
inferior goods

Measuring Consumer Preference

marginal utility
total utility
consumer surplus
producer surplus

Elasticity

elasticity
price elasticity of demand
determinants of demand elasticity (PAID)
elastic
luxury
necessity
unit elastic
inelastic
elasticity of supply
income elasticity of demand
normal goods
inferior goods
cross-price elasticity of demand
complements
substitutes

Factor Markets

marginal revenue product of labor
wage taker
monopsony
marginal factor cost (marginal resource cost)
unions
featherbedding agreements
bilateral monopoly

CHAPTER 7 REVIEW QUESTIONS

See Chapter 9 for answers and explanations.

1. Which of the following could have caused an increase in the demand for ice cream cones?

   (A) A decrease in the price of ice cream cones
   (B) A decrease in the price of ice cream, a complimentary good to ice cream cones
   (C) An increase in the price of ice cream, a complimentary good to ice cream cones
   (D) A decrease in the price of lollipops, a close substitute for ice cream
   (E) An increase in the supply of ice cream cones

2. The total utility from sardines is maximized when they are purchased until

   (A) marginal utility is zero
   (B) marginal benefit equals marginal cost
   (C) consumer surplus is zero
   (D) distributive efficiency is achieved
   (E) deadweight loss is zero

3. If a 3 percent increase in price leads to a 5 percent increase in the quantity supplied

   (A) supply is unit elastic
   (B) demand is inelastic
   (C) demand is elastic
   (D) supply is elastic
   (E) supply is inelastic

4. Normal goods always have a/an

   (A) elastic demand curve
   (B) inelastic demand curve
   (C) elastic supply curve
   (D) negative income elasticity
   (E) positive income elasticity

5. When the cross-price elasticity of demand is negative, the goods in question are necessarily

   (A) normal
   (B) inferior
   (C) complements
   (D) substitutes
   (E) luxuries

6. If a business wants to increase its revenue and it knows that the elasticity quotient of demand of its product is equal to 0.78, it should

   (A) decrease price because demand is elastic
   (B) decrease price because demand is unit elastic
   (C) decrease price because demand is inelastic
   (D) increase price because demand is inelastic
   (E) increase price because demand is elastic

7. A student eats 3 slices of pizza while studying for his Economics exam. The marginal utility of the first slice of pizza is 10 utils, the second slice is 7 utils, and the third slice is 3 utils. Which of the statements below holds true with the above data?

   (A) The student would not eat any more pizza.
   (B) The marginal utility of the fourth slice of pizza will be 0.
   (C) The student should have stopped eating pizza after 2 slices.
   (D) The total utility this student received from eating pizza is 20 utils.
   (E) The total utility decreases after the first slice of pizza because of diminishing marginal utility.

8. Relative to a competitive input market, a monopsony

   (A) pays less and hires more workers
   (B) pays less and hires the same number of workers
   (C) pays more and hires more workers
   (D) pays more and hires fewer workers
   (E) pays less and hires fewer workers

9. Which of the following is NOT among the methods unions use to increase wages?

   (A) Negotiations to obtain a wage floor
   (B) Restrictive membership policies
   (C) Efforts to decrease the prices of substitute resources
   (D) Featherbedding or make-work rules
   (E) Efforts to increase the demand for the product they produce

10. A bilateral monopoly exists when

   (A) a monopsony buys from a monopoly
   (B) a monopoly sells to two different types of consumers
   (C) a monopoly buys from a monopsony
   (D) a monopolist sells two different types of goods
   (E) a monopoly sells at two different prices

Chapter 7 Summary

Understanding and Manipulating Demand

o   The demand curve shifts with
  •   **T**astes and preferences of consumers
  •   the prices of **R**elated goods
  •   the **I**ncome of buyers
  •   the number of **B**uyers
  •   **E**xpectations for the future

Measuring Consumer Preference

o   **Marginal utility** is the additional utility gained from consuming one more unit of a good.

o   **Total utility** is the sum of all marginal utility values gained from each unit consumed.

o   **Consumer surplus** is the value a buyer receives from the purchase of a good *in excess* of what the consumer pays for it; **producer surplus** is the difference between the price a seller receives for a good and the minimum price for which she would be willing to supply a quantity of the good.

Elasticity

o   The **price elasticity of demand** for a given good describes the extent to which consumer behavior will change as the price of the good changes.

o   The elasticity of a good relates to
  •   the **P**roportion of the consumer's income spent on the good
  •   the **A**vailability of close substitutes
  •   the **I**mportance of a good
  •   the ability to **D**elay the purchase of a good

- A good is **elastic** (a **luxury**) if $\%\Delta Q_d > \%\Delta P$

- A good is **unit elastic** if $\%\Delta Q_d = \%\Delta P$

- A good is **inelastic** (a **necessity**) if $\%\Delta Q_d < \%\Delta P$

- Knowing the elasticity of a demand curve tells sellers how much their total revenue will change with a change in price:
    - elastic goods: $P\uparrow \rightarrow TR\downarrow$
    - unit elastic goods: $P\uparrow \rightarrow TR$ constant
    - inelastic goods: $P\uparrow \rightarrow TR\uparrow$

- The **elasticity of supply** measures the responsiveness of the quantity supplied to price changes.

    - Elasticity of supply is calculated by $\dfrac{\%\Delta Q_s}{\%\Delta P}$

Income Elasticity

- **Income elasticity of demand** measures the responsiveness of the quantity demanded to changes in income.

    - Income elasticity is calculated by $\dfrac{\%\Delta Q_d}{\%\Delta \text{Income}}$

- Individuals buy more **normal goods** (positive income elasticity) when their income increases; they buy more **inferior goods** (negative elasticity) when their income decreases.

Cross-Price Elasticity of Demand

- The **cross-price elasticity of demand** measures the responsiveness of the quantity demanded of one good to the price of another.

    - Cross-price elasticity of good x in relation to good y is calculated by $\dfrac{\%\Delta Q_d(x)}{\%\Delta P(y)}$

- When cross-price elasticity is negative, then goods x and y are **complements**; when cross-price elasticity is positive, then goods x and y are **substitutes**.

Deriving the Value of Factors of Demand

o The **marginal revenue product of labor** is the amount of revenue generated by one additional unit of labor; calculate using this formula:

$$MRP_L = MP_L \ P_{output}$$

o The above equation can be used for any of the factors of demand.

Determining Wages and Other Factor Prices

o A **monopsony** occurs when one firm is the sole purchaser of labor services.

o The **marginal factor cost (MFC)** is the additional cost of one more unit of labor.
o
A monopsony will choose an employment level at which $MRP_L = MFC_L$.

Unions

o Workers increase their collective bargaining and lobbying strengths by forming labor unions. They attempt to
  • increase the demand for labor
  • decrease the supply of labor
  • negotiate higher wages

Bilateral Monopoly

o A **bilateral monopoly** occurs when there is only one buyer and one seller in the market.

Chapter 8
Government and Microeconomics

SYSTEMS OF GOVERNMENT AND MICROECONOMIC DECISIONS

The allocation of scarce resources can be largely influenced by the system of government in a country or region. This section provides a brief thumbnail of three forms of government and the prominent decision-making mechanisms they entail.

Communism is a system in which the government owns all the resources in society and answers the three economic questions: what, how, and for whom goods are produced. Communism is designed to minimize imbalance in wealth via the collective ownership of property. Legislators from a single political party—the communist party—divide the available wealth for equal advantage among citizens. The problems with communism include a lack of incentives for extra effort, risk taking, and innovation. The critical role of the central government in allocating resources and setting production levels makes this system particularly vulnerable to corruption.

Socialism is a system in which the government maintains control of sectors of the economy that are particularly prone to market failure, such as energy, education, or health care. Socialism shares with communism the goal of fair distribution and the pitfall of inadequate incentives. Rather than the government controlling wages as under a communist system, wages are determined by negotiations between trade unions and managers. Another difference between socialism and communism is that under socialism, a single political party does not rule the economy.

Capitalism is a system in which individuals and private firms own the resources in society and answer the three economic questions: what, how, and for whom goods are produced. Under a capitalist system, private individuals control the factors of production and operate them in the pursuit of profit. Wages are determined by negotiations between managers and employees or their unions. The market forces of supply and demand largely determine the allocation of scarce resources. Government may regulate businesses and provide tax-supported social benefits. The previous sections describe how product markets can determine prices and quantities for goods and services, and this section describes the influence of various government policies.

BASIC GOVERNMENT INTERVENTIONS

This section studies three basic steps governments can take to manage their economies: a price ceiling, a price floor, and a tax.

Price Ceiling

A **price ceiling** is an artificial cap on the price of a good. Examples include **rent controls** in many U.S. cities and limits on the price of bread in some parts of Europe. In order for a price ceiling to have any effect, the ceiling must be *below* the equilibrium price as in Figure 1.

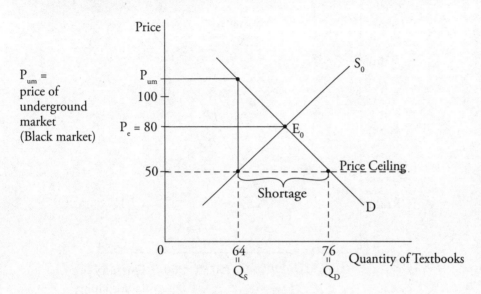

P_{um} = price of underground market (Black market)

Figure 1: Price Ceiling

If the equilibrium price for textbooks was \$80 and a price ceiling of \$100 was imposed, it would have no effect because the price would not be that high anyway. A price ceiling of \$50, however, means that 76 would be demanded and 64 would be supplied, resulting in a shortage of 12 textbooks.

Although price ceilings provide lower prices for those who are able to purchase the good, negative repercussions are common. To purchase the good, buyers may need to wait in line for long periods of time. Because the price of Duke basketball tickets is below the equilibrium price (perhaps due to a self-imposed price ceiling), students wait in line for as long as a week to purchase tickets to individual games. The time they lose waiting in line constitutes a **queuing cost** and would be unnecessary if the price were able to reach equilibrium where the number of buyers equaled the number of tickets available at that price.

Price ceilings can also result in black market activity. Again looking at Figure 1, because the potential buyers of the 65th and subsequent textbooks value them at close to \$100 and the seller(s) could provide them for just over \$50, there is an opportunity for mutually beneficial but illegal transactions, called **black market** transactions. For example, if the 65th book was sold illegally for \$80 by a seller with a marginal cost of \$55 to a buyer who values it at \$99, the seller nets \$25 and the buyer would get \$19 worth of value in excess of what she paid for the textbook. (This assumes they do not get caught.) There are black markets for such goods as tickets to sporting events and concerts, foreign currencies that have a fixed official price (exchange rate), and human organs.

Price Floor

A **price floor** is an artificially imposed minimum price. Since 1938, the government has placed such a floor on the price of labor—the **minimum wage**. In order to have any effect, a price floor must be *above* the equilibrium price as in Figure 2.

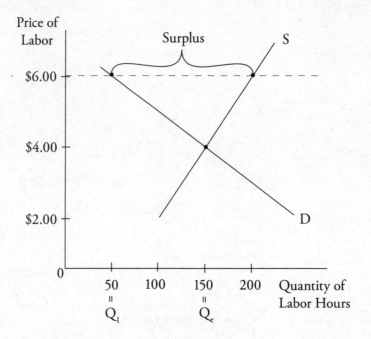

Figure 2: Price Floor

A minimum wage of $2 per hour would be meaningless because even without any intervention, the higher equilibrium wage of $4 would be attained. With a minimum wage of $6 per hour, 200 workers will be supplied, 50 will be demanded, and a surplus of 150 will be unemployed. Notice that this is more than the 100 workers $(Q_e - Q_1)$ that would be employed at $4 but not at $6. The other 50 are from new entrants into the workforce who did not want to work for $4 an hour but do want to work for $6. Clearly the minimum wage helps the 50 workers who are still employed at the higher wage, but hurts those who lost their jobs due to the decreased quantity of labor demanded at $6 an hour.

Tax

Let's examine how a tax on a consumer good interplays with the concepts of supply, demand, elasticity, and surplus. Consider the effect of a tax on the use of hotel rooms. Fictional demand and supply curves for hotel rooms are illustrated in Figure 3.

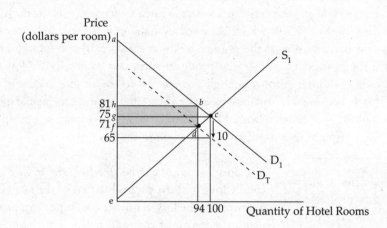

Figure 3

In the absence of a tax, supply is S_1, demand is D_1, and the equilibrium price is $75 per night. Now suppose that a city tax of $10 per night is imposed on hotel guests. The original demand curve (D_1) indicates the quantity of hotel rooms that will be demanded at a given price. Because consumers now have to pay $10 per room to the city, the amount they are willing to pay the hotels goes down by $10 per room, so the demand curve shifts down. The dotted line indicates the new demand curve (D_T) facing hotels, and the new equilibrium is at a price of $71 and a quantity of 94 rooms. Of course, the total amount that consumers pay is $71 *plus the $10 tax*, or $81.

It is important to note that the total payment by the consumers has gone up by only $6—less than the amount of the tax. The amount received by the hotels has gone down by the other $4 of the tax. Thus, the burden of the tax does not depend on who has to pay for it. Rather, it depends on the relative elasticities of supply and demand. If you illustrate this same story with a perfectly inelastic (vertical) supply curve, you will find that the entire burden of the tax would be paid by hotels. That is, the total payment by consumers will be $75 per room just as before the tax, and hotels will receive only $65 per room.

In Figure 3, consumer surplus and producer surplus before the tax are represented by the areas *acg* and *gce*, respectively. The shaded area *hbdf* represents the tax revenue of $10 × 94 rooms = $940, which is carved partially out of the pre-tax consumer surplus and partially out of the pre-tax producer surplus. The areas *abh* and *fde* represent the post-tax consumer and producer surpluses, respectively. Notice that the post-tax consumer surplus goes all the way up to the original demand curve (D_1). This is because D_1 still indicates the most that consumers would pay for various numbers of hotel rooms. D_T illustrates what the consumers would pay minus the portion of that payment that must go to the city.

Tax burden can be a difficult topic for many students. Keep in mind that a tax creates a gap (or a wedge) between what consumers pay and what firms receive. The amount of the gap is exactly equal to the tax. Note that the new price paid minus the original equilibrium price (before the tax) is the consumer tax burden. The original equilibrium price (before the tax) minus the new amount collected (net of the tax) is the share borne by the producer, or the producer tax burden.

The area *bcd* is called the **deadweight loss**, the **efficiency loss**, and the **excess burden** of the tax, because it represents the loss to former consumer and producer surplus in excess of the total revenue of the tax. That is, deadweight loss ultimately stems from the fact that fewer hotel rooms are consumed now than before a tax was imposed. In other words, every portion of the pre-tax consumer and producer surplus either remains as surplus or is captured as tax revenues *except* that triangle, which is lost to everyone. With experimentation you will find that, like the distribution of the tax burden, the size of the deadweight loss is also determined by the elasticity of the supply and demand curves.

Figure 4 illustrates the fact that the outcome is the same if the tax is imposed on the hotels rather than on the consumers.

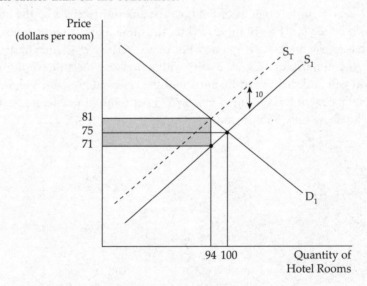

Figure 4: A Tax on Suppliers

A $10 room tax collected from hotels shifts the supply curve facing consumers up by $10. In addition to the minimum the hotels must receive to provide a given number of rooms as indicated by S_1, they now must receive an additional $10 per room to give to the city. Note that the resulting total price that consumers pay, the price that hotels receive after paying the tax, the tax revenue, the quantity, and the deadweight loss are identical to the case in which the consumers paid the tax.

RESPONDING TO MARKET FAILURE

Market Failure

Market failure occurs when resources are not allocated optimally. That is, allocative efficiency is not achieved. This can result from

- imperfect information

- imperfect competition

- externalities

- public goods

Imperfect competition and the resulting potential for unnecessarily high prices, low quantities, inferior quality, and deadweight loss is explained in detail in the previous chapter. The next sections feature more discussion on externalities and public goods. **Imperfect information** means that buyers and/or sellers do not have full knowledge about available markets, prices, products, customers, suppliers, and so forth. For example, imperfect information occurs when buyers pay too much for a product because they do not know about a lower-priced alternative. Another example of this occurs when producers make too much of a specific product, and not enough of another because they don't understand the demand of their customers. Solutions to imperfect information include truth-in-advertising regulations, consumer information services, and market surveys by firms. As another example of available solutions, some countries require restaurants and hotels to post price lists so that potential customers can easily compare prices.

IMPERFECT COMPETITION

In contrast to the allocative, distributive, and production efficiency that are achieved when a perfectly competitive market is in long-run equilibrium, firms with market power can challenge the efficiency of the market if left unchecked. Consider a monopoly as in Figure 5.

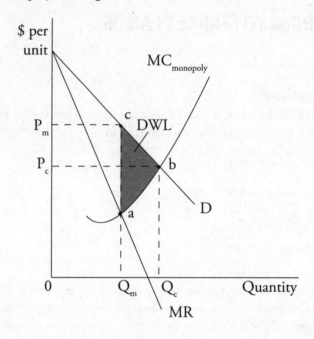

Figure 5

The monopoly price will be P_m, and the monopoly will produce Q_m. To simplify the comparison of monopoly and competitive outcomes, let's assume constant returns to scale, meaning that many smaller firms could produce a fraction (say, one one-thousandth) of the market's output for that same fraction of the cost. The competitive market's supply curve would be the monopoly's MC curve, and the competitive market's equilibrium would be at the intersection of MC and the demand curve. Note that at this intersection, $P_c = MC$ is the condition for allocative efficiency. The competitive price P_c is below the monopoly price P_m, and the competitive quantity Q_c is more than the monopoly quantity Q_m.

Along with the potential for higher prices and lower quantities in a monopoly market comes a welfare loss. In the absence of externalities (to be discussed below), the demand curve reflects the benefits to consumers of additional units of the good, and the marginal cost curve reflects the additional cost of resources needed to provide those benefits. Thus, the area *abc* between the demand curve and the MC curve from Q_m to Q_c represents the deadweight loss (DWL), sometimes called "efficiency loss" (in essence, DWL is lost consumer and producer surplus), due to a monopoly market structure. The potential for monopolies to decrease quality is an added detriment of monopoly power.

Monopolies also have some positive attributes. The potential for sustainable monopoly profits can induce individuals and firms to invent new products. Some argue that the quest for monopoly profits motivates research and development expenditures that result in important drugs and technology. In other situations, competition is not an option. Industries such as power generation and rail service have such high fixed costs that it would be impossible for a particular service area to support more than one firm. Firms in these industries are called **natural monopolies**.

As illustrated in Figure 6, the high fixed costs in natural monopolies cause the average total cost curve to fall throughout the relevant range of production, and the demand curve intersects average total cost while it is still falling. In this case the allocatively efficient price (P_{SO}), at which marginal cost equals demand, would not allow profits because P_{SO} is less than average total cost at the corresponding quantity of Q_{SO}. However, the monopoly price of P_M is also undesirable because it is considerably higher than the socially optimal price and the associated quantity of Q_M is below the socially optimal quantity.

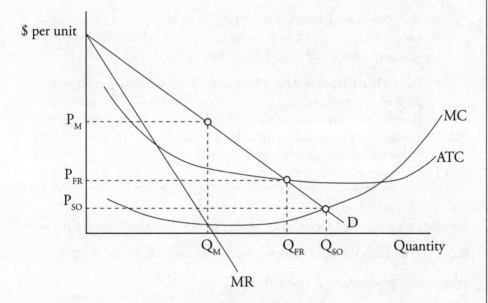

Figure 6: Natural Monopoly

Because competition can't temper prices in this situation, it is common for natural monopolies to be regulated. The challenge, then, is to decide on a regulated price. If a price ceiling is set at P_{SO}, production will satisfy the MB = MC condition for social optimality (assuming there are no externalities), but the monopoly will require financial assistance in order to survive because it will experience a loss of the difference between price and average total cost for every unit sold.

An available compromise is to set a **"fair return" price ceiling** at P_{FR}. This price is equal to average total cost at the corresponding quantity of Q_{FR}. Thus, the firm will break even. The fair return price falls between the monopoly price and the socially optimal price, providing what many regulators see as a desirable middle ground between the resource misallocation caused by higher prices and the losses caused by lower prices.

The threats of excessive prices, limited quantities, and inferior quality have led the government to foster competition in industries in which it is considered beneficial. The primary tool used to restrict market power is antitrust legislation. Congress created the Interstate Commerce Commission (ICC) in 1887 to oversee and correct abuses of market power in the railroad industry; in 1914, Congress created the Federal Trade Commission (FTC) to investigate the structure and conduct of firms engaging in interstate commerce.

A summary of landmark antitrust legislation follows:

- The **Sherman Act (1890)** declared attempts to monopolize commerce or restrain trade among the states illegal.

- The **Clayton Act (1914)** strengthened the Sherman Act by specifying that monopolistic behavior such as price discrimination, tying contracts, and unlimited mergers is illegal.

- The **Robinson-Patman Act (1936)** prohibits price discrimination except when it is based on differences in cost, difference in marketability of product, or a good faith effort to meet competition.

- The **Celler-Kefauver Act (1950)** authorized the government to ban **vertical mergers** (mergers of firms at various steps in the production process from raw materials to finished products) and **conglomerate mergers** (combinations of firms from unrelated industries) in addition to **horizontal mergers** (mergers of direct competitors).

There are several formal measures of market power. The **Herfindahl-Hirschman Index** (HHI) takes the market share of each firm in an industry as a percentage, squares each percentage, and adds them all up. $HHI = \sum_{i=1}^{m} S_i^2$. For example, if one firm holds a 100 percent market share, the HHI = 100^2 = 10,000. If two firms hold 30 percent market shares and one holds a 40 percent market share, the HHI = $30^2 + 30^2 + 40^2$ = 3,400. The HHI increases as the number of firms in the industry decreases or as the firms become less uniform in size. The n-firm **concentration ratio** is the sum of the market shares of the largest n firms in an industry, where n can represent any number. For example, if the four largest firms in the cola industry hold 21, 18, 11, and 6 percent market shares, the four-firm concentration ratio is the sum of these numbers, 56.

Externalities

Externalities are costs or benefits felt beyond or "external to" those causing the effects. Some like to think of these as spillover effects. Inefficiencies arise as the result of externalities because those making decisions do not consider all of the repercussions of their behavior. When your neighbor decides how many dogs to own, she is likely to weigh the price of the dogs, their food, their health care, etc., against the joy she receives from owning them. On the other hand, she might not consider the costs imposed on you due to the dogs' barking and biting, and the droppings left in your yard. This is an example of a **negative externality** because the external effects of your neighbor's dog ownership are hurtful to you. The result of her failure to consider the costs she is imposing on you is that she will buy too many dogs. Negative externalities lead to overconsumption.

On the other hand, when your neighbor decides how many flowers to plant in her yard, she might plant fewer than the optimal amount for society if she does not consider the enjoyment you and others in the neighborhood get out of seeing and smelling them. When you decided whether or not to get a flu shot last winter, did you consider the benefits to others of not getting the flu from you if you were immunized? Flowers and flu shots are sources of **positive externalities,** which lead to underconsumption. It is important to note that externalities are also known as spillover effects: negative externalities are called **spillover costs** and positive externalities are called **spillover benefits**.

Figure 7 illustrates the dog ownership decision for your neighbor, whom we'll call Mary.

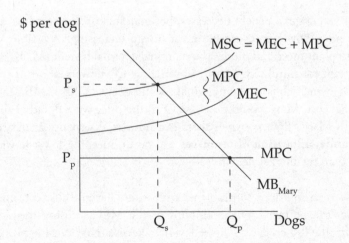

Figure 7: Negative Externalities

Mary's marginal benefit per dog decreases as she acquires more and more dogs, in accordance with the law of diminishing marginal utility. The **marginal private cost** (MPC) per dog (the additional cost Mary pays for each additional dog) is assumed to be constant, although the analysis is the same if it is increasing. The **marginal external cost** (MEC) per dog (the additional cost imposed on the neighbors) might increase because each additional dog not only barks, bites, and makes droppings but also helps provoke the existing dogs to cause even more ruckus. Looking only at her MB and MPC, Mary will own Q_p dogs. To find the optimal quantity for society, add the MEC and the MPC to find the marginal social cost (MSC). The MSC intersects the MB at the socially optimal quantity of Q_s dogs. This is the number of dogs Mary would own if she paid the full marginal social cost of P_s for that particular quantity. As shown with Mary's dog, when there are negative externalities associated with a good, an **over allocation of resources** will occur, meaning more goods will be produced than the market demands.

Figure 8 illustrates the flower-purchasing decision for Mary.

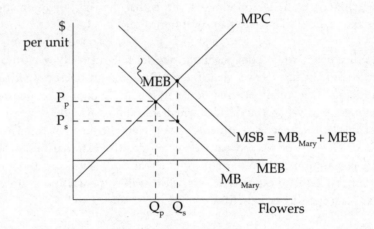

Figure 8: Positive Externalities

While Mary's marginal benefit decreases, her marginal private cost increases as she purchases more flowers because she must forego increasingly valuable alternative activities to plant more and more. The marginal external benefit (MEB) is assumed to be constant for simplicity. Mary will purchase Q_p flowers, short of the socially optimal Q_s, which equates the marginal social benefit (MSB = MB + MEB) and the marginal cost. Mary would purchase Q_s if the price were P_s rather than P_p. As shown with Mary's flowers, when there is a positive externality associated with a good, an **under allocation of resources** will occur, meaning fewer flowers will be produced than the market demands.

There are several solutions to problems with externalities. Those causing negative externalities can be taxed by the amount of the MEC, causing them to feel or "internalize" the full costs of their behavior. Likewise those causing positive externalities can be subsidized by the amount of the MEB so that their private benefit equals the marginal social benefit. This is one reason why it is a good idea to subsidize immunizations and education and tax liquor and gasoline. Ronald Coase suggested that those who are helped or hurt by positive or negative externalities might be able to pay the decision makers to produce more or less of their product. The viability of such payoffs is contingent on the clarity of each side's rights (for example, the right for a firm to pollute), and the ability of the affected parties to organize and collect the necessary funds. Alternative solutions for negative externalities include restricting the output to the socially optimal quantity (Q_s) or imposing a price floor at the socially optimal price (P_s).

Note that an individual's marginal benefit curve is synonymous with his or her demand curve, and the marginal cost curve (above average variable cost) is equivalent to the supply curve for a competitive firm. Don't be confused if you see presentations of the externality story that replace MB and MPC with D and S. Also note that for the purpose of finding the social optimum, it makes no difference whether the MEC is added to the MPC curve or subtracted from the MB curve. Either way, the MEC creates the same sized wedge between MB and MPC, and the resulting socially optimal quantity and price are the same. Likewise, a MEB could be subtracted from the MPC rather than being added to the private MB to yield identical results.

Public Goods

Public goods are those that many individuals benefit from at the same time. They are characterized as being *nonrival in consumption and nonexcludable*. A **nonrival good** is one for which the consumption of that good does not affect its consumption by others. For example, Donna's use of a radio signal does not detract in any way from Dina's use of the same radio signal. Rival goods like food and parking spaces cannot be consumed by multiple users simultaneously.

Once available, **nonexcludable** goods cannot be held back from those who desire access. For example, once a country is protected by a military system, it is impossible to prevent particular individuals within the country from benefiting from that defense. Other examples of public goods include police protection, disease control, clean air, and the preservation of animal species.

Because multiple users benefit from a public good at the same time, the demand curve for society that reflects the marginal benefit from each additional unit of the good is found by adding each individual's demand curve vertically. Figure 9 illustrates a market for police protection that consists of only two individuals, Vernon and Linda.

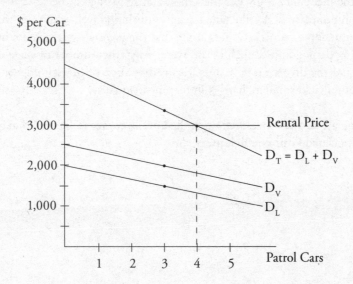

Figure 9: A Public Good

Vernon's annual benefits from the protection of various numbers of police cars are represented by his demand curve, D_V, and Linda's benefits from the same police cars are represented by D_L. The total annual benefit from the third patrol car, for example, is Vernon's $2,000 benefit plus Linda's $1,500 benefit, or $3,500. Their town should purchase police cars until the total social demand, D_T, equals the annual price of renting a police car—$3,000—which occurs with the rental of four police cars.

The problem that arises with public goods is that consumers know that they can benefit from the provision of these goods whether or not they pay for them. Even if each household gains $1,000 per year worth of benefits from military protection, a door-to-door collection to pay for the military would come up short due to the temptation for households to be free riders. A **free rider** is one who attempts to benefit from a public good without paying for it. Given the nonrival and nonexcludable nature of national defense, individuals have little incentive to reveal their true preferences. Instead, they might say they would rather risk invasion than pay for national defense, and then benefit from the protection paid for by others. Another classic example of the free rider problem is the difficulty of getting neighbors to pay for a streetlight in a cul-de-sac. The solution to the free rider problem in most cases is to have some form of government (federal government for national defense, a neighborhood association for streetlights) provide the public goods. Governmental units can collect money in the form of taxes, fees, or dues from everyone who benefits from the public goods and then fund their provision.

Distribution of Income

You've heard it before—the rich are getting richer and the poor are getting poorer. In relative terms, this is correct. The *gap* between rich and poor continues to widen. This is generally true on the basis of the share of income held by the richest and poorest 20 percent of the U.S. population over the past few decades. Some argue that income inequality is greater than these statistics suggest, because the rich also receive nonmonetary perks like fancy meals, housing, travel, and so on that do not show up in income reports. Others argue that the inequality trends are influenced by changing demographics such as the average age, the number of wage earners in a family, and the divorce rate. Comparisons over time of households with similar demographics yield smaller changes in income inequality.

Income equality is often measured using the **Lorenz curve,** as illustrated in Figure 10, and the associated **Gini coefficient**.

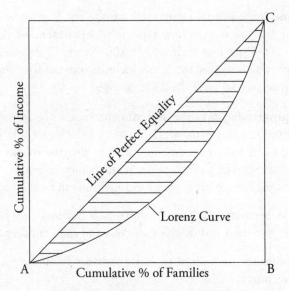

Figure 10: The Lorenz Curve

The vertical axis measures the cumulative percentage of income. The horizontal axis measures the cumulative percentage of families, starting with the poorest and ending with the richest. The straight line from corner to corner represents perfect income equality because the proportion of families equals the proportion of income—the "poorest" 10 percent hold fully 10 percent of the income and so forth. The line below it is the Lorenz curve, which depicts the actual relationship between families and income in the United States. The poorest 20 percent hold only 4 percent of income, the poorest 40 percent hold 14 percent of income, and so on.

The Gini coefficient is the ratio

$$\frac{\text{shaded area}}{\text{area of triangle ABC}}$$

You're nearing the end of the Microeconomics review! Before you dive into Macro, be sure to give yourself some downtime to let your brain absorb the information you've been studying.

If income were divided equally, both the shaded area and the Gini coefficient would be 0. If the richest family made all of the income, the Gini coefficient would be 1. The Gini coefficient in the United States is about 0.48.

The **poverty line** is the official benchmark of poverty. It is set at three times the minimum food budget as established by the Department of Agriculture. The poverty line for a family of four is about $25,100. Nearly 12.3 percent of Americans live below the poverty line. The list below includes some of the programs that seek to redistribute income and assist the disadvantaged.

- With a **progressive tax,** the government receives a larger percentage of revenue from families with larger incomes. In contrast to a progressive tax, which helps redistribute income to the poor, a **regressive tax** collects a larger percentage of revenue from families with smaller incomes. A **proportional tax** collects the same percentage of income from all families.

- The **Social Security** program provides cash benefits and health insurance (Medicare) to retired and disabled workers and their families.

- **Public assistance** or **welfare** typically provides temporary assistance to the very low-income families.

- **Supplemental Security Income (SSI)** assists very poor elderly individuals who have virtually no assets and little or no Social Security entitlement.

- **Unemployment compensation** provides temporary assistance to unemployed workers.

- **Medicaid** provides health insurance and hospitalization benefits to the low-income families.

- The **Supplemental Nutrition Assistance Program (SNAP)**, also known as **Food Stamps**, and **Public Housing** programs provide food and shelter for the low-income families.

KEY TERMS

Systems of Government

communism
socialism
capitalism

Basic Government Interventions

price ceiling
rent controls
price floor
minimum wage
queuing cost
black/underground markets
deadweight loss
efficiency loss
excess burden

Responding to Market Failure

market failure
imperfect competition
natural monopoly
"fair return" price ceiling
Sherman Act
Clayton Act
Robinson-Patman Act
Celler-Kefauer Act
vertical mergers
conglomerate mergers
horizontal mergers
Herfindahl-Hirschman Index
concentration ratio
externalities
public goods
imperfect information
negative externality
positive externality
marginal private cost

marginal external cost (marginal social cost)
public goods
nonrival goods
nonexcludable goods
free rider

Distribution of Income

Lorenz curve
Gini coefficient
poverty line
progressive tax
regressive tax
proportional tax
Social Security
public assistance/welfare
Supplemental Security Income
unemployment compensation
Medicaid
Supplemental Nutrition Assistance Program (SNAP)/ Food Stamps
Public Housing program

CHAPTER 8 REVIEW QUESTIONS

See Chapter 9 for answers and explanations.

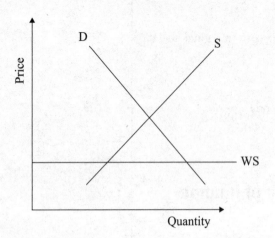

1. Suppose the supply and demand for cotton in the United States are represented by curves S and D respectively in the figure above. Also assume that the world supply for cotton is so large that the United States would be a "price taker" in the world market (as represented by WS). If the United States were to open its cotton market to free trade with the world, then

   (A) the domestic price of cotton would rise, and the United States would export cotton
   (B) the domestic price of cotton would fall, and the United States would export cotton
   (C) the domestic price of cotton would rise, and the United States would import cotton
   (D) the domestic price of cotton would fall, and the United States would import cotton
   (E) there would be no change in the price of cotton in the United States

2. When the labor demand curve is downward-sloping, an increase in the minimum wage is

   (A) beneficial to some workers and harmful to other workers
   (B) beneficial to all workers and harmful to some employers
   (C) harmful to all workers and employers
   (D) beneficial to all workers and employers
   (E) none of the above

3. Because people with relatively low incomes spend a larger percentage of their income on food than people with relatively high incomes, a sales tax on food would fall into which category of taxes?

   (A) Progressive
   (B) Proportional
   (C) Regressive
   (D) Neutral
   (E) Flat

4. If the government regulates a monopoly to produce at the allocative efficient quantity, which of the following would be true?

   (A) The monopoly would break even.
   (B) The monopoly would incur an economic loss.
   (C) The monopoly would make an economic profit.
   (D) The deadweight loss in this market would increase.
   (E) The deadweight loss in this market would decrease.

5. If the government subsidizes producers in a perfectly competitive market, then

   (A) the demand for the product will increase
   (B) the demand for the product will decrease
   (C) the consumer surplus will increase
   (D) the consumer surplus will decrease
   (E) the supply will decrease

6. If corn is produced in a perfectly competitive market and the government placed a price ceiling above equilibrium, which of the following would be true?

   (A) There would be no change in the amount of corn demanded or supplied.
   (B) There would be a shortage created of corn.
   (C) There would be a surplus created of corn.
   (D) The producers of corn would lose revenue due to the decreased price.
   (E) Illegal markets may develop for corn.

7. Which of the following examples would result in consumers paying for the largest burden of an excise tax placed on a producer?

   (A) If the demand curve is price elastic and the supply curve is price inelastic
   (B) If the demand curve is price elastic and the supply curve is perfectly elastic
   (C) If the demand curve is price inelastic and the supply curve is price elastic
   (D) If the demand curve is price inelastic and the supply curve is price inelastic
   (E) If the demand curve is perfectly inelastic and the supply curve is price elastic

Chapter 8 Summary

Systems of Government and Economic Decisions

- **Communism** is a system in which the government owns all the resources in society and answers the three economic questions: what, how, and for whom are goods produced.

- **Socialism** is a system in which the government maintains control of some resources in society, such as energy distribution, education, or health care.

- **Capitalism** is a system in which individuals and private firms own the resources in society and answer the three economic questions: what, how, and for whom are goods produced.

Basic Government Interventions

- A **price ceiling** is an artificial cap on the price of a good.

- A **price floor** is an artificially imposed minimum price.

- **Deadweight loss** (also known as **efficiency loss** or **excess burden**) is the loss to former consumer and producer surplus in excess of total revenue of the tax.

- Calculating the effects of a new tax is tricky: the burden of the tax does not depend on who has to pay for it. Rather, the weight of the tax burden depends on the relative elasticity of the supply and demand curves for the good in question.

Responding to Market Failure

- **Natural monopolies** occur when fixed costs are so high as to prohibit a second firm from entering the market.

- The **Sherman Act**, the **Clayton Act**, the **Robinson-Patman Act**, and the **Celler-Kefauer Act** are important pieces of antitrust legislation.

o   A **vertical merger** is a merger of firms at various steps in the production process.

o   A **conglomerate merger** is a combination of firms from unrelated industries.

o   A **horizontal merger** is a merger of direct competitors.

o   A **market failure** occurs whenever resources aren't allocated optimally. This can result from
  •   imperfect competition
  •   **externalities:** costs or benefits felt beyond those causing the effects
  •   **public goods:** goods that many individuals benefit from at the same time
  •   **imperfect information:** buyers and/or sellers do not have full knowledge about available markets, prices, products, customers, suppliers

o   **Negative externalities** lead to overconsumption; **positive externalities** lead to underconsumption.

o   The **marginal private cost** (MPC) of a good is the cost paid by the consumer for an additional unit of a good; the **marginal external cost** is the cost paid by people other than the buyer for an additional unit of a good.

o   A **nonrival good** is one for which the consumption of that good does not affect its consumption by others.

o   **Nonexcludable** goods cannot be held back from those who desire access.

o   A **free rider** is one who attempts to benefit from a public good without paying for it.

o   The **Gini coefficient** uses the **Lorenz curve** to calculate income inequality.

o   The **poverty line** is the official benchmark for poverty; it is set at three times the minimum food budget as established by the Department of Agriculture.

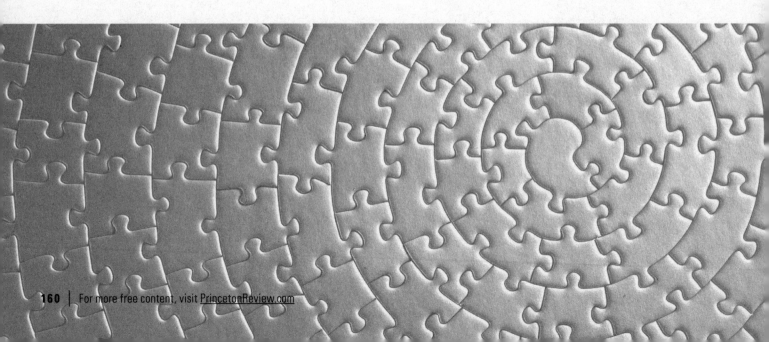

Chapter 9
Microeconomics
Review Questions:
Answers and
Explanations

CHAPTER 5 REVIEW QUESTIONS: ANSWERS AND EXPLANATIONS

1. **A** The question asks about demand, so eliminate any answer choices that focus on supply—eliminate (B), (D), and (E). The Fisher effect relates to monetary supply, so eliminate (C). The demand curve is downward sloping because each additional unit a consumer consumes gives that consumer less utility than the previous one; therefore, the consumer is willing to pay less for additional units, creating a downward sloping demand curve. The answer is (A).

2. **B** The question asks about supply, so eliminate (C) because it focuses on demand. Scale (including decreasing marginal costs) and scope refer to a particular firm, whereas the question asks about the aggregate supply of lawn-mowing services. Eliminate (A), (D), and (E). The supply curve is upward sloping because as the price of lawn-mowing services increases, more suppliers are willing to enter the market as their opportunity cost for supplying these services increases compared to their other economic opportunities. In other words, a physician will take the job of a dishwasher if the pay for washing dishes is higher than the pay for being a physician. The answer is (B).

3. **B** If the supply increases, then at any price point, the quantity of that good increases, and the supply curve shifts to the right. If the demand increases, then at every price point, the quantity demanded increases, and the demand curve shifts to the right (see the figure below). The combination of an increase in both supply and demand will result in an increase in quantity—eliminate (A) and (C). The change in equilibrium price depends on the relative size of the increase in demand and supply, as well as the relative elasticity of supply and demand. The answer is (B).

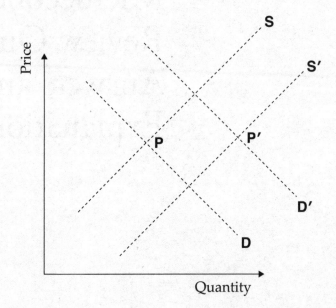

4. **A** When your choices include "None of the above," it is important to eliminate all other choices before settling on your answer. In this case, the change is from point M to point M′ in the figure below. This change necessarily results in a lower equilibrium price, but undetermined equilibrium quantity. Therefore the answer is (A).

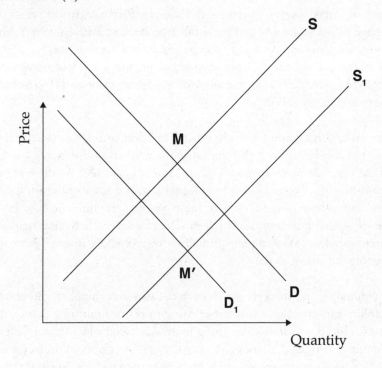

5. **C** According to the graph, Country A can produce 40 TVs or 30 DVD players (or some combination in the middle). Therefore 1 DVD player costs 1.3 TVs in Country A. Similarly, in Country B, 1 DVD player costs 2.0 TVs. Trade would benefit both countries—eliminate (A)—and the opportunity (relative) costs of DVD players to TVs in (D) and (E) don't match the calculations above—eliminate (D) and (E). As DVD players cost less in Country A compared to Country B, Country A has a comparative advantage in DVD players. Therefore the answer is (C).

6. **D** Choices (A), (B), (C), and (E) all refer to factors of production. The cost of the car designer's studio can be considered either land or capital. The car designer's time is labor, and the car designer's creativity can be considered either labor or entrepreneurship. Steel is capital, and rubber is a natural resource. (D) refers to opportunity cost, which is not a factor of production. Therefore, the correct answer is (D).

CHAPTER 6 REVIEW QUESTIONS: ANSWERS AND EXPLANATIONS

1. **E** The long-run average cost curve is always below the short-run average cost curve except at the cost-minimizing point for that short-run average cost curve. To the left of that point, the firm is using too much capital and fixed costs are too high. To the right of this point, the firm is using too little capital and diminishing returns to scale are causing costs to increase. See Figure 4 on page 82. Choices (A), (B), and (C) can be eliminated because the SRAC and LRAC curves will intersect at the quantity for which the amount of capital in question is the cost minimizing amount. Choice (D) can be eliminated because LRAC is below the SRAC due to lack of fixed costs in the long term. Therefore the answer is (E).

2. **B**   If a monopoly faces a straight downward-sloping demand curve, then the marginal revenue for a monopoly is halfway between the demand curve and the vertical axis. See Figure 10 on page 93. Therefore the answer is (B).

3. **D**   The marginal cost curve always intersects the average variable cost curve at its lowest point (see Figure 3 on page 80). Choice (A) can be eliminated because MC intersects MR to find the profit-maximizing quantity. Choices (B) and (E) can be eliminated because the AVC, by definition, represents an average of marginal costs and will not intersect at its minimum and maximum points. Choice (C) can be eliminated because AVC is a parabola with a positive slope and doesn't have a single maximum point. Therefore the answer is (D).

4. **B**   The best approach to this question is to use Process of Elimination. Consider that in oligopoly markets, there are a few (possibly large) firms that dominate the market, so eliminate (D). As perfect competition is reduced, these firms do make economic profit, so eliminate (A). As there are only a few firms that would most probably be subjected to antitrust legislation, and some of the antitrust legislation may have been developed in response to the actions of these oligopolies, eliminate (C). Typically in oligopolistic markets there are several buyers and few sellers. Therefore the sellers have market power, so eliminate (E). While interdependence is not a prerequisite for oligopolistic markets, it is a common feature of such markets. Therefore the answer is (B).

5. **A**   Consider that monopolistic markets are characterized by one supplier and several buyers. The seller thus has the ability to control prices by either fixing prices or limiting quantity. As the firm is limiting quantity to maximize its revenue, it is causing more deadweight loss than a firm ordinarily would in a perfectly competitive market. A monopoly is unlikely to lower prices if in fact it is likely to raise prices, so eliminate (B). A monopoly reduces supply by limiting production, so eliminate (C). A monopoly has only one firm, so eliminate (D). Quality of goods is not discussed, as economics assumes that the goods are identical and meet the minimum quality standards, so eliminate (E). Therefore the answer is (A).

6. **D**   With a question like this one, it is easier to work out the possible outcomes and compare them to the given choices. Let's first look at Company's A strategies: If Company B expands, then Company A does not expand. If Company B does not expand, then Company A does not expand. Therefore no matter what Company B does, Company A's strategy would be to not expand. And therefore Company A has a dominant strategy, so eliminate (B), (C) and (E).

Turning to Company B, if Company A were to expand, Company B would not want to expand. If Company A does not expand, Company B does not expand. Therefore no matter what Company A does, Company B has a dominant strategy of not expanding, so eliminate (A). As both companies have a dominant strategy, the answer is (D). (Note that as both companies benefit from not expanding, a Nash equilibrium also exists.)

7. **C**   As the firm is a price taker in the labor market, wages will not be affected, so eliminate (B) and (D). As marginal product of labor has increased (workers have become more productive), the marginal revenue product (amount earned by each worker) has also increased. This will cause the firm to hire more workers until the marginal cost of labor equals the marginal product of labor, so (A) can be eliminated. Therefore the answer is (C).

8. **D** A competitive firm's demand for labor is determined by that quantity when the marginal productivity of labor is equal to the marginal cost of labor (i.e., when the last worker produces just enough to cover his/her wages). Eliminate (B) because the question is framed in regard to the firm's demand for work, not the employee's willingness to work. Eliminate (C) and (E) because demand for labor is not restricted by physical products produced or the marginal utility and cost. Eliminate (A) because profits alone do not determine demand for labor. Therefore the answer is (D).

9. **B** If the third worker's MP = 10, then that worker generated income of 10 × $3 = $30. As the worker is paid $15, the firm is making economic profit. Therefore it should hire more workers until the productivity of the last worker just equals the revenue generated by that worker. Eliminate (C), (D) and (E). As more workers are hired (and no other investment in the business is made), each subsequent worker will generate lower and lower marginal revenue and MRP_L will decrease. Therefore the answer is (B).

10. **A** When a firm produces at a point where MR = MC, then it is maximizing its profits, which is to say that it is producing at the point at which its revenues most exceed its costs (see pages 88–89). Therefore the answer is (A).

11. **C** Price discrimination occurs when a company can charge different prices to different customers for essentially the same product with the goal of maximizing revenue. Therefore any company that can engage in price discrimination will earn higher revenues than those companies that do not. Therefore the answer is (C).

12. **E** To determine Company A's strategy, suppose Company B opts for a small budget. Company A would opt for a large budget. If Company B opts for a large budget, Company A would opt for a small budget. As Company A opts for either a small or large budget based on Company's B position, Company A does not have a dominant strategy, so eliminate (A), (B), (C) and (D). Let's look at Company B's strategy instead. If Company A opts for a small budget, Company B would opt for a small budget. If Company A were to opt for a large budget, Company B would choose the large budget as well. Therefore there isn't a dominant strategy for either company. Therefore the answer is (E).

13. **B** A monopoly produces less and sells for more than firms in perfect competition, so eliminate (A). As no short-run-versus-long-run data are given, eliminate (C) and (D). Cost data are not given so eliminate (E). Therefore the answer is (B).

14. **E** The quantity a monopoly supplies is determined by that quantity where MR = MC (point D). Therefore the quantity supplied would be G (see the following figure). The total revenue a monopoly receives is area P_2EGO. The cost is area PDGO, and the profit is P_2EDP. Therefore the answer is (E).

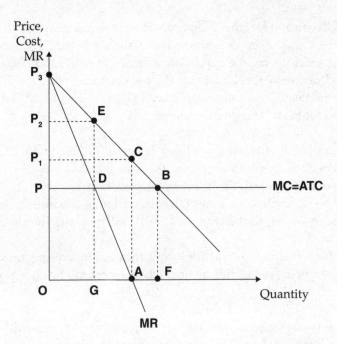

15. **E** For the same quantity, the supply price has increased. This means that the price of producing that good has increased. The answer that states an increase in production price is (E), so the correct answer is (E).

CHAPTER 7 REVIEW QUESTIONS: ANSWERS AND EXPLANATIONS

1. **B** Increase in demand refers to a shift in the demand curve. An increase in the demand for a good could be caused by an increase in real income (assuming that it is a normal good), a drop in price of a complimentary good, or a rise in price of a substitute. Eliminate (A) because a change in price would change the quantity demanded, not cause an overall shift in the curve. Eliminate (C) and (D) because they incorrectly define the effects of changes in compliments and substitutes. Eliminate (E) because a shift in the supply curve does not necessarily affect the demand curve. In this case, the best answer is (B).

2. **A** The question asks about total utility, which refers to consuming sardines. This question focuses on the demand for sardines, so answer choices that refer to supply (D) can be eliminated. As the question does not refer to demand and supply, any answer choices that need the supply and demand curves—(C) and (E)—can be eliminated. Similarly, utility is independent of cost, so (B) can be eliminated. To maximize the total utility of sardines, they need to be consumed until the marginal utility is equal to zero (regardless of the price). Therefore the answer is (A).

3. **D** The question gives data on the supply curve, so answer choices that refer to demand can be eliminated— eliminate (B) and (C). *Elasticity* = $\dfrac{\textit{Percent Change in Quantity}}{\textit{Percent Change in Price}}$ = $\dfrac{5}{3}$ = 1.7 > 1. As the elasticity of supply is greater than 1, the supply is elastic. Therefore the answer is (D).

4. **E** Normal goods are defined with respect to consumer income levels; therefore, answers that do not reference income—(A), (B), and (C)—can be eliminated. As income increases, the demand for a normal good increases. Therefore, the answer is (E).

5. **C** Cross-price elasticity refers to the demand of a good when the equilibrium price of another good changes. Choices (A), (B), and (E) can be eliminated as they are not functions of cross-price elasticity. A negative cross-price elasticity means that the demand of a good has decreased when the equilibrium price of another good increases. This means that the two goods are complements. For example, the quantity for rental skis decreases when ticket prices for ski resorts increases. The answer is (C).

6. **D** If the elasticity quotient of demand is less than 1, the demand is inelastic. Choices (A), (B), and (E) can be eliminated as they incorrectly define elasticity in terms of the demand price elasticity given in the question, 0.78. Because of the direct relationship between price and total revenue for inelastic goods, the firm should increase its price, as it will increase its revenue. The answer is (D).

7. **D** As the question makes no prediction of the utility derived from eating more than three slices of pizza, any answer that mentions consequences after the third slice or makes a non-economic judgment on pizza eating—(A), (B), and (C)—can be eliminated. Total utility increases with the consumption of each subsequent slice, as the marginal utility for the three slices is positive, so eliminate (E). The total utility is the sum of the utility received from consuming each slice. In this case it is 10 + 7 + 3 = 20. Therefore, the total utility from consuming three slices of pizza is 20 utils. The answer is (D).

8. **E** A monopsony occurs when there is only one buyer for a specific good (for example, a large company in a small town is virtually the only buyer of labor). As the buyer is interested in maximizing its own revenue, the net result is that wages are depressed and fewer workers are hired. Eliminate (C) and (D) because they incorrectly define changes in payment. Eliminate (A) and (B) because they incorrectly describe changes in the firm's hiring pattern. Therefore the answer is (E).

9. **C** Unions are interested in increasing their members' wages. They do this through collective bargaining, wage floors, featherbedding, increasing the demand for their goods (the "Buy American" campaign, for example), and other such tactics. One way to approach this question is through Process of Elimination (which is probably the most efficient way as the tactics listed are all union tactics). Another is to realize that decreasing the price of substitute resources makes those resources more attractive and therefore would hurt union wages. Therefore the answer is (C).

10. **A** A bilateral monopoly exists when a monopsony buys from a monopoly—i.e., there is only one seller and one buyer of a good or service. See page 135. Remember that "mono" in "monopoly" means "one," so (B) can be eliminated because it references two different buyers. Eliminate (D) and (E) because what is sold is irrelevant in determining a bilateral monopoly. Eliminate (A) because the term "monopsony" is specific to buyers. Therefore the answer is (A).

CHAPTER 8 REVIEW QUESTIONS: ANSWERS AND EXPLANATIONS

1. **D** Before trade, the price and quantity of cotton would be P and Q respectively (as shown in the figure below). As the world price is below the domestic equilibrium price, the domestic price would fall to P′ and the equilibrium quantity would rise to Q′. As domestic producers would not be able to produce the higher quantities at the lower price, the United States would become a net importer of cotton. The answer is (D).

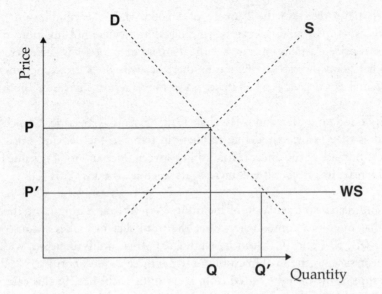

2. **A** The best approach is to draw the supply and demand for labor (see the figure below). As the minimum wage increases from W to W′, the wages rise, but the quantity of labor needed drops. Therefore, increasing the minimum wage would be beneficial for some workers (for those who are employed at the higher wage), but detrimental for others (those who were employed at the lower wage, but are no longer employed). The answer is (A).

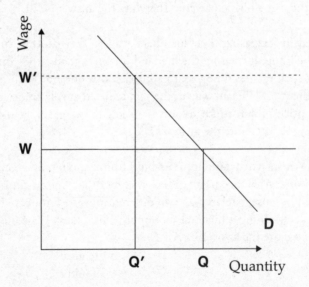

3. **C** Extracting proportionally more tax income from the poor is by definition a regressive tax (see page 156). Therefore the answer is (C).

4. **E** As the question does not give any information on the profits the monopoly is making, one cannot comment on them, so eliminate (A), (B) and (C). Regulating a monopoly to allocative efficiency is a measure designed to reduce deadweight loss. Therefore the answer is (E).

5. **C** As the demand curve does not change, answers focusing on demand—(A) and (B)—can be eliminated. A subsidy increases supply, so eliminate (E). Consumer surplus is the area under the demand curve between the equilibrium price and the vertical axis (see the following figure). The consumer surplus before the subsidy is shown by region A, and after the subsidy, consumer surplus increases to include regions B and C. Therefore the answer is (C).

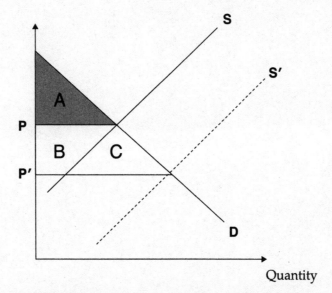

6. **A** The best way to approach this question is to draw the supply and demand curves (see the following figure). Remember that a price ceiling sets a maximum price a producer may charge. Since the price ceiling (PC) is above the equilibrium price, the equilibrium price and quantity do not change as a result of the price ceiling. Therefore the answer is (A).

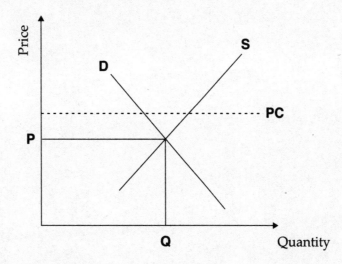

7. **E** The side with the more relative inelasticity would bear the greater tax burden. If consumers are to bear the majority of the tax burden, then the demand curve should be inelastic and the supply curve should be elastic. Therefore the answer is (E).

Review of
Macroeconomics
Concepts

Chapter 10
Basic
Macroeconomics
Concepts

Economics is the study of how to allocate scarce resources among competing ends. **Macroeconomics** is the branch of economics that deals with the whole economy and issues that affect most of society. These issues include inflation, unemployment, gross domestic product, national income, interest rates, exchange rates, and so on. **Microeconomics** is the branch of economics that looks at decision making at the firm, household, and individual levels and studies behavior in markets for particular goods and services. For example, it models a firm's decision of how much to produce and what price to charge for its goods or services.

The concepts of scarcity, opportunity costs, production possibilities, specialization and comparative advantage, functions of an economic system, demand, supply, and price determination are important to both microeconomic and macroeconomic analysis. Because there is overlap, these concepts are covered only once, in the section on microeconomics.

MEASUREMENT OF ECONOMIC PERFORMANCE

Gross Domestic Product, National Income, and Net Domestic Product

A country's annual **Gross Domestic Product** (GDP) is the total value of all final goods and services produced in a year within that country. The expression "*final goods and services*" indicates that to avoid double counting, GDP does not include the value of intermediate goods like lumber and steel that go into the production of other goods like homes and cars, or the repurchase of used goods, which were included in GDP in the year in which they were first produced. Also excluded from the calculation of GDP are financial transactions such as the buying and selling of stocks and bonds, since there is no productive activity associated with them to measure. Public and private transfer payments also are not considered in GDP, nor are underground economic activities (both legal and illegal) and home production. The media is prone to use changes in GDP as indicators of societal well-being. Although an increase in this measure might reflect an increase in the standard of living, GDP also increases with expenditures on natural disasters, deadly epidemics, war, crime, and other detriments to society. Unless "bads" such as these are subtracted, be cautious in interpreting changes in GDP.

National income (NI) is the sum of income earned by the factors of production owned by a country's citizens. It includes wages, salaries, and fringe benefits paid for labor services, rent paid for the use of land and buildings, interest paid for the use of money, and profits received for the use of capital resources. **Personal income** (PI) is the money income received by households before personal income taxes are subtracted, and **disposable income** (DI) is personal income minus personal income taxes.

Be Careful!

Some textbooks ignore the intermediate step of personal income and just mention national income and disposable income. If the intermediate step is not used, then you would have to deduct taxes and add back in government transfers to go from national income to disposable income.

There are two primary methods for calculating GDP—the expenditure approach and the income approach. The **expenditure approach** adds up spending by households, firms, the government, and the rest of the world using the following formula:

$$GDP = C + I + G + (X - M)$$

Here **C** represents personal consumption expenditures by households, such as purchases of durable and nondurable goods and services. **I** represents investment in new physical capital, new construction (both commercial and residential), and additions to business inventories. **G** represents government purchases, **X** represents exports, and **M** represents imports.

The **income approach** makes use of the fact that expenditures on GDP ultimately become income. National income can thus be modified slightly to arrive at GDP. To begin with, depreciation must be added to national income. **Depreciation** is the decline in the value of capital over time due to wear or obsolescence. Depreciation expenses are subtracted from corporate profits before the NI calculation, so they must be re-added to capture the value of output needed to replace or repair worn-out buildings and machinery. **Subsidy payments** made by the government to farmers (for example) are part of the farmers' income but are not made in exchange for goods or services, so they are not part of GDP. Thus, they must be subtracted from NI to find GDP.

Finally, we must add the income of foreign workers in the country whose GDP is being calculated, and we also must subtract the income of citizens working abroad. This addition of the **net income of foreign workers** accounts for the fact that NI includes the income of all citizens everywhere, whereas GDP includes the value of goods produced domestically by anyone. If George Lucas makes a film in France, his income will be part of the U.S. national income because he is a U.S. citizen, but his foreign-made film is part of France's GDP. We must subtract his income from NI when calculating the U.S. GDP. The opposite is true for citizens of France, for example, who produce in the United States. In summary

$$GDP = NI + Depreciation - Subsidies + Net\ income\ of\ foreigners$$

Net domestic product is GDP minus depreciation. This indicates how much output is left over for consumption and additions to the capital stock after replacing the capital used up in the production process.

Inflation and Price Indices

Inflation is a sustained increase in the overall price level. An increase in the price of one good is not necessarily inflation, although it might be part of a broader increase in the general price level that would constitute inflation. The opposite of inflation—a sustained decrease in the general price level—is called **deflation**. If all prices, wages, salaries, rents, and so forth increase by the same percentage, the real effects of inflation might be minimal. For example, suppose Ted's salary is $10 per day and he uses it to buy a pizza for $6 and two mochas for $2 each.

With inflation at the rate of 100 percent per day, all prices and salaries are doubled by the next day. Ted earns $20, pizzas cost $12 and mochas cost $4. In economic terms, Ted's **nominal salary** (the actual number of dollars) has increased, but his **real salary** (the purchasing power of the dollars) has remained the same. There should be no real effect because Ted can still purchase exactly what he did before with his salary—one pizza and two mochas. If Ted notes the increase in his salary but does not notice the similar increase in all prices, he might think he is better off. This is called **money illusion,** and can lead to excessive spending. Other detrimental effects of inflation include the following:

- Stores must change price listings on signs, shelves, computers, and wherever else they are recorded to keep up with inflation. The costs of such changes are called **menu costs,** a name that originated with the classic example of restaurants having to print new menus after price changes.

- Fixed incomes and incomes that increase at a rate less than the inflation rate decrease in value, imposing a burden on the recipients.

- The value of interest payments that do not increase in step with inflation decreases, hurting lenders and savers.

- Social tensions tend to increase with inflation, in part due to the uncertainty and redistribution of income that it entails.

- Increased shoe leather costs are the cost of time and effort that people spend trying to counteract the effects of inflation. Examples of this include holding less cash on hand and having to make frequent trips to the ATM.

- The unit of account (the standard monetary unit of measurement of value/costs of goods, services assets) is unstable because of inflation.

There are also benefits from inflation. Those who borrowed money at fixed interest rates pay back amounts that are worth less in real terms due to inflation. Suppose the interest rate on Stephanie's $100 loan is fixed at five percent, meaning that she makes a nominal interest payment of $5 per year. If the price of apples is $1 this year, the real purchasing power of her interest payment is five apples. If inflation takes the price of apples up to $1.25, the real value of her interest payment decreases to the equivalent of four apples.

Price indexes are used to measure inflation and adjust nominal values for inflation to find real values. The **Consumer Price Index** (CPI) is the government's gauge of inflation. It is used, for example, to adjust tax brackets and social security payments for inflation. To find it, the Bureau of Labor Statistics checks the prices of items in a fixed representative "market basket" of thousands of goods and services used by typical consumers in a base year.

The CPI is calculated as

$$CPI = \frac{\text{Cost of base year market basket at current prices}}{\text{Cost of base year market basket at base year prices}} \times 100$$

The inflation between years Y and Z (Z being the more recent year) can be calculated using the following formula:

$$\text{Inflation between years Y and Z} = \left[\frac{\text{CPI in Year Z}}{\text{CPI in Year Y}} - 1 \right] \times 100$$

And any year's nominal GDP (or any other nominal figure) can be converted into real base year dollars using the following formula:

$$\text{Real GDP} = \frac{\text{Nominal GDP}}{\text{CPI for the same year as the nominal figure}} \times 100$$

The CPI may overestimate the inflation rate, primarily due to its inflexible dependency on the base year market basket. If the price of concert tickets goes up considerably, you might substitute movies for concerts. Because the CPI relies on a fixed market basket, such substitutions for less expensive goods and services are not accounted for in its measure of inflation. Quality improvements and price changes in new products that were not in the base year basket are also excluded from CPI inflation estimates.

The **Producer Price Index** (PPI) is similar in calculation to the CPI, but it applies to the prices of wholesale goods such as lumber and steel. The PPI is sometimes a good predictor of future inflation because producers often pass their cost increases on to consumers.

The **Gross Domestic Product Deflator** is an alternative general price index that reflects the importance of products in current market baskets, rather than in base year market baskets, which become less relevant over time. Its formula is

$$\text{GDP Deflator} = \frac{\text{Cost of current year market basket at current prices}}{\text{Cost of current year market basket at base year prices}} \times 100$$

This formula differs from the CPI calculation in that current year quantities are used. The value of the GDP Deflator can be substituted for CPI values in the formulas for inflation and real GDP above. Because the GDP Deflator reflects both price changes and substitutions away from goods that have become relatively expensive, it generally registers a lower inflation rate than the CPI.

The primary causes of inflation are discussed in the section on aggregate demand.

Unemployment

The **labor force** includes employed and unemployed adults. To be considered **unemployed**, a labor force participant must be willing and able to work, and must have made an effort to seek work in the past four weeks. The **labor force participation rate** is the number of people in the labor force divided by the working-age population. The **unemployment rate** is the number of unemployed workers divided by the number in the labor force, then multiplied by 100 to get the percent. The various categories of unemployment are defined below.

- **Frictional unemployment** occurs as unemployed workers and firms search for the best available worker-job matches. Included in this category are new labor force entrants looking for their first jobs and workers who are temporarily between jobs because they are moving to a new location or occupation in which they will be more productive.

- **Structural unemployment** is the result of a skills mismatch. As voice recognition software is perfected, skilled typists may find themselves out of work. The same was true for blacksmiths skilled at making horseshoes after the advent of the automobile made horse-drawn buggies obsolete. Poorly educated people may find themselves structurally unemployed because they lack marketable skills.

- **Cyclical unemployment** results from downturns in the business cycle. During recessions and depressions, firms are likely to hire fewer workers or let existing workers go. When the economy recovers, many of these cyclically unemployed workers will again find work.

- **Seasonal unemployment** is the result of changes in hiring patterns due to the time of year. Ski instructors and lifeguards are the classic examples of workers who lose their jobs because of the season.

Discouraged workers are those who are willing and able to work, but become so frustrated in their attempts to find work that they stop trying. Because they are not making an effort to find a job at least once every four weeks, discouraged workers are not counted among the unemployed in official statistics, and are a reason why the unemployment rates might understate the true unemployment problem. On the other hand, **dishonest workers** bias the unemployment figures upward. These individuals claim to be unemployed in order to receive unemployment benefits when, in fact, they do not want a job or are working for cash in an unreported job.

The **natural rate of unemployment**, about 5 percent in the United States, is the typical rate of unemployment in a normally functioning economy and is often thought of as the sum of frictional and structural unemployment. **Full employment** is *not* 100 percent employment, but the level of employment that corresponds with the natural rate of unemployment. With full employment there is no cyclical unemployment.

Some unemployment can be a good thing. Frictional unemployment often allows workers to move into new jobs that are more satisfying for both the worker and the employer than a previous matching. But high rates of unemployment can be devastating, leading to personal loss of self-confidence, crime, the breakup of families,

Employ This Tip to Remember Unemployment

You can remember the categories of unemployment using the following irreverent initialism:

Fire–Frictional

Some–Structural

Cut–Cyclical

Some–Seasonal

and suicide. There are also losses to output and income. Economists, including the late Arthur Okun, have estimated that for every one percentage point increase in the unemployment rate above the natural rate, output falls by 2 to 3 percentage points. This is called **Okun's law.**

NATIONAL INCOME AND PRICE DETERMINATION

Aggregate Supply

The **aggregate supply** (AS) curve indicates the total value of output that producers are willing and able to supply at alternative price levels in a given time period, holding other influences constant. Aggregate supply lives on the same graph as **aggregate demand** (AD), which is total demand for goods and services in the economy. Do not confuse the aggregate supply curve and the firm supply curve. The vertical axis of the aggregate supply curve measures the price level, not the price, of any particular good. Think of the **price level** as the average level of all prices—essentially what a price index like the CPI or the GDP Deflator measures. The horizontal axis measures the real value of all goods and services produced domestically in a given period—real GDP. Remember from above that expenditures on output (GDP) ultimately become income (NI), so the horizontal axis can be considered a measure of national output and income. Because it is the *real* value of GDP, it changes only when the quantity of goods and services produced changes, and not when only the price level changes.

It is important to remember that while aggregate supply and demand curves appear and behave in similar ways to individual market supply and demand curves, they illustrate fundamentally different relationships in the economy.

- When graphing individual markets, the *y* axis represents the price of an individual good or service in the market.

- When graphing aggregate markets, the *y* axis represents the price level, a quantity that considers the collective value goods and services produced by one nation, usually in an international marketplace.

- When graphing individual markets, the *x* axis represent the quantity of a specific good or service.

- When graphing aggregate markets, the *x* axis represents the real GDP.

Figure 1 illustrates a typical **short-run aggregate supply** curve (labeled AS). It has a flat depression range (sometimes called the "Keynesian stage"), a positively sloped intermediate range, and a vertical physical limit (sometimes called the "Classical stage").

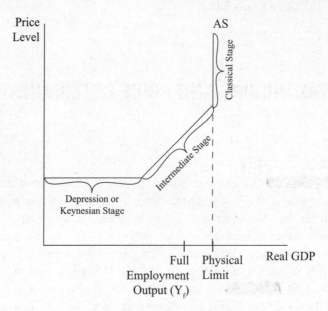

Figure 1: Aggregate Supply

During a depression, firms have large inventories and excess capacity and would be glad to sell more output at the existing price level. Likewise, workers and other factors of production are plentiful and the economy can increase its output without placing upward pressure on prices or wages. This results in the horizontal segment of the aggregate supply curve. In other words, during a depression, changes in aggregate demand affect real GDP but not the price level.

The economy normally operates in the intermediate range of the AS curve, which is why many diagrams illustrate only this positively sloped segment of the curve. At these intermediate levels of output, there are no excessive inventories, and firms are closer to their productive capacities. Expansions in output require firms to hire additional inputs and work their plants and equipment at a faster pace, actions that require a profit incentive. While firms demand higher prices for increased output, wages and other input prices are relatively slow to adjust due to long-term contracts. If output prices increase faster than input prices, real factor prices (the buying power of payments to factors of production) decrease and the profit per unit of output increases. This gives firms the incentive they need to increase employment and produce more goods and services. Of course, the opposite of the above analysis is true for decreases in the price level and output. So changes in aggregate demand affect both price level and GDP in the intermediate range of the AS curve.

A change in the price level can also cause firms to produce more or less as the result of short-run misperceptions. If a firm sees the price of its product going up and does not realize that all prices are increasing at the same time, the firm might think that the relative value of its good has increased and be fooled into producing more.

As the economy reaches full employment, it becomes more difficult for firms to find new workers at the existing wage rate, and firms must increase wages (among other factor prices) in order to hire more inputs and increase output. The price level required to induce additional output then escalates until the economy reaches its physical limit for output. When factories cannot run any faster and workers cannot work any more overtime, the short-run AS cannot increase any more, and increases in aggregate demand simply increase the price level.

The AS curve shifts in response to changes in input prices and availability, technology, public policy, and other macro disturbances.

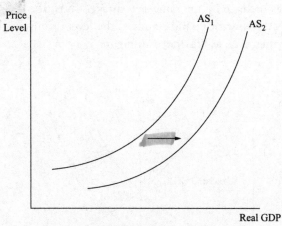

Figure 2: Shifting Aggregate Supply

More specifically, the AS will shift to the right, as in Figure 2, when

- Inputs become cheaper, more productive, or more plentiful, as with
    - New discoveries of raw materials
    - Increases in the labor supply
    - Decreases in wages or other input prices
    - Improvements in education or training
    - Decreased inflationary expectations
    - Increased investment (more capital)
    - Technological advances
    - Predictable or beneficial weather conditions

- Government policies reduce production costs, as with
    - Tax cuts
    - Deregulation
    - Reform in welfare or unemployment insurance programs

- Macro disturbances, such as wars and natural disasters, cease

The *opposite* of each of the above influences would cause the short-run AS curve to shift to the *left*.

Long-Run Aggregate Supply

In the long run, wages and other input prices will adjust in accordance with output prices, and vice versa. This eliminates the incentive to produce more or less output at higher or lower price levels, because the purchasing power of per-unit profits has not changed. For example, suppose a firm sells phones for $100 each, has production costs of $60 per phone, and uses its $40 in profits per phone to buy two $20 CDs. If all prices and production costs increase by 10 percent, this firm will sell its phones for $110, spend $66 per phone on production, and make $44 in profits with which it can buy two $22 CDs. There is no reason to produce more just because all values increase by the same percentage. Thus, the **long-run aggregate supply curve** (LAS) is vertical, and stands at the level of output that corresponds with full employment, Y_f, as illustrated in Figure 3.

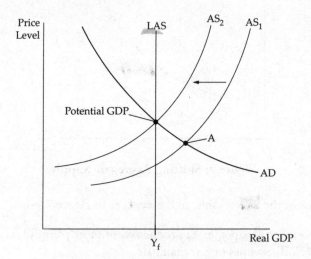

Figure 3: Long-Run Aggregate Supply

The LAS curve is located at Y_f because at real GDP levels greater than Y_f there is no cyclical unemployment and increases in output place upward pressure on wages and other input prices. In Figure 3, consider an economy operating at point A, the short-run equilibrium of aggregate supply (AS_1) and aggregate demand (described in detail in the next chapter). Because real GDP exceeds Y_f, upward pressure on input prices will shift the short-run AS curve to the left until it resembles AS_2 and equilibrium real GDP equals Y_f. Likewise at output levels less than Y_f, excess capacity and unemployment lead to decreases in wages and other input prices that shift the short-run AS curve to the right until real GDP again equals Y_f.

The LAS curve and Y_f will shift to the right as the result of improved skill levels due to education and training, increased capital levels thanks to investment in previous periods, improved technology resulting from research and development, or increased resource availability due to new discoveries or population increases.

Classical Analysis

Classical economists theorize that wages, prices, and interest rates fluctuate quickly, clearing (bringing to equilibrium) labor and capital markets, and allowing input and output prices to stay in line with each other. Classical economists also believe in **Say's law**—the idea that supply creates its own demand. In other words, when supplying goods, workers earn money to spend or save, and savings end up being borrowed and spent on business investments. There should be no problem finding demand for the goods and services produced, because the income from making them will be spent purchasing them. This supports the classical contention that the government does not need to concern itself with policies that maintain demand at a desirable level.

Critics of Say's law argue that savings might not equal investment, because the interest rate does not fluctuate freely enough to clear the capital market (see Figure 4).

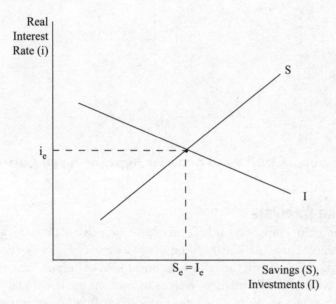

Figure 4: The Capital Market

John Maynard Keynes (see next page) argued that investment demand depends more on expectations about the prosperity of the economy than on interest rates. If savings exceed investment, some of the nation's real GDP will not be purchased and firm inventories will expand, resulting in layoffs and subsequent production below full employment output. Likewise, if savings are less than investment, expenditures will exceed real GDP and firm inventories will deplete, resulting in inflation and production beyond full employment output.

The general description of the long-run aggregate supply curve above explains that real GDP rests at Y_f in the long run after wage adjustments have had a chance to catch up with price adjustments. If wages can adjust quickly, as classical theory suggests, they will remain in line with prices, and changes in the price level will not result in changes in real GDP even in the short run. The assumption of flexible wages thus corresponds with a vertical aggregate supply curve as in the left side of Figure 5. One result of a vertical AS is that increases in aggregate demand (due to expansionary policy or otherwise) will increase the price level while having no effect on real GDP.

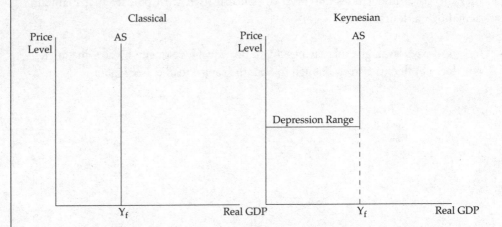

Figure 5: Classical and Keynesian Aggregate Supply Curves

Keynesian Analysis

British economist John Maynard Keynes had a somewhat different view of the aggregate supply curve. As illustrated on the right side of Figure 5, the Keynesian AS curve is horizontal until the full-employment level of output, where it becomes vertical, as classical theory predicts. Keynes focused on the horizontal "depression range" of AS where excess capacity and unemployment allow increases in output and income without forcing the price level to increase.

Keynes blamed the existence of unemployment and the inability of the economy to self-adjust to full-employment output largely on "sticky" wages, particularly in the downward direction. Keynesians argue that wage contracts are typically adjusted no more than once a year, and such influences as unions, tradition, and a reluctance to threaten company morale effectively prohibit decreases in wages. If wages cannot adjust to match changes in price levels, deviations from full employment output might persist until the government steps in with monetary or fiscal policy (explained in Chapter 12) to bolster or tame the economy. This is in contrast with the classical economists' preference for laissez-faire (hands-off) governmental policy.

Rational Expectations

The theory of **rational expectations** suggests that people learn to anticipate government policies designed to influence the economy, thereby making the policies ineffectual. With an understanding of the true sources of inflation, and using all available information, workers and consumers respond quickly to policies unless they are somehow caught off guard or fooled. For example, if the government predictably attempts to boost real GDP by increasing the money supply or government spending (and thus aggregate demand) as in Figure 6, people will anticipate the resulting inflation and build it into their wage and price demands.

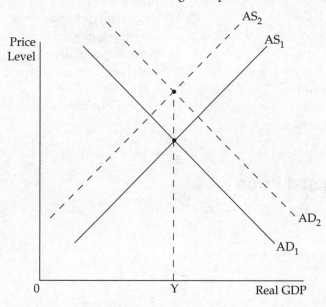

Figure 6

The increased wages will shift AS back from AS_1 to AS_2 and the government policy will have no real effect on output or income. In concert with the classical theory discussed above, the rational expectations theory assumes that wages, prices, and interest rates adjust quickly to keep real GDP at the full-employment level. Unemployment is seen as a temporary result of random shocks, because on average, wages and prices are set at the levels that equate supply and demand in both the goods and labor markets. The bottom line of the rational expectations theory is that government intervention is not necessary or useful for stabilizing the economy.

KEY TERMS

Measurement of Economic Performance
Gross Domestic Product
national income
personal income
disposable income
expenditure approach
income approach
depreciation
subsidy payments
net foreign income
net domestic product

Inflation and Price Indices
inflation
deflation
nominal salary
real salary
money illusion
menu cost
Consumer Price Index
Producer Price Index
Gross Domestic Product Deflator

Unemployment
labor force
unemployed
labor force participation rate
unemployment rate
frictional unemployment
structural unemployment
cyclical unemployment
seasonal unemployment
discouraged worker
dishonest worker
natural rate of unemployment
full employment
Okun's law

National Income and Price Determination
aggregate supply
aggregate demand
price level
short-run aggregate supply
long-run aggregate supply
classical economists
Say's law
Keynesian analysis
rational expectations

CHAPTER 10 REVIEW QUESTIONS

See Chapter 14 for answers and explanations.

1. Gross Domestic Product is a close approximation of

   (A) national income
   (B) societal welfare
   (C) the consumer price index
   (D) the GDP deflator
   (E) the current account balance

2. The government measures inflation using the

   (A) GNP
   (B) URL
   (C) CPI
   (D) FED
   (E) GDP

3. If global warming raises temperatures so high that snow can never again exist anywhere, snow ski instructors will experience which type of unemployment?

   (A) Structural
   (B) Frictional
   (C) Seasonal
   (D) Institutional
   (E) Cyclical

4. Long-run aggregate supply is most likely to increase as the result of

   (A) an increase in the real interest rate
   (B) increased investment in capital
   (C) an increase in aggregate demand
   (D) an increase in the unemployment rate
   (E) an increase in the exchange rate

Goods	Quantity	Year 1 price per unit	Year 2 price per unit
Pizza	5	$12.00	$11.00
Soda	10	$2.00	$1.25
Napkins	100	$.05	$.15

5. The diagram above shows data about the change in prices for a variety of goods. What happened to the CPI for this consumer from year 1 to year 2?

   (A) It rose by 3%.
   (B) It fell by 3%.
   (C) It fell by one-third.
   (D) It rose by one-third.
   (E) It remained unchanged.

6. Which of the following would be classified under C when calculating GDP?

   (A) A homeowner mowing her own lawn
   (B) $50.00 spent eating out at a restaurant
   (C) The purchase of new computer software by an accounting firm
   (D) Flour purchased by a baker to make donuts
   (E) Donating old clothing to charitable causes

7. Which transactions will NOT be counted in GDP?

   (A) Pirated DVDs entering the nation illegally
   (B) The services of a physician
   (C) A retiree's social security benefits
   (D) A and C
   (E) B and C

Chapter 10 Summary

Measurement of Economic Performance

o   A country's annual **Gross Domestic Product** (GDP) is the total value of all final goods and services produced in a year within that country. GDP is calculated using either the **expenditure approach** or the **income approach**.

o   **National income** (NI) is the sum of income earned by the factors of production owned by a country's citizens.

o   **Personal income** (PI) is the money income received by households before personal income taxes are subtracted, and **disposable income** (DI) is personal income minus personal income taxes.

o   **Depreciation** is the decline in the value of capital over time due to wear or obsolescence.

o   **Inflation** is a sustained increase in the overall price level. **Deflation** is a sustained decrease in the overall price level.

o   One's **nominal** salary is the actual number of dollars that person earns; one's real salary is the purchasing power of those dollars.

o   The **Consumer Price Index** (CPI) is the government's gauge of inflation.

o   Calculate CPI using the following formula:

$$\text{Inflation between years Y and Z} = \left[\frac{\text{CPI in Year Z}}{\text{CPI in Year Y}} - 1 \right] \times 100$$

o   The **Producer Price Index** (PPI) measures changes in the prices of wholesale goods such as lumber and steel.

o   The **Gross Domestic Product Deflator** is an alternative general price index that reflects the importance of products in current market baskets, rather than in base year market baskets, which become less relevant over time.

o The **labor force** includes employed and unemployed adults. To be **unemployed**, a labor force participant must be willing and able to work, and must have made an effort to seek work in the past four weeks.

o The **labor force participation rate** is the number of people in the labor force divided by the working-age population.

o **Discouraged workers** are those who are willing and able to work, but become so frustrated in their attempts to find work that they stop trying; **dishonest workers** claim to be unemployed to receive benefits, but are able to work or working for cash in an unreported job.

o **Full employment** is the level of unemployment that corresponds with the natural rate of unemployment (about 5% in the United States).

o **Okun's Law** states that for every one percentage point increase in the unemployment rate above the natural rate, output falls by 2 to 3 percentage points.

National Income and Price Determination

o The **aggregate supply** (AS) curve indicates the total value of output that producers are willing and able to supply at alternative price levels in a given time period, holding other influences constant.

o **Aggregate demand** (AD) is the total demand for goods and services in the economy.

o The **price level** is the average level of all prices.

o The **long-run aggregate supply curve** (LAS) is vertical and stands at the level of output that corresponds with full employment.

o **Say's law** is the idea that supply creates its own demand.

o British economist John Maynard Keynes theorized a flat AS curve in the depression range and argued that wages cannot adjust to match changes in prices levels. Further, he argued that deviations from full employment output might persist until the government steps in with monetary or fiscal policy.

o The theory of **rational expectations** suggests that people learn to anticipate government policies designed to influence the economy, thereby making the policies ineffectual.

Chapter 11
Aggregate Demand

CIRCULAR FLOW

It is useful to visualize the flow of resources through the economy with a diagram such as Figure 1.

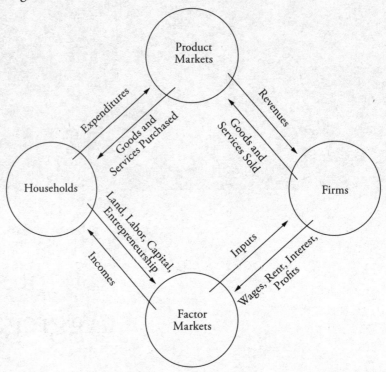

Figure 1

> Questions regarding figures such as Figure 1 have shown up on past AP exams, so be sure to take the time to study and draw the circular flow diagram yourself.

Goods flow from firms to households through the product markets, and inputs flow from households to firms through the factor markets. This simplified model highlights the interdependence between firms and households and the equality of aggregate income and expenditure. If the payments from firms to households for inputs differ from the payments from households to firms for goods and services, the owners of the firms experience profits or losses. Because the firm owners themselves represent households, the full value of expenditures, including any profits or losses, ends up as household income. As for GDP, whether production is valued at what is paid for it or what is paid to produce it doesn't matter because of the equality of **aggregate income** and **aggregate expenditure**.

Aggregate income = Aggregate expenditure = GDP

These equalities hold even when the government and international transactions are included in the model, as discussed on the following page.

Before we move on, let's get even broader and look at a larger circular-flow diagram to see how money flows throughout the economy at large:

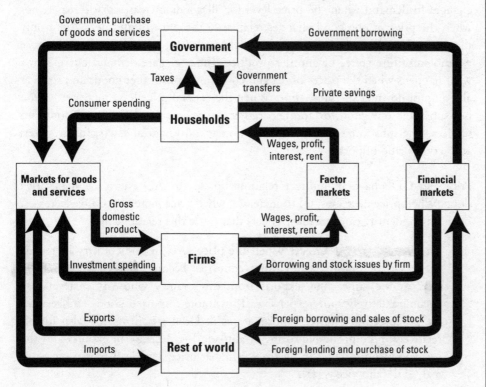

Model 1: Expanded Circular-Flow Diagram

COMPONENTS OF AGGREGATE DEMAND

Aggregate demand is the total demand for goods and services in the economy. Economists are interested in aggregate demand (AD) because, in the same way the market demand curve illustrates microeconomic patterns, the AD curve illustrates macroeconomic patterns such as inflation, unemployment, or the relative value of national currencies. The curve as depicted in Figure 2 is the relationship between real GDP and the price level.

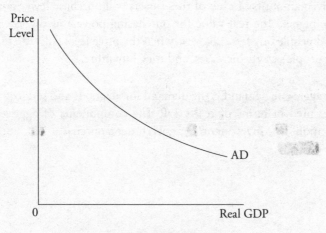

Figure 2: Aggregate Demand

It is not a simple aggregation of individual demand curves for particular goods, and it is not a market demand curve. The difference is that the AD curve reflects changes in demand when the price level for all goods increases or decreases, not when the price of one good changes relative to the price of another. When only the price of tea goes up, it is clear that the demand for tea will go down because we can substitute coffee or another product. The aggregate demand curve shows what happens when the prices of tea and coffee and most other goods and services all go up or down at the same time. When the general price level increases, we do not substitute one good for another; rather, we as a nation buy fewer goods and services. The substitutes in this case are money and financial assets, future goods and services, and imports.

Price and GDP have an indirect relationship, so the AD curve has a negative slope. When price decreases, GDP increases; when price increases, GDP decreases. Economists identify three primary effects that cause this relationship.

- **The Foreign Trade Effect:** When the price level in one country increases, the prices of imports from other countries become relatively less expensive. At the same time, exports from the country whose price level rose become relatively more expensive. Thus, more imported goods and services are purchased and fewer exports are sold. Domestic firms will also find it relatively more profitable to invest abroad. The decrease in exports and the increase in imports resulting from a higher price level lead to a decrease in real GDP (and vice versa).

- **The Interest Rate Effect:** When the price level increases, the real quantity of money (its purchasing power) decreases. People need more money even to continue their current consumption levels. This increases the demand for money in the form of loans, and decreases the supply of loanable funds. To reach equilibrium in the money market, the interest rate (which is effectively the price of money) must increase. The higher interest rate leads to a decrease in real GDP as households and firms put off major purchases and investment until future periods when the interest rate might be lower. Likewise, a decrease in the price level decreases interest rates and increases real GDP.

- **The Real Wealth Effect (or Real Balances Effect):** When the price level increases, the value of assets such as cash and checking-account balances falls. Given amounts of each of these assets will purchase fewer goods when prices are higher. The real value (or purchasing power) of the assets thus declines, and people buy less. Likewise when the price level falls, the purchasing power of people's assets increases, and they buy more.

Because aggregate demand is the demand for all goods and services in the economy, it is measured in terms of real GDP. The components of aggregate demand are consumption (C), investment (I), government purchases (G), and exports minus imports (X – M).

A Memorable Relationship

You can remember the effects that cause the indirect relationship between price and GDP using the following uplifting acronym:

Friends—Foreign Trade Effect

Inspire—Interest Rate Effect

Relationships—Real Wealth Effect

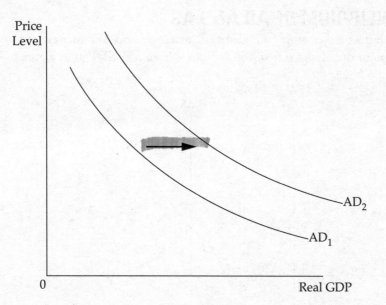

Figure 3: Shifting Aggregate Demand

The AD curve will shift to the right, as in Figure 3, when the following changes occur for reasons other than a change in the price level:

- Consumption increases due to
  - Expectations of inflation or shortages in the future
  - Increased incomes or wealth
  - Optimism about jobs and income

- Investment increases due to
  - Interest rates dropping
  - Investors gaining optimism

- Government carries out expansionary policy such as a(n)
  - Increase in spending
  - Increase in the money supply
  - Decrease in taxes

- Net exports increase because
  - The exchange rate decreases (imports decrease)
  - Foreign income increases (exports increase)

Of course, the opposite of each of these effects would shift the AD curve to the left.

EQUILIBRIUM OF AD AND AS

As with the market supply and demand curves, AS and AD intersect at an equilibrium point that designates an equilibrium level of real GDP as in Figure 4.

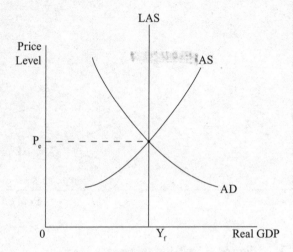

Figure 4: Long-Run Equilibrium

When the price level is above equilibrium, surpluses lead to a decrease in the price level. When the price level is below equilibrium, shortages bring increases in the price level. Because aggregate supply is vertical at full-employment output in the long run (or sooner, according to classical theory), the long-run equilibrium will occur at full-employment output regardless of the position of AD. Note that when AD intersects AS but not on the LRAS, you have only short-term equilibrium.

The behavior of AS and AD determines both real GDP and the price level, and studying AS and AD can give economists more information about inflation. Inflation can result from decreases in AS or increases in AD. When prices rise due to an increase in the costs of the factors of production, this is called **cost-push** or **supply-side inflation**. Graphically, this is illustrated by shifting the AS curve to the left.

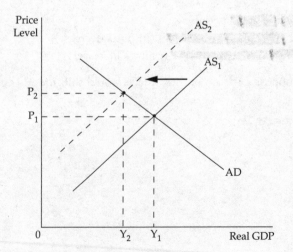

Figure 5: Cost-Push Inflation

Notice that this inflation is accompanied by a decrease in real GDP. **Stagflation** occurs when inflation is concurrent with relatively high unemployment and a reduction in GDP. **Demand pull inflation** is the result of the AD curve shifting out to the right relative to the AS curve for any of the reasons explained earlier in this section. Inflation that remains steady for a long period at a low rate is sometimes called **creeping inflation**. Unsteady inflation that exceeds 10 percent per year and grows month after month is sometimes called **galloping inflation**. Very rapid price increases in excess of 50 percent per year are sometimes called **hyperinflation**.

The Multiplier

Common economic problems can occur when equilibrium between AS and AD occurs above or below LAS.

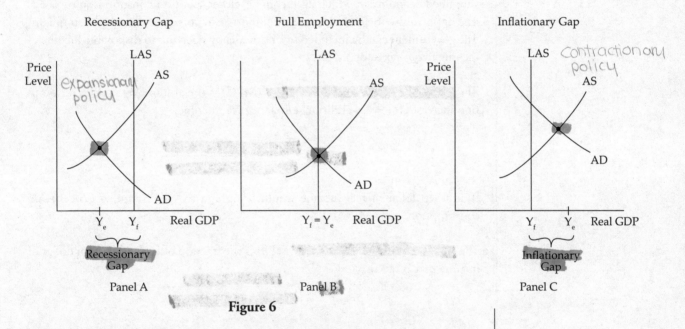

Figure 6

In Panel A of Figure 6, the equilibrium real GDP level, Y_e, is below the full employment output level, Y_f. When $Y_e < Y_f$, a **recessionary gap** exists as the amount by which equilibrium real GDP would have to increase to reach Y_f. In Panel B, equilibrium occurs at Y_f. This is a long-run equilibrium that can persist without recession or inflation, because there is no cyclical unemployment (see explanation on previous page) and no need to raise wages and overextend the labor force as would be necessary to produce beyond Y_f. In Panel C, equilibrium occurs at a real GDP level above Y_f. When $Y_e > Y_f$, an **inflationary gap** exists as the amount by which equilibrium real GDP would have to decrease to reach Y_f.

Classical theory suggests that when a recessionary gap exists, the surplus of workers and other inputs will cause wages and other input prices to fall, thus shifting AS to the right, lowering the price level, and increasing real GDP until equilibrium is at Y_f. Likewise, according to classical theory, an inflationary gap will quickly be cured as production beyond Y_f necessitates high wages that lead AS to shift left, the price level to increase, and real GDP to fall until $Y_e = Y_f$. Keynesian theory counters that wages are not flexible enough to respond quickly to inflationary and recessionary pressures, and government intervention may be called for.

If the government wants to resolve inflationary and recessionary gaps with changes in expenditures, it becomes increasingly important to understand the effect on real GDP of each additional dollar of government purchases (or other types of spending). This is where the spending multiplier comes in. An additional dollar of spending adds more than a dollar to real GDP. This is because the initial dollar ends up in someone's pocket as income, and that person will turn around and spend some of it, creating more income and more spending and so on. The **spending multiplier** is the number by which the initial amount of new spending should be multiplied to find the total resulting increase in real GDP.

At the introductory level, the spending multiplier is discussed in the context of a simplified economy in which all income is either spent on consumption or saved. The opportunity to spend income on imports is ignored for the sake of simplicity. The government can be included in this model by referring to disposable income—income net of taxes, or $Y - T$.

The **marginal propensity to consume** (MPC) is the amount by which consumption increases for every additional dollar of real income.

$$MPC = \frac{\text{change in consumption}}{\text{change in real income}}$$

If another dollar of real income would bring you to spend another 76 cents on consumption, your MPC is 0.76.

The **marginal propensity to save** (MPS) is the fraction of each additional dollar of income that is saved.

$$MPS = \frac{\text{change in saving}}{\text{change in real income}}$$

When the government and foreign trade are omitted, or when income means disposable income, the marginal propensity to save is the complement to the marginal propensity to consume.

$$MPC + MPS = 1$$
$$\text{or}$$
$$MPS = 1 - MPC$$

The formula for the **spending multiplier** or **expenditure multiplier** is

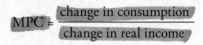

$$\text{Multiplier} = \frac{1}{1 - MPC} = \frac{1}{MPS}$$

The derivation of the multiplier formula is beyond the scope of the AP exam, but an example might convince you of its strength. Suppose spending (C, I, or G) increases by $100. This $100 will end up in people's pockets as income. If

spending multiplier
$$\frac{1}{1 - MPC} \text{ or } \frac{1}{MPS}$$

the marginal propensity to consume is 0.75, 75 percent of the initial spending increase—or $75—will be spent and becomes new income. Of that $75, 75 percent—or $56.25—will again be spent, and so on until 75 percent of the final amount of additional income won't buy a piece of penny candy. This process is carried out through nine rounds of spending in Table 1.

Spending Round	Increase in Spending	Cumulative Increases in Real GDP
1	$100.00	$100.00
2	$75.00	$175.00
3	$56.25	$231.25
4	$42.19	$273.44
5	$31.64	$305.08
6	$23.73	$328.81
7	$17.80	$346.61
8	$13.35	$359.95
9	$10.01	$369.97
:	:	:
All others	$30.03	$400.00

Table 1

In the end, real GDP increases by a total of $400. With an initial expenditure of $100 and a multiplier of $\frac{1}{(1-0.75)} = \frac{1}{0.25} = 4$, this is exactly what the multiplier would predict: 4 $100 = $400. Likewise, when expenditures decrease, the resulting total decrease in real GDP is found by multiplying the amount of the initial decrease by the spending multiplier.

ONE LAST THING

The transition from short-run equilibrium to long-run equilibrium as the economy "self" corrects is summarized in this handy series of figures:

Initially, the economy is at equilibrium at E_1, where AD_1 and $SRAS_1$ intersect and the price level is at P_1.

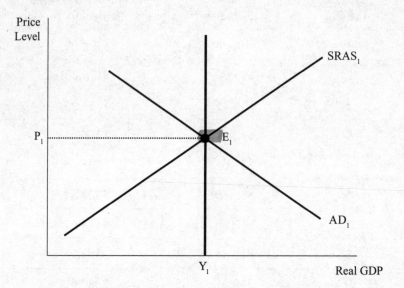

Figure 7

An initial negative demand shock decreases the aggregate demand to the left to AD_2.

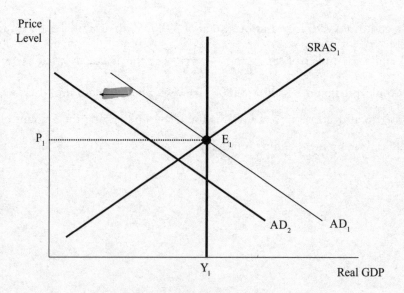

Figure 8

This reduces the price level to P_2 and aggregate output to Y_2, leading to higher unemployment in the short run and shifting equilibrium to E_2.

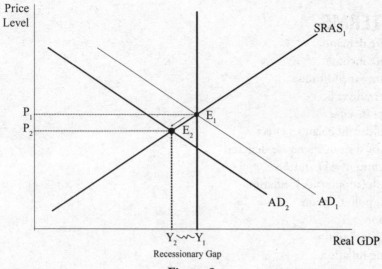

Figure 9

The reduction in price level leads to a decrease in nominal wages in the long run, which increases short-run aggregate supply to SRAS$_2$, bringing the economy into equilibrium at E$_3$, at which point, aggregate output is back to potential output at Y$_1$.

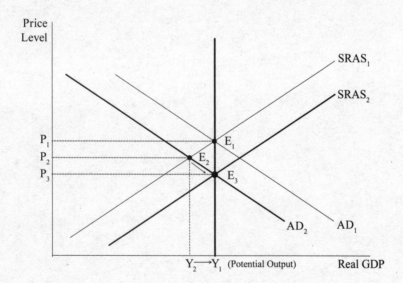

Figure 10

KEY TERMS

aggregate demand
aggregate income
aggregate expenditures
foreign trade effect
interest rate effect
real wealth/real balances effect
causes for shift in aggregate demand
equilibrium of AD and AS
cost push (supply-side) inflation
demand pull inflation
stagflation
creeping inflation
galloping inflation
hyperinflation
recessionary gap
inflationary gap
expenditure/spending multiplier
marginal propensity to consume
marginal propensity to save

CHAPTER 11 REVIEW QUESTIONS

See Chapter 14 for answers and explanations.

1. Operating in the intermediate range of the aggregate supply curve, an increase in aggregate demand results in an increase in

   (A) price level only
   (B) real GDP only
   (C) neither price level nor real GDP
   (D) nominal GDP only
   (E) price level and real GDP

2. If the marginal propensity to consume is 0.8, what is the largest total increase in GDP that can result from $500 of new spending?

   (A) $400
   (B) $500
   (C) $625
   (D) $2,500
   (E) $5,000

3. Stagflation occurs when

   (A) the price level rises for two consecutive quarters
   (B) the price level rises and output falls
   (C) the price level stays the same and output increases
   (D) the price level stays the same and output decreases
   (E) the price level and output both fall

4. A recessionary gap exists when the short-run equilibrium level of real GDP

   (A) decreases over time
   (B) equals the full-employment level of real GDP
   (C) is above the full-employment level of real GDP
   (D) is below the full-employment level of real GDP
   (E) increases over time

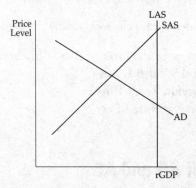

5. On the graph of the aggregate supply and demand model above, a recessionary gap exists, and the economy is in

   (A) neither short-run nor long-run equilibrium
   (B) long-run, but not short-run, equilibrium
   (C) short-run equilibrium
   (D) both long- and short-run equilibrium
   (E) long-run, but not short-run, equilibrium

Chapter 11 Summary

Circular Flow

o   Aggregate income = Aggregate expenditure = GDP

Components of Aggregate Demand

o   **Aggregate demand** is the total demand for goods and services in the economy.

o   Three effects cause the inverse relationship between price and GDP.
  • **The Real Wealth Effect**
  • **The Foreign Trade Effect**
  • **The Interest Rate Effect**

Equilibrium of AD and AS

o   **Cost-push** or **supply-side inflation** occurs when inflation results from an increase in resource costs that shifts the AS curve to the left.

o   **Stagflation** is defined by the combination of rising prices and falling output.

o   **Demand pull inflation** is the result of the AD curve shifting out to the right relative to the AS curve.

o   Inflation that remains steady for a long period at a low rate is called **creeping inflation**.

o   Unsteady inflation that exceeds 10 percent per year and grows month after month is **galloping inflation**.

o   **Hyperinflation** is very rapid price increases in excess of 50 percent per year.

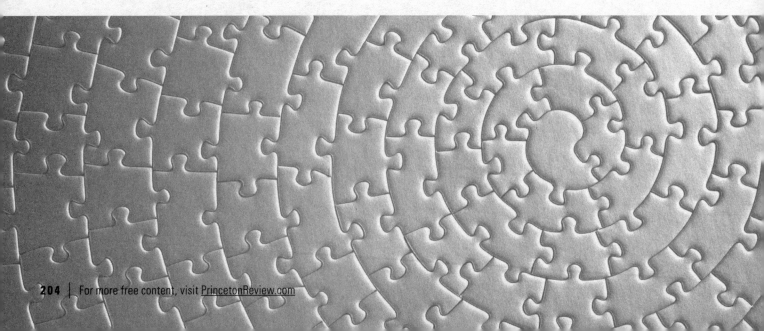

o   A **recessionary gap** exists as the amount by which equilibrium real GDP would have to increase to reach LAS.

o   An **inflationary gap** exists as the amount by which equilibrium real GDP would have to decrease to reach LAS.

o   The **spending multiplier** is the number by which the initial amount of new spending should be multiplied to find the total resulting increase in real GDP.

o   The **marginal propensity to consume** (MPC) is the amount by which consumption increases for every additional dollar of real income.

$$\text{MPC} = \frac{\text{change in consumption}}{\text{change in real income}}$$

o   The **marginal propensity to save** (MPS) is the fraction of each additional dollar of income that is saved.

$$\text{MPS} = \frac{\text{change in saving}}{\text{change in real income}}$$

o   The formula for the **spending multiplier** or **expenditure multiplier** is

$$\text{Multiplier} = \frac{1}{1 - \text{MPC}} = \frac{1}{\text{MPS}}$$

Chapter 12
Money and Fiscal Policy

MONEY AND BANKING

Defining Money and Measuring Wealth

Money is any commonly recognized item used to exchange goods and services within an economy. Though the word *money* is commonly used to refer to anything exchanged between individuals and having value, the formal definition is more rigorous. For an item to formally be considered money, it must have the following characteristics:

- Portability: money must be easily transferred between individuals

- Durability: money must endure and hold value through time

- Divisibility: money must be broken down into smaller units to make change

- Fungibility: money must carry interchangeable value across place and time (in other words, a buyer and seller must agree on the value of the item being used as money, and future buyers and sellers must agree, too)

Many items have been used as money throughout history with varying degrees of success. Economists generally agree that precious metals have been some of the most effective monies humans have used, pointing to the gold and silver exchanged in ancient Egypt that is still used as money today. Other items have been less successful. For example, because packs of cigarettes are portable and easily divided, they have been used as money in prisons. However, cigarettes do not function well as money in the larger economy. Cigarettes aren't fungible; individuals who don't smoke don't think they have value. Nor are cigarettes durable: if set on fire or dropped in a puddle, a cigarette is obsolete.

Money has three primary functions.

1. **Medium of exchange**. Without money, we would have to barter for everything. This is hard enough when there is a **double coincidence of wants**, meaning that the person who owns the goods or services you want (for example, flour) has a desire for what you have to barter with (for example, chickens). But if you have chickens, you want flour, and the flour owner wants a shovel, you will have to try to trade your chickens for a shovel that you can trade for flour. If the shovel maker doesn't want chickens, the complexity grows. A common medium of exchange greatly simplifies such transactions.

2. **Store of value.** If the goods or services you produce are perishable, you will benefit from a nonperishable item that will hold the value of past production into the future. The output of a tomato farmer or a ski instructor will have little value six months after production. By exchanging this output for something that carries value across place and time, the benefits of production can be transferred into the future. (Note: storing value is the key characteristic that distinguishes money from currency.)

3. Unit of account. Money provides a standard unit for price listings and comparisons. If there were no common unit of account, price listings would be in terms of arbitrary units (three chickens per shovel, two sacks of flour per telephone) and price comparisons would involve a complex set of conversions. The recent adoption of the euro as a standard unit of account in the European Union was largely an attempt to eliminate the burden of reconciling the many different measures of value there.

Money is commonly confused with two other concepts: wealth and currency. **Currency** is an item that is used as money but does NOT act as a store of value or carry intrinsic value. Consider, for example, the difference between a silver coin and paper cash that are both worth one US dollar. If the U.S. ceases to exist, the silver coin would still have value; people in other countries would want to use it as money or perhaps melt it down into jewelry. The silver coin carries intrinsic value beyond that of the US dollar. The paper cash, however, would be worthless and have no value beyond that of scratch paper. As a result, silver coins are money and paper cash is currency. (Another way to conceptualize this relationship: all money is currency, but not all currency is money.)

Because confusion between money and currency is so common, economists sometimes use the terms **commodity money** and **fiat money** to describe the same relationship. **Commodity money** refers to any raw material with intrinsic value that is used in exchange for other goods in an economy (such as a silver coin), while **fiat money** refers to currency without intrinsic value (such as paper cash).

Wealth is the value of the total assets owned by an individual or entity. While there are a variety of ways to measure and think about wealth, it is most commonly the sum of one's assets, minus any debts.

The **Federal Reserve Bank** (the Fed) is responsible for monitoring the wealth and money supply in the United States. Confusingly, the term "money supply" does not refer to the supply of money within the United States; the **money supply** refers to the supply of *currency* and other liquid assets held within the U.S. The term **liquidity** refers to how easily an asset can be transferred into currency; in other words, liquidity refers to how easily an asset can be sold for its cash value. The Fed tracks money supply totals in categories ranked in decreasing order of liquidity:

- **M1** is the sum of coin and paper money plus checking deposits and travelers' checks.

- **M2** is M1 plus savings deposits, small-time deposits (deposits less than $100,000 with a fixed term of maturity such as CDs), money market mutual funds, and Eurodollar deposits (overnight, dollar-denominated deposits in European banks).

The United States has a **fractional reserve banking system** in which only a fraction of total deposits is held on reserve and the rest is lent out. The ratio of a bank's reserves to its total deposits is called the **reserve ratio**.

$$\text{Reserve ratio} = \frac{\text{bank reserves}}{\text{total deposits}}$$

The Fed sets a minimum reserve ratio for all banks. Banks earn profits by lending the amount of their deposits beyond the required reserves out to borrowers who pay an interest rate higher than the interest rate the banks pay to their depositors.

Central to the accounting practices of a bank is a **balance sheet** called a **T account,** as shown in Figure 1.

Panel A

Assets		Liabilities	
Required Reserves	10	Deposits	100
Excess Reserves	10		
Loans	80		
	100		100

Panel B

Assets		Liabilities	
Required Reserves	6	Deposits	60
Excess Reserves	0		
Loans	54		
	60		60

Panel C

Assets		Liabilities	
Required Reserves	6	Deposits	60
Excess Reserves	0	Borrowed Reserves	26
Loans	80		
	86		86

Figure 1

The **assets** side includes required reserves, excess reserves that can be loaned out, and loans. The **liabilities** side includes deposits and reserves that can be borrowed from the Fed. The two sides of the T account must always balance, so when something changes the total on one side of the T account, there must also be a change on the other side. Consider a bank with assets and liabilities as in Panel A (in millions of dollars). This bank has $100 million in deposits, and with a reserve ratio of 10 percent, its required reserves are $10 million. Loans could increase from $80 million to $90 million by reducing excess reserves from $10 million to zero. Now suppose a major depositor reduced her deposits by $40 million. The required reserves are now 10 percent of the remaining $60 million in deposits, or $6 million. There are several options for how the bank can come back into balance.

It could call in $26 million in loans, bringing assets and liabilities to $60 million, as shown in Panel B. It could also borrow $26 million in reserves from the Fed as in Panel C, balancing each side of the T account with $86 million.

The fractional reserve banking system enables what economists call **money creation**. Money creation is the generation of assets caused when an initial deposit to a bank is held partially in reserve and partially redistributed as a loan over and over again. Suppose $100 million of new deposits enters a banking system which, for simplicity, we will assume has no initial holdings and loans out all of its excess reserves. We will also assume there are no cash holdings, meaning that all loans are either deposited in a bank or paid to people who deposit them in a bank. When the $100 million deposit enters the first bank, 10 percent must be held as reserves, and $90 million is loaned out. That $90 million is deposited in another bank and 90 percent of that, or $81 million, is loaned out. The $81 million is deposited and enables a $72.9 million loan, which is deposited and enables a $65.61 million loan and so on. In the end, as illustrated in Figure 2, the entire $100 million initial deposit is held as reserves; there are $900 million in loans stemming from this deposit; and total deposits are $1,000 million, or $1 billion.

Bank 1	Reserves	10	Deposits	100
	Loans	90		
Bank 2	Reserves	9	Deposits	90
	Loans	81		
Bank 3	Reserves	8.1	Deposits	81
	Loans	72.9		
Bank 4	Reserves	7.29	Deposits	72.9
	Loans	65.61		
•	•		•	
•	•		•	
•	•		•	
Total	Reserves	100	Deposits	1000
	Loans	900		

Figure 2

The total amount of deposits resulting from an initial deposit that is ultimately held as reserves is conveniently found using the **money multiplier**.

$$\text{Money multiplier} = \frac{1}{\text{required reserve ratio}}$$

In the above example, the required reserve ratio was 0.10, so the money multiplier was $\frac{1}{0.10} = 10$, and the $100 million new deposit created a total of $10 \times \$100$ million = $1 billion in deposits.

Tools of Central Bank Policy

The central bank—the Federal Reserve Bank (or simply the Fed) in the United States—has three primary tools with which to control the money supply.

- Adjustments in the required reserve ratio

- Adjustments in the discount rate paid by banks to borrow from the Fed

- Open market operations (buying and selling of government securities)

As was explained in the previous section, the required reserve ratio is a key factor in the process of money creation. If the required reserve ratio is high, banks must hold a large portion of their deposits as reserves and lend out less. This makes the multiplier smaller, so each new deposit ultimately creates a smaller amount of total deposits. If the Fed wants to increase the money supply, it can decrease the required reserve ratio and thereby require banks to hold less money in reserves. This increases the money multiplier and expands the money creation process.

The **discount rate** is the interest rate banks pay to borrow money from the Fed. When the rate is low, banks are more likely to borrow from the Fed when the banks' excess reserves do not satisfy their demand for loans. The Fed can thus increase the money supply by decreasing the discount rate or vice versa.

Open market operations involve the Fed's purchase and sale of government securities. When the government runs a deficit (G > T), the Treasury (not the Fed) borrows money by selling government securities—bonds, bills, and notes—on the open market. Congress has authorized the Fed to buy and sell these government securities just like individuals and other institutions, which enables it to inject money into the economy or remove it from circulation. When the Fed sells a bond for $1,000, it is effectively giving a piece of paper to the buyer that says "bond" on it and taking in the buyer's money. This removes money from circulation. It may also have a multiplied effect if the $1,000 to buy the bond is withdrawn from a bank account, bringing the bank's reserves below the required level and causing the bank to call in loans from others who will subsequently remove deposits from other banks and cause further contraction. To expand the money supply, the Fed can buy securities. If the Fed buys a bond, it gives money to someone in exchange for a piece of paper. This new money in the economy is likely to be deposited into someone's bank account, where most of it will be lent out again, and the whole multiplier process works its magic once more.

FISCAL POLICY

The government exercises **fiscal policy** when it tries to counter fluctuations in aggregate expenditure with changes in purchases, transfer payments (e.g., unemployment insurance, social security, or welfare), or taxes. **Expansionary fiscal policy** involves increasing government purchases, increasing transfers, or decreasing taxes in order to shift aggregate demand to the right and boost real

GDP. **Contractionary fiscal policy** involves decreasing purchases, decreasing transfers, or increasing taxes, thus shifting aggregate demand to the left, which will lower the price level and decrease real GDP.

Because government purchases are a component of autonomous expenditures, the **government spending multiplier** is the same as the autonomous spending multiplier.

$$\text{Government spending multiplier} = \frac{1}{1-MPC} = \frac{1}{MPS}$$

% change in saving / change in real income

If the MPC is 0.5 and equilibrium real GDP exceeds full employment real GDP by $1 trillion, the government can use the multiplier formula to determine the amount by which its purchases should decrease to bring Y_e down to Y_f.

The multiplier in this case is $\dfrac{1}{(1-0.5)} = \dfrac{1}{0.5} = 2$, meaning that for every dollar that G decreases, Y_e will decrease by two dollars. Thus a decrease in G by $500 billion will decrease Y_e by the desired $1 trillion.

When the government changes taxes or transfer payments, the multiplier is a bit smaller, because for each $1 decrease in taxes or increase in transfers, a fraction (the MPS) is saved, and only the MPC is initially spent. This is in contrast to a $1 increase in government spending, all of which falls into the hands of the initial sellers of goods and services. The tax multiplier is negative because tax increases lead to expenditure decreases, and vice versa. The **tax multiplier**, which indicates the total change in real GDP resulting from each $1 change in taxes, is thus:

$$\text{Tax multiplier} = -\frac{MPC}{MPS}$$

The multiplier for transfer payments is the same except the MPC is positive.

The above multipliers apply only when government spending, transfers, or taxes are changed. If an increase in government spending is accompanied by an equivalent increase in taxes, or likewise both G and T decrease in order to balance the budget, the government spending multiplier and the tax multiplier are combined to form the **balanced budget multiplier**.

$$\text{Balanced budget multiplier} = \frac{1}{1-MPC} + \left(\frac{-MPC}{1-MPC}\right) = \frac{1-MPC}{1-MPC} = 1$$

Thus, the change in real GDP resulting from an equivalent change in G and T is no different from the initial change in G and T.

There are both direct and indirect effects of fiscal policy. Consider the repercussions of an increase in government purchases. The expenditure increase will increase real GDP as can be illustrated with the AE diagram in Figure 3. In macroeconomics, we often use a 45 line as a guide. In Figure 3, the 45 line signifies the point at which AE = real GDP. The economy achieves equilibrium when AE intersects the 45 line.

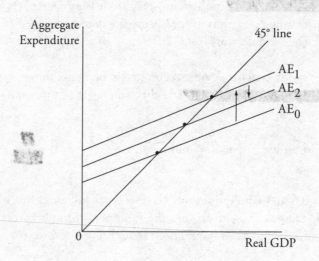

Figure 3

With an increase in real GDP, more money will be demanded for the purpose of making the additional expenditures. Figure 4 illustrates the demand and supply of money.

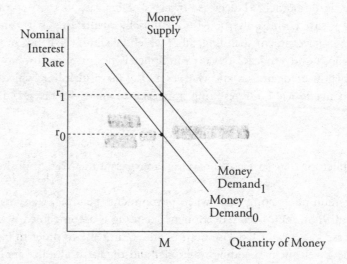

Figure 4: The Money Market

We assume that the supply of money is vertical. The increase in the demand for money drives up the equilibrium interest rate. Investment decreases as interest rates rise, thus bringing AE back down to AE_2 on Figure 3.

The decrease in real investment stemming from higher interest rates (r) due to government purchases is called **crowding out**. The effect of crowded-out investment on real GDP is most likely smaller than the initial increase in real GDP due to the purchases, in which case we call it **partial crowding out**. If the decrease in investment eliminates the entire boost in real GDP from the increased purchases, this is called **complete crowding out**. To summarize the effects of expansionary fiscal policy

$$G \uparrow \text{or } T \downarrow \Rightarrow AD \uparrow \Rightarrow Y \uparrow \Rightarrow Md \uparrow \Rightarrow r \uparrow \Rightarrow I \downarrow \Rightarrow Y \downarrow$$

(typically falling by less than the initial increase in Y)

The effects of contractionary fiscal policy are summarized as

$$G \downarrow \text{or } T \uparrow \Rightarrow AD \downarrow \Rightarrow Y \downarrow \Rightarrow Md \downarrow \Rightarrow r \downarrow \Rightarrow I \uparrow \Rightarrow Y \uparrow$$

(typically increasing by less than the initial decrease in Y)

Fiscal Policy in an Open Economy

The U.S. has an **open economy**, meaning it trades with other nations to acquire goods that cannot be supplied within its borders and sells goods in international markets. By contrast, countries that don't engage in foreign trade are considered to have **closed economies**. In open economies, the effects of fiscal policy on interest rates can have additional implications on international trade. For example, expansionary fiscal policy can cause the following chains of events, leading to a decline in net exports:

Government (G) spending increases or Taxes (T) decrease ⇒

Higher interest rates (the crowding-out effect) ⇒

Increased demand for the domestic currency for investment purposes (e.g. Treasury bonds) ⇒

Appreciation of the domestic currency relative to foreign currencies ⇒

Exports (X) decrease and Imports (M) increase

- Net Exports (X – M) decrease, partially offsetting the effects of the expansionary policy

Likewise, **contractionary fiscal policy** can cause the following events leading to an increase in net exports:

Government (G) spending decreases or Taxes (T) increase ⇒

Lower interest rates (due to the government demanding fewer loanable funds) ⇒

Decreased demand for the domestic currency for investment purposes (e.g. Treasury bonds) ⇒

Depreciation of the domestic currency relative to foreign currencies ⇒

Exports (X) increase and Imports (M) decrease ⇒

- Net Exports (X – M) increase, partially offsetting the effects of the contractionary policy

The Loanable Funds Market

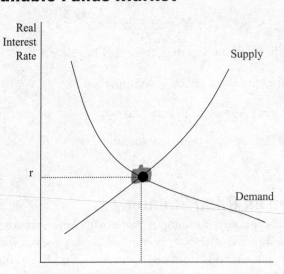

Figure 5: The Loanable Funds Market

An exam question might ask you to illustrate the loanable funds market rather than the money market. The workings of these markets are similar, although the loanable funds market has a positively sloped supply curve. This is because higher interest rates don't increase the total money supply, but they do increase the supply of loanable funds. As interest rates increase, households become more willing to forgo current consumption and make their money available to banks and borrowers. Considering the two graphs side by side can offer further comparison:

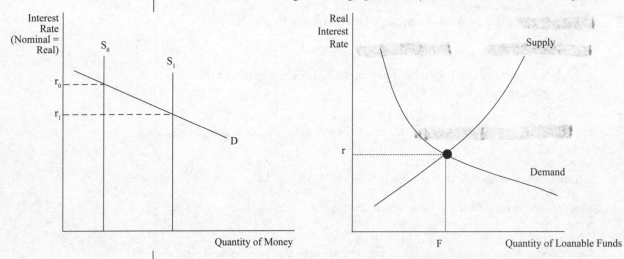

Figure 6: The Money Market

Both of these graphs serve a similar function: to find the equilibrium point between the quantity of money demanded and the quantity of money supplied to determine the interest rate, which is used as a measure of the value of money. However, they each illustrate fundamentally different relationships. The money market graph illustrates how actions by a central bank affect the interest rate in the short run. For example, Figure 6 illustrates how increasing the supply of money through open market operations decreases the interest rate. On the other hand, the loanable funds market illustrates only the market specific to loans from financial institutions over the long run. In the short run, the money market can be used to assess the interest rate as normal and real interest rates are held equal; in the long run, only the real interest rate applies, thus the need to utilize the loanable funds market instead. Generally speaking, the money market graph is used to determine the value of money the short run, and the loanable funds market is used to determine the value of money in the long run.

It can be helpful to simply remember that the money supply is held constant in the short run. When you're taking the AP exam, read the exam questions carefully. If a question refers to the money market, draw a vertical money supply curve. If the question refers to the loanable funds market, draw the loanable funds supply curve with a positive slope to reflect the sensitivity of loanable funds to the interest rate.

Supply-Side Fiscal Policy

Supply-side economists believe that changes in tax rates will affect aggregate supply as well as aggregate demand. These are their primary arguments.

- With lower taxes, households will save more and businesses will invest more. The investment will increase capital levels and make workers more productive.

- Lower income-tax rates increase the take-home pay of workers and thus increase the incentive for individuals to enter the workforce or increase their work hours.

- Entrepreneurship involves many risks. Lower tax rates increase the after-tax rewards to successful entrepreneurs and may encourage them to take risks with new products and technologies.

If a tax cut prompted both an increase in aggregate demand and an increase in aggregate supply, the supply-side effect would bolster the increase in real GDP caused by the increase in aggregate demand. Inspired by the work of Arthur Laffer, supply-side economists also argue that tax cuts might actually lead to increases in tax revenue. The idea is that although the tax rate is lower, increases in production (for the reasons given above) might increase the tax base by more than enough to compensate for the lower tax rate.

Critics of supply-side economics contend that tax rates in the United States are already low relative to many industrialized nations, that any supply-side effects are likely to be smaller and longer in coming than supply-siders suggest, and that the results of supply-side tax cuts in the 1980s were unconvincing.

Monetary Policy

Monetary policy is the use of money and credit controls to influence interest rates, inflation, exchange rates, unemployment, and real GDP. In other words, when economists talk about changes in monetary policy, they are talking about changes in the amount of money available on the market. Specific methods of changing the money supply are discussed in the previous section on "tools of central bank policy." Here we will examine the effects of monetary policy.

Figure 7 illustrates the direct effects of **expansionary monetary policy**.

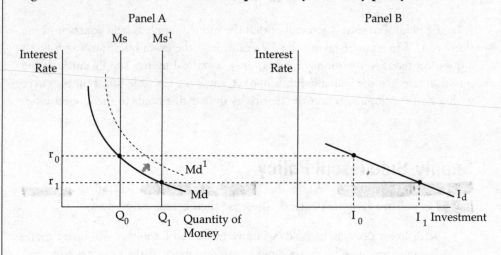

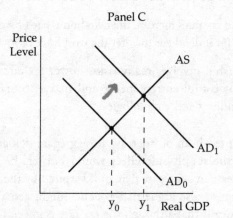

Figure 7

In Panel A, the money supply increases, resulting in a lower interest rate. In Panel B, the lower interest rate is seen to induce an increase in the quantity of investment demanded. Panel C illustrates the result of the increase in I on AD, and the resulting increase in real GDP, including multiplier effects, as explained above.

As is the case for fiscal policy, an increase in real GDP due to expansionary monetary policy spurs a second round of effects. With more output being purchased and more income being earned, the demand for money increases from Md to Md1 in Panel A of Figure 7. This will increase the interest rate and decrease investment. However, the magnitude of these second-round effects is likely to be smaller than that of the direct effects, so the end result of expansionary monetary policy will be a decrease in the interest rate and an increase in real GDP.

In summary, the effects of expansionary monetary policy are

$$M_s \uparrow \Rightarrow r \downarrow \;\Rightarrow\; I \uparrow \Rightarrow AD \uparrow \Rightarrow Y \uparrow \Rightarrow M_d \uparrow \Rightarrow r \uparrow$$

(but not enough to counteract the previous effects)

The effects of contractionary monetary policy are summarized as

$$M_s \downarrow \Rightarrow r \uparrow \;\Rightarrow\; I \downarrow \Rightarrow AD \downarrow \Rightarrow Y \downarrow \Rightarrow M_d \downarrow \Rightarrow r \downarrow$$

(but not enough to counteract the previous effects)

FISCAL-MONETARY MIX

Interaction of Fiscal and Monetary Policies

Fiscal and monetary policy need not operate in isolation. By combining the two types of policy into an orchestrated policy mix, a preferable macro outcome may result. For example, expansionary fiscal policy may boost output at the expense of higher interest rates that crowd out investment. To expand the problem, when investment in capital resources goes down in the current period, future output is sacrificed because there is less capital for use in production (reread this sentence twice—this point is often missed on AP exams!). In order to limit or eliminate the crowding out of investment that may result from expansionary fiscal policy, it can be combined with expansionary monetary policy that will increase the money supply and decrease the interest rate.

Monetarist-Keynesian Controversy

Part of learning macroeconomics is understanding the variety of ideas put forth about the behavior of the economy and the different policy prescriptions that result. Here we will contrast some of the most extreme views of Keynesian and monetarist theory. Of course, the truth and most economists' views are somewhere in the middle.

As illustrated in the top section of Figure 8 (shown on the next page), Keynesians believe that changes in the money supply will have little effect on interest rates because the demand curve for money is relatively flat. If it is perfectly flat, a **liquidity trap** exists, meaning that changes in the money supply will have no effect on interest rates. Notice that as the money supply increases from M_s to M_s^1 in the top left graph, there is no change in the equilibrium interest rate and therefore no change in real investment. Even if interest rates were to change, Keynesians believe that the investment demand curve is relatively inelastic (steep), making it largely unresponsive to changes in the interest rate. As a result, Keynesians see little place for monetary policy in spurring the economy, and favor fiscal policy measures instead.

Keynesian View

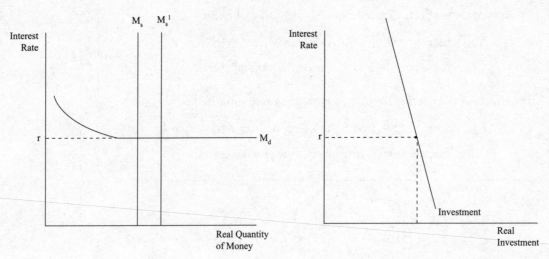

Monetarist View

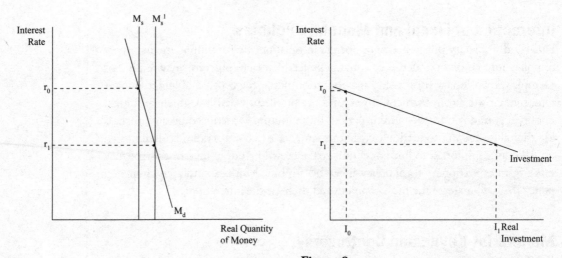

Figure 8

In contrast, monetarists believe that the demand for money is very sensitive to the interest rate. As shown in the lower half of Figure 8, the result of a steep demand curve for money is that an increase in the money supply lowers interest rates substantially. Monetarists further believe that investment demand is relatively elastic, making it very responsive to decreases in the interest rate. Given this, the money supply is a useful tool for keeping the economy on an even keel. Monetarists believe that the economy is inherently stable and recommend a steady increase in the money supply proportional to the increase in real GDP. At the same time, this theory does not favor fiscal policy, both because it can be ill-timed, and due to the problem of crowding out when investment is sensitive to the interest rate. If either the demand curve for money is vertical (totally unresponsive to the interest rate) or the investment demand curve is horizontal, complete crowding out occurs. In this case, fiscal policy has no effect because any increase in government spending increases the demand for money and induces an increase in interest rates that eliminates an equivalent amount of investment.

Monetarists also explain the power of monetary policy using the **equation of exchange**. According to the following equation, the money supply (M) times the velocity of money (V) equals the average price (P) times the quantity of goods and services sold in a period (Q):

$$MV = PQ$$

The **velocity of money** is the number of times per period (typically a year) that the average dollar is spent on final goods and services. The same dollar will bounce around the economy several times each year. Mike will spend $20 to purchase groceries from David, and then David will spend the same $20 to purchase CDs from Lauren the banker, and then Lauren will loan the same $20 out to Megan for home improvements, and so forth. Simply put, the equation of exchange states that the number of dollars multiplied by the number of times they are used per year must equal the total number of dollars spent in a year.

If one item in the equation of exchange changes, another item must change to maintain the balance. Thus, if M changes, either V, P, or Q must also change. Monetarists claim that velocity is stable, so increases in M must increase P and/or Q and thus increase total spending (P Q). Classical economists and some monetarists also subscribe to the **quantity theory of money**, which states that in addition to V being stable, Q is stable. This implies that increases in M will have no effect other than to increase the price level. All of these direct linkages between the money supply and expenditures are in contrast with the Keynesian view, which is that the money supply has a small and indirect influence on expenditures by affecting interest rates that affect investment, which affects aggregate expenditures.

Keynesians and monetarists also differ in their approach to inflation and interest rates. Real interest rates are adjusted for anticipated inflation.

Real interest rate = nominal interest rate − anticipated inflation, and likewise,

Nominal interest rate = real interest rate + anticipated inflation

Keynesians advocate fighting inflation by decreasing the money supply to drive up both real and nominal interest rates and to reduce consumption and investment. Monetarists believe that there is a fairly stable **natural rate of real interest**, in which case fluctuations in the nominal interest rate simply reflect changes in anticipated inflation. From their perspective, the real interest rate must change in order to influence investment. If market participants can predict that the Fed will counter inflation by reducing money supply growth, anticipated inflation and nominal interest rates will begin to fall, not rise, when the Fed tightens the money supply. This is called the **Fisher effect**.

A summary of classical, Keynesian, and monetarist views appears in Table 1.

Monetarists	Monetarists see the money supply as the primary tool to bring economic stability. For stability, they suggest following a strict "monetary rule," such as increasing the money supply at a rate equal to the average growth in real output. They believe that fiscal and monetary policy, intended for fine-tuning, threaten to destabilize the economy. They also feel that changes in government spending will crowd out private spending and have little or no effect on aggregate spending, prices, real output, or real interest rates. Unemployment and output are expected to tend toward their natural rates without active intervention.
Classical Economists	Classical economists agree with monetarists that the economy is fairly stable and will naturally adjust to full employment. They feel that attempts to fine-tune the economy are ineffective because individuals come to anticipate the government's actions and act to offset them. Classical economists emphasize that the velocity of money is constant, meaning that an increase in the money supply has a direct effect on total spending.
Keynesians	Keynesians view the economy as inherently unstable and blame inadequate demand for periods of stagnation. They recommend active government policy to respond to inflationary and recessionary gaps. They feel that changes in government spending can affect aggregate spending, real interest rates, and real output. Keynesians also believe that changes in the money supply have a relatively small and indirect effect on output. Changes in the money supply affect interest rates, which affect investment, which affects aggregate expenditures, which affect income and output.

Table 1

DEFICITS

The **budget deficit** is the difference between federal government spending and tax collections (G – T) in one year. The **national debt** is the accumulation of past deficits—the total amount that the federal government owes at a given time. The Keynesian emphasis on fiscal policy to spur and cool the economy has an associated requirement for deficit spending during recessions, which can be balanced with budget surpluses during booms. The government finances deficits by selling Treasury bonds, bills, and notes on the open market. Although the United States has had a multi-trillion-dollar debt since the early 1980s, there is little agreement over how much debt is too much. Some adhere to the **Ricardian Equivalence theory** that deficit financing is no different from tax financing because if the former is chosen, people will simultaneously increase their savings by the amount they would have been taxed in preparation for the inevitable repayment of the debt at a later time. Others worry that government spending crowds out private economic activity and feel that debt or deficit ceilings should be in place to limit the burden of repayment.

When governments use expansionary fiscal policy, they increase spending, decrease taxes, or a combination of both. These expansionary policies will move an economy toward deficit, as now the government will be spending more and/or receiving less. On the other hand, when a government imposes a contractionary fiscal policy, the decreased spending/increased taxes will move an economy toward surplus, as now the revenue will be greater and total spending less.

Deficits can be financed by either borrowing or creating money. When the government borrows, it competes with private borrowers and bids up the interest rate. This can crowd out private investment and interest-sensitive consumption. By creating money, the government can spend money without raising interest rates, but this is likely to cause inflation.

In September 2018, the U.S. national debt was $21.5 trillion, or just about $65,600 per person. Defenders of high debt levels argue that it is wise to borrow now for educational programs, national defense, infrastructure, and research if the benefits to present and future generations exceed the eventual costs to those same parties. They also note that much of the debt is held domestically, meaning that we simply owe money to ourselves.

Those who wish to pay off the debt sooner argue that most of the benefits will be received by present generations and paid for by future generations. They note that few individuals have squirreled away $65,600 for debt repayment as the Ricardian Equivalence theory would predict. And they state that by crowding out private investment in capital, research, and development, the government reduces labor productivity, incomes, and living standards for the same future generations that will be saddled with repaying the debt.

KEY TERMS

Defining Money and Measuring Wealth

money
commodity money
fiat money
medium of exchange
double coincidence of wants
store of value
unit of account
money supply
liquidity
Federal Reserve Bank
M1
M2
fractional reserve banking system
reserve ratio
balance sheet
T account
assets
liabilities
money creation
money multiplier
discount rate
open market operations

Fiscal Policy

fiscal policy
expansionary fiscal policy
contractionary fiscal policy
government spending multiplier
tax multiplier
balanced budget multiplier
crowding out
partial crowding out
complete crowding out
open economy
closed economy
loanable funds market
money market
supply-side economist
monetary policy
expansionary/easy money policy
contractionary/tight money policy

Fiscal-Monetary Mix

monetarist
liquidity trap
equation of exchange
velocity of money
quantity theory of money
real interest rate
nominal interest rate
natural rate of interest
Fisher effect

Deficits

budget deficits
national debt
Ricardian Equivalence theory
structural shocks
inflationary expectations

CHAPTER 12 REVIEW QUESTIONS

See Chapter 14 for answers and explanations.

1. Which of the following statements is correct in regard to the federal budget deficit and the federal debt?

    (A) When the debt is negative, the deficit decreases.
    (B) When the debt is positive, the deficit decreases.
    (C) The deficit is the accumulation of past debts.
    (D) When the deficit is negative, the debt decreases.
    (E) When the deficit is negative, the debt increases.

2. There is relatively more crowding out as the result of expansionary fiscal policy when

    (A) expansionary monetary policy accompanies the fiscal policy
    (B) the investment demand curve is inelastic
    (C) government spending improves profit expectations among businesses
    (D) aggregate supply is vertical
    (E) the investment demand curve is elastic

3. Which of the following would be considered contractionary monetary policy?

    (A) The purchase of bonds
    (B) The sale of bonds
    (C) An increase in taxes
    (D) An increase in government spending
    (E) A decrease in the discount rate

4. In what ways is contractionary fiscal policy in the United States likely to affect domestic interest rates and the international value of the dollar?

    (A) Interest rates increase and the dollar depreciates.
    (B) Interest rates decrease and the dollar appreciates.
    (C) Interest rates increase and the dollar appreciates.
    (D) Interest rates decrease and the dollar is not affected.
    (E) Interest rates decrease and the dollar depreciates.

5. Which of the following policies might the Fed adopt to counter a recession?

    (A) A decrease in taxes
    (B) An increase in government spending
    (C) An increase in the discount rate
    (D) An increase in the required reserve ratio
    (E) The purchase of bonds

6. Which of the following statements would "supply-side" economists disagree with?

    (A) Tax changes cause shifts in aggregate supply that work against shifts in aggregate demand, thus reducing the effect of the tax change on real GDP.
    (B) A tax cut is likely to increase aggregate supply by boosting saving, investment, and thus capital accumulation.
    (C) A tax increase is likely to decrease aggregate supply by decreasing after-tax wages and thus providing disincentives to work.
    (D) A tax cut is likely to increase aggregate supply by providing greater rewards for risk taking.
    (E) A decrease in tax rates does not necessarily result in a decrease in tax revenues.

7. The Fed decides to sell bonds on the open market. How is this likely to affect interest rates and the value of the dollar?

    (A) The interest rate decreases, and the value of the dollar decreases.
    (B) The interest rate decreases, and the value of the dollar increases.
    (C) The interest rate increases, and the value of the dollar increases.
    (D) The interest rate increases, and the value of the dollar decreases.

8. How will an increase in investment from businesses and consumers affect aggregate demand?

    (A) Investment from businesses and consumers doesn't affect aggregate demand.
    (B) Aggregate demand will increase.
    (C) Aggregate demand will decrease.
    (D) Aggregate will spike before equalizing.

Chapter 12 Summary

Money and Banking

o   **Money** is anything that is commonly accepted as a means of payment for goods and services.

o   Money has three functions.
   - Medium of exchange
   - Store value
   - Unit of account

o   **Currency** is any item that is used as money that does NOT act as a store of value or carry intrinsic value.

o   **Commodity money** is any raw material with intrinsic value that is used in exchange for other goods in an economy (such as a silver coin).

o   **Fiat money** is a currency without intrinsic value (such as paper cash). Fiat money is also known as currency.

o   **Wealth** is the value of the total assets owned by an individual or entity.

o   **Money supply** is the amount of money available on the market; **liquidity** refers to how easily that money can be accessed.
   - **M1** is the sum of coin and paper money plus checking deposits and travelers' checks.
   - **M2** is M1 plus investments.

o   The United States has a **fractional reserve banking system** in which only a fraction of total deposits is held on reserve and the rest is lent out.

$$\text{Reserve ratio} = \frac{\text{bank reserves}}{\text{total deposits}}$$

o **Money creation** is the generation of assets caused by an initial deposit to a bank being held partially in reserve and partially redistributed as a loan over and over again.

o The **money multiplier** is the total amount of deposits resulting from an initial deposit that is ultimately held as reserves.

$$\text{Money multiplier} = \frac{1}{\text{required reserve ratio}}$$

o The **discount rate** is the interest rate banks pay to borrow money from the Fed.

o **Open market operations** involve the Fed's purchase and sale of government securities.

Fiscal Policy

o The government exercises **fiscal policy** when it tries to counter fluctuations in aggregate expenditure with changes in purchases, transfer payments, or taxes.

o **Expansionary fiscal policy** involves increasing government purchases, increasing transfers, or decreasing taxes in order to shift aggregate demand to the right and boost real GDP. To summarize the effects

$$G \uparrow \text{ or } T \downarrow \Rightarrow AD \uparrow \Rightarrow Y \uparrow \Rightarrow Md \uparrow \Rightarrow r \uparrow \Rightarrow I \downarrow \Rightarrow Y \downarrow$$

o **Contractionary fiscal policy** involves decreasing purchases, decreasing transfers, or increasing taxes, thus shifting aggregate demand to the left, which will lower the price level and decrease real GDP.

$$G \downarrow \text{ or } T \uparrow \Rightarrow AD \downarrow \Rightarrow Y \downarrow \Rightarrow Md \downarrow \Rightarrow r \downarrow \Rightarrow I \uparrow \Rightarrow Y \uparrow$$

o Because government purchases are a component of autonomous expenditures, the **government spending multiplier** is the same as the autonomous spending multiplier.

$$\text{Government spending multiplier} = \frac{1}{1 - MPC} = \frac{1}{MPS}$$

o The **tax multiplier** is the total change in real GDP resulting from each $1 change in taxes.

$$\text{Tax multiplier} = -\frac{\text{MPC}}{\text{MPS}}$$

o **Crowding out** is the decrease in real investment stemming from higher interest rates due to government purchases.

o **Monetary policy** is the use of money and credit controls to influence interest rates, inflation, exchange rates, unemployment, and real GDP.

o The effects of expansionary monetary policy are

$$M s \uparrow \Rightarrow r \downarrow \ \Rightarrow \ I \uparrow \Rightarrow AD \uparrow \Rightarrow Y \uparrow \Rightarrow M d \uparrow \Rightarrow r \uparrow$$

o The effects of contractionary monetary policy are

$$M s \downarrow \Rightarrow r \uparrow \ \Rightarrow \ I \downarrow \Rightarrow AD \downarrow \Rightarrow Y \downarrow \Rightarrow M d \downarrow \Rightarrow r \downarrow$$

Fiscal-Monetary Mix

o A **liquidity trap** exists when the demand for money is perfectly flat, meaning that changes in the money supply will have no effect on interest rates.

o The **equation of exchange** states that the number of dollars multiplied by the number of times they are used per year must equal the total number of dollars spent in a year.

$$MV = PQ$$

o The **velocity of money** (V) is the number of times per period that the average dollar is spent on final goods and services.

o The **quantity theory of money** states that Q is stable in addition to V.

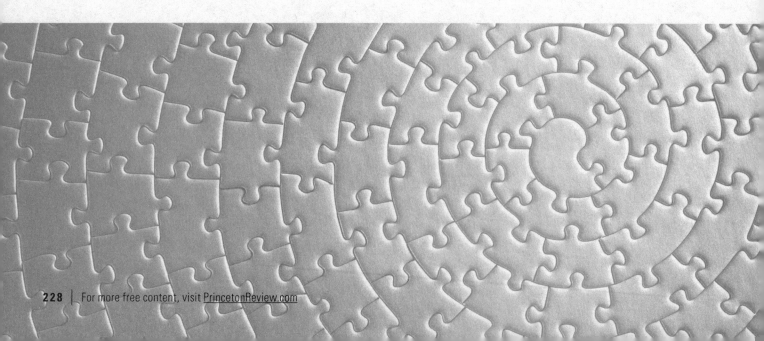

o   Monetarists believe that there is a fairly stable **natural rate of real interest**, in which case fluctuations in the nominal interest rate simply reflect changes in anticipated inflation.

o   The **Fisher effect** occurs when market participants can predict that the Fed will counter inflation by reducing money supply growth, causing anticipated inflation and nominal interest rates to fall when the Fed tightens the money supply.

Deficits

o   The **budget deficit** is the difference between federal government spending and tax collections in one year.

o   The **national debt** is the accumulation of past deficits—the total amount that the federal government owes at a given time.

o   The **Ricardian Equivalence theory** states that deficit financing is no different from tax financing because if the former is chosen, people will simultaneously increase their savings by the amount they would have been taxed in preparation for the inevitable repayment of the debt at a later time.

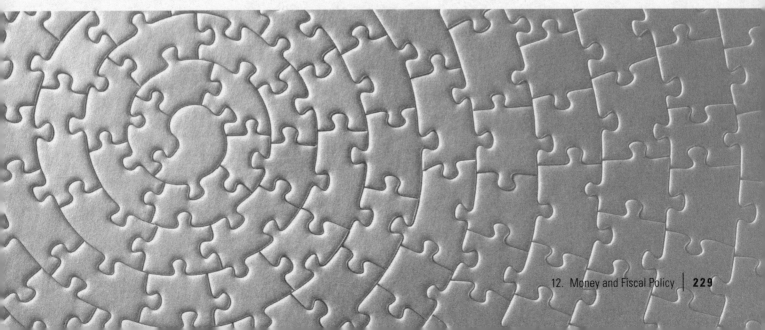

Chapter 13
Currency Exchange, Inflation, and Growth

INTERNATIONAL CURRENCY EXCHANGE

International currency markets exist so nations with different currencies can trade with each other. To purchase merchandise, services, capitals, or financial assets from other nations, buyers must first purchase that nation's currency. An international market for US dollars exists when:

- International citizens want to purchase US goods or services
- International citizens want to invest in US firms
- International citizens want to give monetary gifts to individuals in the U.S.

Though the market for foreign currency exchange has unique characteristics, the market behavior can be illustrated using supply and demand curves like any other commodity. Figure 1 illustrates the market for US dollars in Japan:

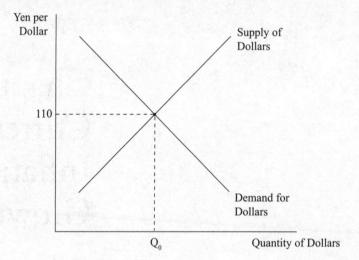

Figure 1: The Currency Market

As the value of yen per dollar increases, the quantity of dollars demanded goes down and the quantity of dollars supplied goes up. The reasoning behind this is the same as for the dollar-zucchini market—at a higher price, consumers desire fewer zucchinis and farmers are willing to produce more. Likewise, when dollars increase in value relative to the the yen, fewer dollars are demanded for purchase of U.S. imports, travel, securities, and so forth in Japan. More people are willing to exchange dollars for yen when they receive more yen per dollar.

The equilibrium in the dollar-yen market determines the **exchange rate**—the rate at which dollars are exchanged for yen, or more generally, the value for which one nation's currency can be exchanged for another. In Figure 2, the exchange rate is 110 yen per dollar.

Pay particular attention to the price of dollars on the y axis: Japanese yen per US dollar. In the foreign exchange market, one national currency is purchased with another, creating a reciprocal relationship between the two currencies. When someone in Japan demands (or purchases) US dollars, they inherently create a supply of Japanese yen in the international currency market. Consider Japanese travelers newly arrived in the U.S.: they supply their yen to the teller in the airport and ask for dollars. Because the transaction inherently involves both currencies, when the value of the dollar changes, the relative value of the yen changes in an equal and opposite amount.

Though the interconnectedness of currencies makes calculating the absolute value of any given currency highly complex, relative relationships therein can be illustrated with the supply and demand curve(s) like any other commodity. Compare Figure 2 on the left with Figure 3 on the right; in Figure 3, the demand curve for US dollars has shifted to the right, reflecting an increase in demand:

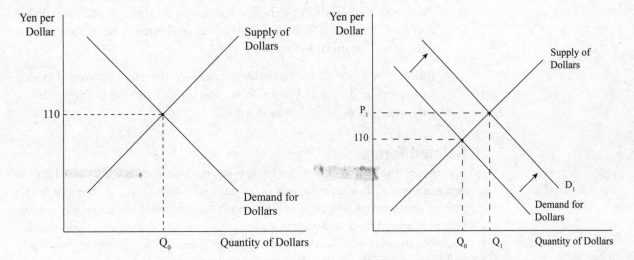

Figure 2: The Currency Market   **Figure 3: Increased Demand for Dollars**

While there isn't enough information to calculate the value of P_1, the graph illustrates that the price of yen per US dollar will increase with demand like any other commodity. In other words, the US dollar has increased in value relative to the yen and therefore costs more yen to purchase. It is critical to remember that the basic laws of supply and demand apply to the relative value of currency when analyzing international currency exchange.

The following factors will cause the demand for the US dollar (or any currency) to shift in the market for international currency exchange:

- Change in relative income levels between countries. Because imports are often normal goods, an increase in another nation's income will increase the demand for US goods and the dollars with which to buy them.

- Change in relative inflation rates. If inflation occurs at a lower rate in the US, then US exports are slower than others to increase in price in the international market. This means US products are less expensive than international competitors, and therefore in higher demand.

- Change in consumer preferences for US goods. If US goods are more popular than those of international competitors, they will be in higher demand.

- Increase in national confidence. Investors are more likely to invest in nations with strong, stable economies and minimal conflict.

Consider the following scenarios and try to predict the effect on the value of the US dollar relative to the Japanese yen:

- Japan has a bumper crop of food, importing less and demanding fewer dollars. (The dollar loses value.)

- Interest rates increase in the United States relative to Japan, and depositors increase the demand for dollars in order to put their funds into U.S. banks. (The dollar increases in value.)

- Prices rise relatively fast in the United States, and the demand for dollars decreases. The supply of dollars increases as consumers purchase more goods elsewhere. (The dollar loses value.)

- Incomes in Japan increase relative to those in the United States, Japanese consumers tend to spend more, increasing the demand for U.S. exports and currency. (The dollar increases in value.)

Related Terms

A currency that **depreciates** or becomes weaker is one that falls in value relative to other currencies. It takes relatively more units of a depreciated currency to buy a unit of another country's currency. For example, if it cost 110 yen to buy a dollar yesterday and today a dollar costs 120 yen, the yen has depreciated. Depreciation decreases imports because they become more expensive for domestic consumers, and increases exports because they become relatively less expensive for foreigners to purchase. A weaker currency thus helps exporting industries and domestic tourism while hurting importing industries and citizens traveling abroad. As a result, currency depreciation makes a trade deficit smaller (or a trade surplus larger).

Appreciation is the opposite of depreciation, and results in a stronger currency. When a currency appreciates or becomes stronger, it takes fewer units of that currency to buy a unit of another currency. For example, if it cost 110 yen to buy a dollar yesterday and it costs 100 yen to buy a dollar today, the yen has appreciated. Appreciation increases imports because they become less expensive, and decreases exports because they become more expensive. A stronger currency thus helps importing industries and citizens traveling abroad, while hurting exporting industries and domestic tourism. As a result, currency appreciation leads to a larger trade deficit (or a smaller trade surplus).

Arbitrage is the practice of buying at a low price and selling at a high price for a certain profit. Arbitrage will prevent exchange rates from being different in one place than in another for any significant period. If Shigeyuki can purchase dollars in Osaka for 90 yen and sell them in Kyoto for 110 yen, he will do so, thus increasing the supply of dollars in Kyoto and increasing the demand for dollars in Osaka until the exchange rate is equalized between the two locations.

Exchange Rate Policy

There are several options for the management of exchange rates, as illustrated in Figure 4.

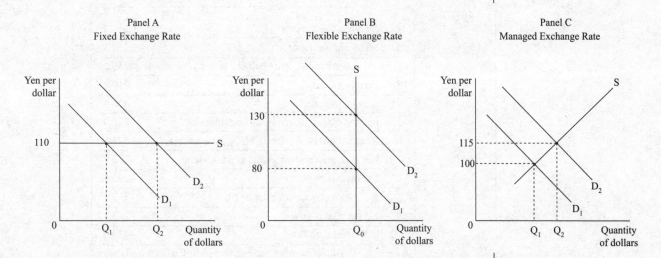

Figure 4

Most central banks hold reserves in each of the major currencies that can be increased or decreased to influence the exchange rate. The central bank can set a **fixed exchange rate** as in Panel A, in which case changes in demand affect only the quantity of dollars purchased, or the central bank can fix the quantity of assets denominated in the home currency and permit a **flexible exchange rate** that changes with demand as in Panel B. Or the central bank can have a **managed exchange rate** as in Panel C. In this case, changes in demand result in changes in the exchange rate, but the exchange rate fluctuations are dampened by a positively sloped supply curve.

The Balance of Payments

As markets become increasingly global, international transactions have a large bearing on virtually every economy. The **balance of payments** is a statement of all international flows of money over a given period, as illustrated in Figure 5.

U.S. Balance of Payments, 2015	
Item	Amount (Billions)
1. Merchandise exports	1,513.5
2. Merchandise imports	−2,272.8
Merchandise trade balance (lines 1–2)	−759.3
3. Service exports	710.2
4. Service imports	−490.6
5. Income from U.S. overseas investments	776.0
6. Income outflow for foreign U.S. investments	−574.5
7. Net U.S. government grants and transfers	−132.0
8. Net private transfers	−267.6
Current-account balance (items 1–8)	−737.8
9. U.S. capital inflow	242.2
10. U.S. capital outflow	−426.0
Financial account balance (items 9–10)	−183.8
11. Statistical discrepancy	274.9
Net balance (items 1–11)	−830.5

Source: U.S. Department of Commerce, Bureau of Economic Analysis, http://www.bea.gov/international

Figure 5

There are three balances within the balance of payments statement. The **merchandise trade balance** is

Merchandise trade balance = merchandise exports – merchandise imports

A merchandise **trade deficit** exists when imports exceed exports, which is typically the case in the United States. The opposite of a trade deficit is a **trade surplus.** Merchandise trade deficits or surpluses must be offset elsewhere in the **current-account** or **financial account balances**.

The current-account balance includes the merchandise trade balance plus the trade of services and transfers between countries.

Current-account balance = trade balance + services balance + transfers

The financial account balance considers other types of assets that change ownership across international borders, including securities, currency, capital (such as machinery), and land. In the equation below, "home" refers to the home country for which the financial account balance is made.

Financial account balance =
foreign purchases of home assets – home purchases of foreign assets

Trade-Offs Between Inflation and Unemployment

Long Run Versus Short Run

Currency exchange provides another lens through which to view inflation: inflation occurs when the value of one nation's currency drops relative to other nations'.

When there is an oversupply of one nation's currency, that nation will experience monetary inflation, increased prices due to the decreased purchasing power of currency. Though slow rates of monetary inflation are accepted by most nations, if one nation experiences inflation at a higher rate their currency will purchase fewer goods in the international market than other nations, and citizens of that nation will face higher prices.

Economists use aggregate supply and demand curves to illustrate the relationship between inflation and unemployment. Changes use aggregate supply and demand curves to illustrate the relationship between inflation and unemployment. Changes in output and associated unemployment fluctuations resulting from shifts in the AD curve suggest an inverse relationship between inflation and unemployment. As the AD curve shifts to the right in Figure 6, the price level increases and unemployment decreases.

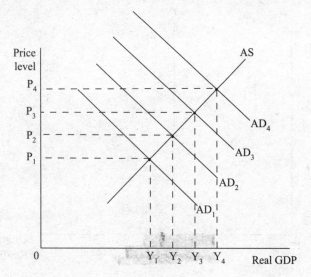

Figure 6

Shifts to the left in AD result in lower price levels but higher unemployment. This inverse relationship between inflation and unemployment is portrayed in Figure 7 in what is called a short-run **Phillips curve**, named after English economist A.W. Phillips.

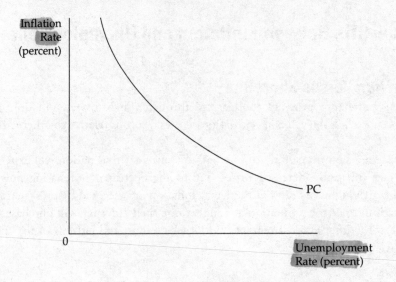

Figure 7: Short-Run Phillips Curve

A fixed output level in the long run at full employment output corresponds with unemployment at the natural rate of unemployment, explained in chapter 10 as the sum of frictional and structural unemployment. This implies a vertical long-run Phillips curve, as illustrated in Figure 8.

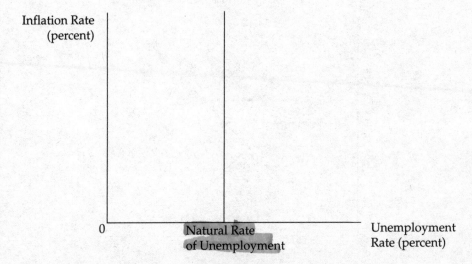

Figure 8: Long-Run Phillips Curve

Supply Shocks

This trade-off between inflation and unemployment that Phillips suggested is supported by real-world data from the 1960s, but data from the 1970s exhibit stagflation—an increase in both the price level and unemployment. Stagflation is caused by shocks to supply that shift AS leftward and result in a rightward shift in the Phillips curve, as illustrated in Figure 9.

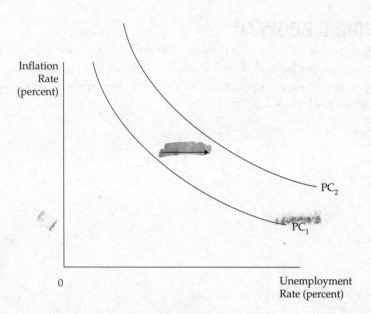

Figure 9

Supply shocks can be caused by natural disasters such as droughts, technical snafus such as computer viruses, or restrictions on the use of resources, as occurred with oil in the 1970s.

Modern Keynesian theory notes that wages and prices are particularly "sticky" in the downward direction (firms are reluctant to lower wages and prices) and that the structure or composition of AD changes over time. When some components of AD become more popular, their prices increase. When other components of AD fall out of favor, rather than lowering their prices and decreasing the payments to their inputs, firms respond with cutbacks and layoffs. The result of these **structural shocks** to the composition of AD is unemployment and inflation. Expansionary policies can increase AD and thereby cure the unemployment but fan the inflation. Alternatively, contractionary policies can reduce price levels but increase unemployment. There lies the trade-off between unemployment and inflation.

The Role of Inflationary Expectations

Shifts in the Phillips curve can result from changes in expectations about inflation. Expectations about inflation are a self-fulfilling prophecy. If inflation is expected, workers and firms build these expectations into their wage and price contracts, and these higher wages and prices result in inflation. Expectations of inflation thus increase the inflation rate for any given level of unemployment, causing a shift to the right in the Phillips curve. If prices are expected to rise more slowly in the future, inflation will decrease for any given unemployment rate and the Phillips curve will shift to the left.

ECONOMIC GROWTH

Economic growth is measured in terms of annual increases in real GDP or real GDP per capita (per person). Growth can be modeled as a rightward shift in the long-run aggregate supply curve or as an outward shift in the production possibility frontier, as illustrated in Figure 10.

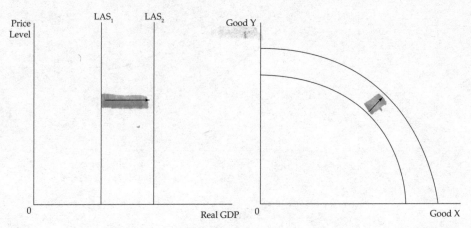

Figure 10: Models of Economic Growth

Sources of growth include

- **Increased investments in human capital,** which come from education, training, practice, and experience. For example, as more people receive training in solar panel installation, more solar panels can be purchased and installed.

- **Increased investments in physical capital.** For example, with more tractors, farmers can harvest more grain from a given area of land.

- **Improvements in technology,** as can result from research and development efforts. For example, the use of robots in automobile manufacturing plants permits assembly lines to move more rapidly.

- **Enhanced resource utilization.** This results from better management and distribution of productive resources. For example, if there is underutilized capital or labor in an economy, better use of those resources will allow production levels to increase. This type of growth can be illustrated on the production possibilities frontier graph by a movement from a point lying below the production possibilities frontier toward a point on the frontier.

Government policies to promote economic growth include support for education systems, vocational training, research grants, and development programs, which can increase the output levels achievable with a given set of resources. As explained in the section on monetary policy, the central bank can promote growth with actions that lower interest rates and thereby increase investments in capital.

Economic growth permits expanded consumption levels and lessens the burden of scarcity. The Reverend Thomas Malthus put forth perhaps the most famous concern about economic growth. He suggested that output, and food in particular, would grow at an **arithmetic rate**—adding a constant amount each period— while population would grow at a **geometric rate**— increasing by a constant proportion each period. The eventual result would be a population that far exceeded its supplies of food. Fortunately, technological improvements in food and other types of production have provided geometric output growth that meets or exceeds population growth.

Beyond fears of starvation, there are additional constraints on population and output growth that may be more binding. Resources that exist in fixed supply are unlikely to disappear completely because prices will become prohibitively high before the resources vanish.

However, as the availability of fossil fuels, clean air and water, life-sustaining forests, and similar limited resources diminishes, we will have to make due with alternatives, some of which may be inferior. This is what makes economics—the allocation of scarce resources among competing ends—so important for you to study.

More Great Books

Check out The Princeton Review's test prep titles for ACT and SAT: *Cracking the ACT Premium Edition, Cracking the SAT Premium Edition,* and many more!

KEY TERMS

International Currency Exchange

merchandise trade balance
trade deficit
trade surplus
current account balance
financial account balance
currency market
exchange rate
depreciate
appreciation
arbitrage
fixed exchange rate
flexible exchange rate
managed exchange rate
monetary inflation

Economics Growth

economic growth
arithmetic rate
geometric rate
Phillips curve
balance of payments

CHAPTER 13 REVIEW QUESTIONS

See Chapter 14 for answers and explanations.

1. Depreciation of the dollar is most likely to

   (A) increase imports
   (B) increase travel abroad
   (C) increase exports
   (D) decrease a trade surplus
   (E) increase a trade deficit

2. The short-run Phillips curve indicates a

   (A) direct relation between unemployment and inflation
   (B) direct relation between price and quantity demanded
   (C) inverse relation between price and quantity demanded
   (D) inverse relation between unemployment and inflation
   (E) vertical relation between unemployment and inflation

3. Income in Japan grows at a faster rate than income in the U.S. How does this affect the demand for the US dollar and the value of the US dollar?

   (A) Demand for the dollar will increase, and the dollar will depreciate.
   (B) Demand for the dollar will increase, and the dollar will appreciate.
   (C) The supply of the dollar increases, and the dollar appreciates.
   (D) Demand for the dollar decreases, and the dollar will appreciate.

4. A crisis in the U.S. causes investors to prioritize opportunities in Europe and Japan. How does this affect the demand for the US dollar?

   (A) Demand for the dollar increases, and the value depreciates.
   (B) Demand for the dollar increases, and the value appreciates.
   (C) Demand for the dollar decreases, and the value depreciates.
   (D) Demand for the dollar decreases, and the value appreciates.

5. Japan decides to reduce taxes, causing growth. How does this affect the US dollar?

   (A) Reducing taxes in Japan has no effect on the US dollar.
   (B) Reducing taxes in Japan increases the demand of the US dollar.
   (C) Reducing taxes in Japan decreases the demand for the US dollar.
   (D) Reducing taxes in Japan causes the Fed to reduce taxes in the U.S.

Chapter 13 Summary

International Currency Exchange

o   When a central bank sets a **fixed exchange rate**, changes in demand affect only the quantity of dollars purchased; with a **flexible exchange rate**, a central bank can fix the quantity of assets denominated in the home currency.

o   The **balance of payments** is a statement of all international flows of money over a given period.

o   A **trade deficit exists** when imports exceed exports; the opposite is a **trade surplus**.

o   A currency that **depreciates** or becomes weaker is one that falls in value relative to other currencies; **appreciation** occurs when a currency gains value relative to others.

o   **Arbitrage** is the practice of buying at a low price and selling at a high price for a certain profit.

o   **Monetary inflation** occurs when prices increase due to an oversupply of currency

Economic Growth

o   Sources of growth include
   • increased investments in human capital
   • increased investments in physical capital
   • improvements in technology
   • enhanced resource utilization

o   A **Phillips curve** illustrates the inverse relationship between the inflation rate and unemployment.

Chapter 14
Macroeconomics
Review Questions:
Answers and
Explanations

CHAPTER 10 REVIEW QUESTIONS: ANSWERS AND EXPLANATIONS

1. **A** GDP measures the worth of a country's goods and services. Eliminate (C) and (D) because they are indicators of inflation. Eliminate (E) because it is vague, and the question doesn't reference a specific account. Eliminate (B) because societal welfare is broader in scope than just GDP. Therefore the answer is (A).

2. **C** Eliminate (B) and (D) because they are irrelevant and misleading. Eliminate (A) and (E) because they exist independently from inflation. Inflation is measured by the Consumer Price Index (CPI); therefore, the answer is (C).

3. **A** Structural employment occurs when workers have to either move to new industries or learn new skills (types of unemployment are summarized on page 178). Eliminate (C) because the question indicates that snow loss is permanent, not seasonal. Therefore the answer is (A).

4. **B** Long-run aggregate supply increases when industry can produce more. This can happen if the country invests in equipment (i.e., capital). Therefore the answer is (B).

5. **B** The cost of goods for Year 1: 5 × $12.00 + 10 × $2.00 + 100 × $0.05 = $60 + $20 + $5 = $85.00. The cost of goods for Year 2: 5 × $11.00 + 10 × $1.25 + 100 × $0.15 = $55 + $12.5 + $15 = $82.50. As the cost of goods decreased, CPI must have dropped, so eliminate (A), (D), and (E). The change in CPI is $\frac{85-82.5}{85} \times 100 = \frac{2.5}{85} \times 100 \approx 3\%$. Therefore the answer is (B).

6. **B** C is the consumption that gets captured in the GDP calculation. Non-monetary transactions are not captured by the GDP, so eliminate (A) and (E). Goods purchased by a company for producing goods and services are not counted as consumed goods, so eliminate (C) and (D). Therefore the answer is (B).

7. **D** Transactions that do not include an exchange of goods or services (such as transfer payments) and transactions not reported to the government (such as off-the-book payments or illegal activities) are not counted in GDP. Therefore the answer is (D). Side note: Some countries are trying to estimate and include parallel market transactions in their GDP calculations!

CHAPTER 11 REVIEW QUESTIONS: ANSWERS AND EXPLANATIONS

1. **E** The best strategy for this question is to sketch the intermediate range of the AS and AD curves with price on the vertical axis and GDP on the horizontal axis (See Figure 3 on page 195). Shift the AD curve to the right as indicated in the question. Visually, you can see that this will cause both price and GDP to increase. Therefore the answer is (E).

2. **D** The largest increase in GDP = multiplier × $500. Multiplier = $\frac{1}{MPS} = \frac{1}{1-MPC} = \frac{1}{1-0.8} = \frac{1}{0.2} = 5$. Therefore the maximum increase in GDP is 5 × $500 = $2,500. Therefore the answer is (D).

3. **B** Stagflation occurs when an increase in prices is concurrent with a decrease in output and, usually, employment. By definition, the correct answer is (B). Stagflation is often caused by cost-push inflation. This increase in cost of resources causes the aggregate supply curve to shift to the left (AS$_1$ in the figure below), causing prices to increase and GDP to fall. Therefore, a correctly drawn graph also reveals that the answer is (B).

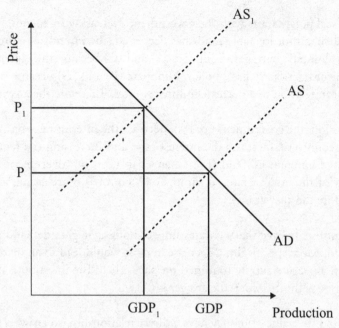

4. **D** Eliminate (A) and (E) because the recessionary gap refers to the relationship between short-run equilibrium and LAS, a function of the full-employment level of real GDP. A recessionary gap occurs when the equilibrium GDP is below full employment level. Therefore the answer is (D).

5. **C** The equilibrium GDP is where the short-term aggregate supply (SAS) curve and the aggregate demand (AD) curve intersect. The GDP at this level is lower than the GDP of where AD and LAS intersect. The economy is, therefore, not at long-run equilibrium, so eliminate answers (B), (D) and (E). As the economy is in short-run equilibrium, the answer is (C).

CHAPTER 12 REVIEW QUESTIONS: ANSWERS AND EXPLANATIONS

1. **D** The deficit is the difference between government spending and tax revenue (G − T) for a given year. The debt is the accumulation of past deficits (an accounting of total difference between government spending and tax revenues). The sign of debt gives no information on deficit, as it is changes in debt that the deficit measures, so eliminate (A) and (B). Choice (C) is reversed in that debt is the accumulation of past deficits, so eliminate (C). When the deficit is negative, then tax revenues exceed government spending. This leads to a decrease in debt. Therefore the answer is (D).

2. **E** Crowding out is a decrease in real investment as a result of government purchases. Government purchases are part of the fiscal policy, so eliminate (A). Impact of government purchases is felt on the demand side, so eliminate (D). When the investment demand curve is elastic, a small increase in government purchases will have a larger reduction in demand for money. Therefore the answer is (E).

3. **B** Contractionary monetary policy is when the government's actions reduce the overall money supply in the economy. Purchasing bonds, increasing taxes (and spending the additional tax revenue), increasing government spending, and decreasing the discount rate all increase the supply of money, so eliminate (A), (C), (D) and (E). Selling bonds reduces the overall money supply in the economy; therefore, the answer is (B).

4. **E** Contractionary fiscal policy starts with the government decreasing its spending (or increasing taxes). As the government demand for loanable funds has decreased, the interest rate drops, leading to a decrease in demand of the domestic currency. Eliminate (A) and (C) because they incorrectly define the interest rate in relation to contractionary fiscal policy. Eliminate (B) and (D) because they incorrectly define the value of the dollar in relation to a decrease in interest rates. Therefore the answer is (E).

5. **E** To counter a recession, the government needs to decrease the interest rates or increase the money supply. Increasing the discount rate increases the interest rate, and increasing the required reserve ratio lowers the money supply. Eliminate (C) and (D). Changes in taxes or government spending may not affect the money supply or the interest rate, so eliminate (A) and (B). Purchasing bonds increases the money supply, and therefore the answer is (E).

6. **A** Supply-side economists believe that tax rates impact both aggregate demand and aggregate supply (in the same direction). More specifically, a decrease in taxes would lead to an increase in aggregate demand and an increase in aggregate supply (outlined on page 217). The question is asking what these economists would disagree with; therefore, the answer is (A).

7. **C** The interest rate and the value of money have a direct relationship, so answers (B) and (D) can be eliminated. Selling bonds decreases the money supply, shifting the supply curve to the left. As a result, the interest rate and the value of money both increase. Choice (C) is correct.

8. **B** An increase in investment from businesses and consumers causes aggregate demand to increase. (A) and (C) are incorrect. There is not enough information to determine the rate at which aggregate demand will change, so (D) is incorrect. Choice (B) is correct.

CHAPTER 13 REVIEW QUESTIONS: ANSWERS AND EXPLANATIONS

1. **C** Depreciation of the dollar will make American goods cheaper to export, and will make imports more expensive for Americans. A direct consequence is that American companies will export more, and demand for foreign goods in America will decrease. Eliminate (D) and (E) because depreciation alone won't necessarily affect the amount of national debt. Eliminate (A) and (B) because they describe effects of appreciation of the dollar. Therefore the answer is (C).

2. **D** The short-run Phillips curve illustrates the inverse relationship between unemployment and inflation rate (illustrated in Figure 7 on page 238). Therefore the answer is (D).

3. **B** When incomes abroad increase faster than those in the U.S., the demand for the dollar will increase and the dollar will appreciate. Most imports are normal goods, so when incomes increase so does the demand for imports. Choice (A) is incorrect because increased demand for dollars causes dollars to appreciate, not depreciate. Choice (C) incorrectly addresses supply instead of demand. Choice (D) confuses the relationship between demand and appreciation; therefore, the answer is (B).

4. **C** When investors pull their money from the U.S., the demand for the dollar decreases and the value depreciates. Choices (A) and (D) incorrectly describe the relationship between demand and value. Choice (B) incorrectly describes the demand for US dollars after the crisis; therefore, the answer is (C).

5. **B** Reducing taxes in Japan will increase the supply of yen in the market, increasing demand for imports from the U.S. and therefore increasing the demand for the US dollar. The correct answer is (B).

Part V
Practice Tests

Chapter 15
Microeconomics
Practice Test

AP® Economics
Micro Exam

DO NOT OPEN THIS BOOKLET UNTIL YOU ARE TOLD TO DO SO.

At a Glance

Total Time
1 hour, 10 minutes
Number of Questions
60
Percent of Total Grade
66.7%
Writing Instrument
Pencil required

Instructions

Section I of this examination contains 60 multiple-choice questions. Fill in only the ovals for numbers 1 through 60 on your answer sheet.

Indicate all of your answers to the multiple-choice questions on the answer sheet. No credit will be given for anything written in this exam booklet, but you may use the booklet for notes or scratch work. After you have decided which of the suggested answers is best, completely fill in the corresponding oval on the answer sheet. Give only one answer to each question. If you change an answer, be sure that the previous mark is erased completely. Here is a sample question and answer.

Sample Question   Sample Answer

Chicago is a

(A) state
(B) city
(C) country
(D) continent
(E) village

Use your time effectively, working as quickly as you can without losing accuracy. Do not spend too much time on any one question. Go on to other questions and come back to the ones you have not answered if you have time. It is not expected that everyone will know the answers to all the multiple-choice questions.

About Guessing

Many candidates wonder whether or not to guess the answers to questions about which they are not certain. Multiple-choice scores are based on the number of questions answered correctly. Points are not deducted for incorrect answers, and no points are awarded for unanswered questions. Because points are not deducted for incorrect answers, you are encouraged to answer all multiple-choice questions. On any questions you do not know the answer to, you should eliminate as many choices as you can, and then select the best answer among the remaining choices.

GO ON TO THE NEXT PAGE.

This page intentionally left blank.

GO ON TO THE NEXT PAGE.

MICROECONOMICS
Section I
Time—70 Minutes
60 Questions

Directions: Each of the questions or incomplete statements below is followed by five suggested answers or completions. Select the one that is best in each case and then fill in the corresponding oval on the answer sheet.

1. Which of the following constitute the fundamental questions every economic system must answer?

 I. What goods and services will be produced?
 II. How will they be produced?
 III. When will they be produced?
 IV. For whom will they be produced?
 V. Where will they be produced?

 (A) I, III, and V only
 (B) I, II, and IV only
 (C) I, II, and V only
 (D) II, IV, and V only
 (E) II, III, and IV only

2. Labor, human capital, entrepreneurship, natural resources, and physical capital are all examples of which of the following?

 (A) Public goods
 (B) Inferior goods
 (C) Factors of production
 (D) Outputs
 (E) Substitutes in production

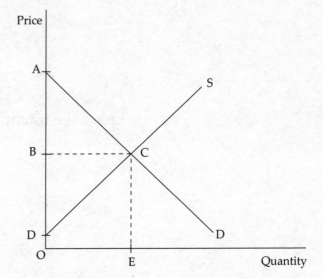

3. In the figure above, consumer surplus is represented by the area

 (A) OACE
 (B) BCD
 (C) ACD
 (D) ABC
 (E) BCEO

4. The law of diminishing marginal utility is most useful for explaining the

 (A) law of supply
 (B) law of demand
 (C) curvature of the total cost curve
 (D) shape of the production possibilities frontier
 (E) diminishing marginal product of capital

GO ON TO THE NEXT PAGE.

Number of Workers	Total Gyros per Hour
1	4
2	10
3	17
4	22
5	25

5. The table above provides the total number of workers and the resulting total output of Gyros Unlimited per hour, holding all other inputs constant. Which of the following statements can be made with certainty based on the available information?

(A) The firm faces decreasing returns to scale.
(B) Diminishing marginal returns begin when the second worker is hired.
(C) The firm faces increasing returns to scale.
(D) The firm should not hire five workers.
(E) Diminishing marginal returns begin when the fourth worker is hired.

6. The owner of a competitive firm making zero economic profit

(A) should consider shutting down because she could make more elsewhere
(B) is making less than normal profits
(C) is making exactly what she would make in her next best alternative job
(D) will most likely make more profits in the long run
(E) is making serious resource allocation errors

7. Which of the following is more likely to result from a competitive market structure than from a monopoly making the same product?

(A) Price equal to marginal cost
(B) Relative welfare loss
(C) Relatively high price
(D) Relatively low quantity
(E) Relatively inferior quality

8. Which of the following is likely to have the most elastic demand?

(A) A good with a vertical demand curve
(B) Cigarettes
(C) All types of soda pop
(D) Sprite
(E) Life-sustaining pills

9. What are the effects on the supply and demand curves for Frisbees if a new procedure reduces the cost of making Frisbees?

	Demand Curve	Supply Curve
(A)	Shifts right	Shifts right
(B)	No change	Shifts left
(C)	No change	Shifts right
(D)	Shifts left	Shifts right
(E)	Shifts right	Shifts left

10. Which of the following statements is true for a firm in a perfectly competitive industry?

(A) Total revenue increases and then decreases.
(B) Marginal revenue is decreasing.
(C) Average revenue is initially negative and then becomes positive.
(D) Marginal revenue is increasing.
(E) Average revenue equals marginal revenue.

11. Which of the following will shift the supply curve for textbooks to the left?

(A) A decrease in the demand for a substitute in production
(B) A decrease in the number of buyers
(C) An increase in printing costs
(D) Expectations of future surpluses
(E) A decrease in taxes on textbook suppliers

12. Consider the following scenarios: imperfect competition, externalities, public goods, and imperfect information. Without government intervention, each of these scenarios would result in:

(A) Demand curves that should be added vertically
(B) Market failure
(C) Prices that are too low
(D) Quantities of output that are too high
(E) An excess of pollution

GO ON TO THE NEXT PAGE.

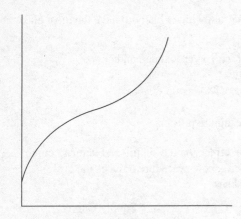

13. The line in the figure above is the most similar to a typical

    (A) total cost curve
    (B) total product curve
    (C) marginal product curve
    (D) average product curve
    (E) marginal cost curve

14. Firms with the following market structure(s) maximize profits by producing where marginal cost equals marginal revenue, if at all.

    I. Perfect competition
    II. Oligopoly
    III. Monopoly
    IV. Monopolistic competition

    (A) I only
    (B) I and II only
    (C) I and III only
    (D) I, III, and IV only
    (E) I, II, III, and IV

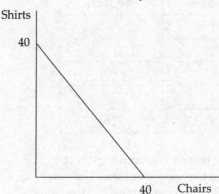

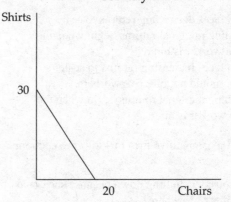

15. The simplified PPFs for countries A and B appear in the figures above. Both countries have the same resources to work with. Which of the following statements is correct?

    (A) Country A has a comparative advantage in both goods.
    (B) Country A has a comparative advantage in chairs, and country B has a comparative advantage in shirts.
    (C) Country B has an absolute advantage in shirts.
    (D) Country A has a comparative advantage in shirts, and country B has a comparative advantage in chairs.
    (E) Country A has an absolute disadvantage in chairs.

GO ON TO THE NEXT PAGE.

16. Which of the following was NOT a landmark antitrust act?

    (A) The Wagner Act
    (B) The Sherman Act
    (C) The Clayton Act
    (D) The Robinson-Patman Act
    (E) The Celler-Kefauver Act

17. In the same period there is a drought affecting the supply of pineapples and a discovery that eating pineapples may assist in the avoidance of cancer. How will this combination of events affect the equilibrium price and quantity of pineapples?

	Equilibrium Price	Equilibrium Quantity
(A)	Increases	Decreases
(B)	Increases	Indeterminate
(C)	Indeterminate	Increases
(D)	Decreases	Indeterminate
(E)	Increases	Increases

18. Which of the following statements accurately describes the relationship between average product (AP) and marginal product (MP) of labor?

    (A) AP rises when MP is above it and falls when MP is below it.
    (B) MP intersects AP at the maximum of MP.
    (C) AP and MP are always parallel to each other.
    (D) AP and MP are either both rising or both falling at all levels of labor.
    (E) AP is always rising when MP is falling and vice versa.

19. Which of the following goods is likely to provide both the largest total utility and the smallest marginal utility?

    (A) Plastic
    (B) Automobiles
    (C) Computers
    (D) Spam
    (E) Air

20. In order to find the market supply curve for a particular good, one would

    (A) aggregate the firm marginal revenue curves horizontally
    (B) aggregate the firm supply curves vertically
    (C) aggregate the firm marginal cost curves vertically
    (D) aggregate the firm marginal revenue curves vertically
    (E) aggregate the firm supply curves horizontally

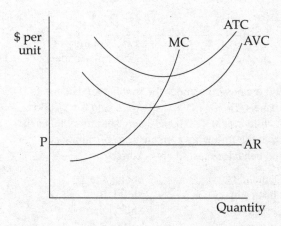

21. A competitive firm facing the demand and cost curves in the figure above should

    (A) shut down immediately
    (B) produce where marginal cost equals marginal revenue
    (C) stay open in the short run but not the long run
    (D) stay open in the short run and long run
    (E) produce where marginal cost equals average revenue

22. A loud party in the neighborhood is disturbing people living nearby who would like to sleep. Which of the following is most likely to lead to an efficient solution to the problem?

    (A) Ban parties
    (B) Permit people to throw parties as they please
    (C) Place a tax on parties equal to the value of the lost sleep that results
    (D) Permit parties only on Tuesdays and Saturdays
    (E) Place a tax on parties equal to the value party-goers receive from their parties

GO ON TO THE NEXT PAGE.

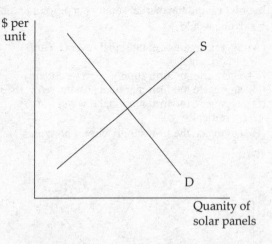

$ per unit

S

D

Quanity of solar panels

23. The figure above illustrates the supply and demand for solar panels. In 2002, 50 panels were sold for $1,000 each, while in 2003, 50 panels were sold for $900 each. Which of the following combinations of supply and demand behavior most likely occurred?

	Demand Curve	Supply Curve
(A)	Shift right	Shift left
(B)	Shift left	Shift right
(C)	Shift right	Shift right
(D)	Shift left	No change
(E)	No change	Shift right

24. Unlike a perfectly competitive firm, a monopoly

(A) will charge the highest price it can on the demand curve
(B) has a horizontal marginal revenue curve
(C) has an upward sloping total revenue curve
(D) faces a downward sloping demand curve
(E) faces a horizontal demand curve

25. Every time Mr. Hamm makes another pizza in his shop, he places $0.45 worth of sauce on top. For Mr. Hamm, the cost of pizza sauce is a component of which of the following?

I. Total Fixed Costs
II. Total Variable Costs
III. Marginal Cost
IV. Total Costs

(A) I and IV only
(B) II and III only
(C) II and IV only
(D) III and IV only
(E) II, III, and IV only

26. If the government wants to establish a socially optimal price for a natural monopoly, it should select the price at which

(A) average revenue equals zero
(B) marginal revenue equals zero
(C) the marginal cost curve intersects the demand curve
(D) the average total cost curve intersects the demand curve
(E) marginal revenue equals marginal cost

27. Which of the following will increase wages for tuba makers?

(A) An increase in the number of graduates at tuba maker training school
(B) An increase in the price of tubas
(C) An increase in the price of tuba lessons
(D) An increase in the tax on tubas
(E) An effective price ceiling for tubas

28. After Julia received a raise in her income, she began purchasing more ice cream cones and fewer popsicles. For Julia, popsicles

(A) disobey the law of demand
(B) are a joint product
(C) are a complementary good with ice cream
(D) are a normal good
(E) are an inferior good

29. When the opportunity for price discrimination arises,

(A) market segments with relatively elastic demand pay higher prices
(B) market segments with relatively inelastic demand pay lower prices
(C) consumer surplus decreases
(D) demand is horizontal
(E) demand is vertical

GO ON TO THE NEXT PAGE.

30. When a perfectly competitive labor market is in equilibrium,

(A) everyone who wants to work has the opportunity to do so
(B) individual firms face downward sloping labor demand curves
(C) unemployment can reach as high as 10-15 percent
(D) individual firms face upward sloping labor demand curves
(E) individual firms are considered "price makers"

Basketball	TC
1	103
2	105
3	109
4	114

31. On the basis of the information in the table above, and the assumption that total fixed costs are 100, which of the following is a correct statement about the costs of basketball production?

(A) The marginal cost of the fourth basketball is 14.
(B) The marginal cost curve falls and then rises.
(C) The total variable cost when three units are produced is 17.
(D) The marginal cost of the first basketball is 103.
(E) The marginal cost curve rises and then falls.

32. A production possibility frontier will be a straight line when

(A) efficiency is achieved
(B) the goods on the axes are perfect substitutes in consumption
(C) utility is maximized
(D) resources are not specialized
(E) the marginal product functions for all inputs are straight lines

33. An industry with three firms selling a standardized or differentiated product would be called

(A) a competitive industry
(B) a monopolistically competitive industry
(C) an oligopoly
(D) a duopoly
(E) a monopoly

34. Which of the following are associated with public goods?

I. Free riders
II. Adding demand curves vertically to find the demand curve for society
III. Nonrivalry in consumption
IV. Nonexcludability

(A) I and II only
(B) I and IV only
(C) II and III only
(D) I, III, and IV only
(E) I, II, III, and IV

Workers	Total Product
1	5
2	9
3	12
4	14
5	15

35. Loony Spoons corporation sells silverware in a competitive market at a constant price of $2 per piece. A competitive labor market sets the wage at $5 per hour. The table above indicates the total product per hour using various numbers of workers. How many workers should Loony Spoons hire per hour?

(A) 1
(B) 2
(C) 3
(D) 4
(E) 5

36. Which of the following statements about a price ceiling is accurate?

(A) An effective price ceiling must be at a price below the equilibrium price.
(B) A price ceiling will increase the quantity of the good supplied.
(C) A price ceiling will cause a shift in the demand curve for the good.
(D) A price ceiling will have no effect on the quantity of the good supplied.
(E) Surpluses in the supply of the good are among the results of a price ceiling.

GO ON TO THE NEXT PAGE.

37. If a decrease in income of 10 percent would cause Alec's consumption of vitamins to increase by 15 percent, which of the following statements is the most likely to be correct?

    (A) Alec's income elasticity of demand is 1.5.
    (B) Vitamins would be categorized as a normal good for Alec.
    (C) Alec's income elasticity of demand is $\frac{2}{3}$.
    (D) Vitamins would be categorized as a necessity for Alec.
    (E) Alec's income elasticity of demand is 150.

	2 workers	4 workers	6 workers
1 shovel	3 trees	4 trees	5 trees
2 shovels	5 trees	6 trees	7 trees
3 shovels	6 trees	8 trees	9 trees

38. The table above indicates the number of trees that can be planted per hour using different combinations of inputs. All of the relevant numbers in the table are consistent with

    (A) constant returns to scale
    (B) increasing marginal returns
    (C) constant marginal returns
    (D) economies of scale
    (E) increasing returns to scale

Tom

		high	low
Bob	high	B: 1 T: 3	B: 5 T: 2
	low	B: 4 T: 6	B: 1 T: 3

39. In the payoff matrix in the figure above, a dominant strategy equilibrium

    (A) is for Bob to go high and Tom to go low
    (B) is for both Bob and Tom to go low
    (C) is for Bob to go low and Tom to go high
    (D) is for both Bob and Tom to go high
    (E) does not exist

40. In the long run, a monopolistically competitive firm

    (A) earns zero economic profit
    (B) earns positive economic profit
    (C) earns negative economic profit
    (D) faces a vertical demand curve
    (E) faces a horizontal demand curve

41. Which of the following is most likely to result in a shift to the right in the demand curve for orange juice?

    (A) A bumper crop of oranges in Florida
    (B) A decrease in the price of Tang
    (C) Expectations of lower future prices for orange juice
    (D) A law permitting orange pickers to be paid less than the minimum wage
    (E) Expectations of higher future income among juice drinkers

42. The market demand curve for labor would shift to the left as the result of

    (A) an increase in the price of the good which the labor is producing
    (B) an increase in demand for the good which the labor is producing
    (C) an increase in the wage rate paid to workers
    (D) a decrease in the marginal product of labor
    (E) a decrease in the number of workers willing to work

43. The industry that makes plastic army figures uses a small fraction of the plastic demanded for all purposes. On this basis, we can conclude that the army-figures industry is most likely a(n)

    (A) increasing-cost industry
    (B) constant-cost industry
    (C) decreasing-cost industry
    (D) profit-making industry
    (E) loss-making industry

GO ON TO THE NEXT PAGE.

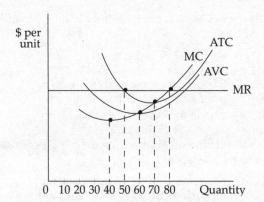

44. Given the cost and revenue curves in the figure above, how many units of output should be produced in order to maximize profit?

   (A) 40
   (B) 50
   (C) 60
   (D) 70
   (E) 80

45. The concentration ratio for a monopoly is

   (A)   0
   (B)   5
   (C)   10
   (D)   100
   (E) 1,000

46. At a Nash equilibrium,

   (A) the supply curve intersects the demand curve
   (B) neither party has an incentive to deviate from his or her strategy
   (C) the marginal revenue curve intersects the marginal cost curve
   (D) the equilibrium is unstable and each party would like to switch strategies
   (E) no additional output could possibly be produced

47. The condition that P = MC is the direct requirement for which type of efficiency?

   (A) Distributive efficiency
   (B) Technical efficiency
   (C) Efficiency in production
   (D) Efficiency in exchange
   (E) Allocative efficiency

48. In order for a firm to successfully carry out price discrimination, which of the following conditions must hold?

   I. The firm cannot face a downward-sloping demand curve.
   II. The firm must have market power.
   III. Buyers with differing demand elasticities must be separable.
   IV. The firm must have motives beyond profit maximization.
   V. The firm must be able to prevent the resale of its products.

   (A) I, III, and V only
   (B) III and IV only
   (C) I and IV only
   (D) II, III, and V only
   (E) II and V only

49. Which of the following is characteristic of a perfectly competitive firm's demand curve?

   (A) Average revenue is less than price at all levels of output.
   (B) Marginal revenue is equal to marginal cost at all levels of output.
   (C) Price and marginal revenue are equal at all levels of output.
   (D) It is the same as the market demand curve.
   (E) Demand is inelastic at all levels of output.

50. The relationship between the marginal revenue curve and the demand curve for a monopoly is most similar to the relationship between the marginal factor cost curve and what curve for a monopsony?

   (A) Labor demand
   (B) Labor supply
   (C) Marginal external cost
   (D) Total cost
   (E) Marginal cost

GO ON TO THE NEXT PAGE.

51. What could the government do to most effectively avoid a free rider problem?

    (A) Enact stricter antitrust legislation
    (B) Provide more complete information about the relevant goods
    (C) Supply public goods using tax dollars
    (D) Tax those creating negative externalities
    (E) Subsidize those creating positive externalities

52. The necessity for a monopoly to lower its price in order to sell more units of its product explains why

    (A) monopolies are common among public utilities
    (B) the marginal revenue curve is below the demand curve for a monopoly
    (C) the marginal cost curve for a monopoly slopes upward
    (D) monopolies are able to maintain market power
    (E) monopolies differ from monopolistically competitive firms

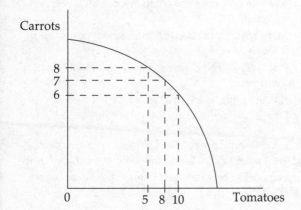

53. Based on the PPF in the figure above, the opportunity cost of producing the seventh carrot is

    (A) 2 tomatoes
    (B) 3 tomatoes
    (C) 5 tomatoes
    (D) 8 tomatoes
    (E) the slope of the PPF

54. The market demand curve for labor will shift to the right when

    (A) the number of firms increases
    (B) the price of output decreases
    (C) the labor supply curve shifts to the right
    (D) the labor supply curve shifts to the left
    (E) the marginal product of labor decreases

55. Patents, control of resources, economies of scale, and exclusive licenses are

    (A) all requirements for price discrimination
    (B) required in order for a firm to earn short-run profits
    (C) all sources of elastic demand
    (D) all barriers to entry
    (E) all detriments to market power

56. Which of the following statements is accurate in regard to a perfectly competitive firm?

    (A) Demand is downward-sloping.
    (B) The demand curve lies above the marginal revenue curve.
    (C) Price is determined by the equilibrium in the entire market.
    (D) Average revenue differs from price.
    (E) Marginal revenue differs from average revenue.

57. Which of the following indicates that two goods are complements?

    (A) A positive income elasticity
    (B) A horizontal demand curve
    (C) A negative cross-price elasticity
    (D) A demand elasticity greater than 1
    (E) A positive cross-price elasticity

58. Education makes Chris a better worker, voter, parent, and citizen. Because the benefits from education go beyond those that Chris enjoys himself, education provides

    (A) increasing marginal utility and should be subsidized
    (B) externalities and should be taxed
    (C) decreasing marginal utility and should be taxed
    (D) externalities and should be subsidized
    (E) an example of a good with inelastic supply

GO ON TO THE NEXT PAGE.

59. When a negative externality exists as the result of the production of a good, the socially optimal quantity of output could be achieved by

    (A) free market capitalism
    (B) placing limits on the quantity that can be produced
    (C) government purchases of the good
    (D) setting a minimum on the quantity that can be produced
    (E) subsidizing the good's production

60. The demand curve for labor is derived from

    (A) the market labor demand curve
    (B) the demand curve for the output produced by labor
    (C) the labor supply curve for the firm
    (D) the equilibrium wage in the labor market
    (E) the market labor supply curve

END OF SECTION I

GO ON TO THE NEXT PAGE.

MICROECONOMICS
Section II
Planning time—10 minutes
Writing time—50 minutes

You will have 10 minutes to read the exam questions. Spend this time reading through all of the questions, practicing graphs, noting possible problem-solving approaches, and otherwise planning your answers. It's fine to make notes on the green question insert, but be sure to write your answers and anything else that might be worth partial credit in the pink answer booklet—the graders will not see the green insert. After 10 minutes you will be told to break the seal on the pink Free-Response booklet and begin writing your answers in that booklet.

Directions: You have 50 minutes to answer all three of the following questions. It is suggested that you spend approximately half your time on the first question and divide the remaining time equally between the next two questions. In answering the questions, you should emphasize the line of reasoning that generated your results; it is not enough to list the results of your analysis. Include correctly labeled diagrams, if useful or required, in explaining your answers. A correctly labeled diagram must have all axes and curves clearly labeled and must show directional changes. Use a pen with black or dark blue ink.

1. In the country of Kold, the marginal cost of producing gloves is constant at \$1 per pair, regardless of the industry structure.

   (a) Draw a correctly labeled graph of the glove market that includes a downward-sloping demand curve. Suppose that the market is controlled by a monopolist. Label as P_m and Q_m the price and quantity that would maximize profits.
   (b) On the same graph drawn for part (a), label as P_c and Q_c the price and quantity that would prevail in the long run if the glove market were perfectly competitive.
   (c) On the same graph drawn for parts (a) and (b), shade the area that represents the efficiency loss (or deadweight loss) associated with the monopoly. Explain what efficiency condition is violated by the monopoly.
   (d) Explain how and why the relationship between the demand curve and the marginal revenue curve differs between an unregulated monopoly and a perfectly competitive firm.

GO ON TO THE NEXT PAGE.

Ally

	Baseball	Soccer
Lee — Baseball		
Lee — Soccer		

2. Both Ally and Lee plan to attend either the soccer game or the baseball game after taking their AP exams. They prefer to meet at the same event, but before the exams they are too preoccupied to determine which event to attend, and the exams let out at different times, so they don't run into each other afterward. The events are on opposite sides of town and Lee and Ally must each choose one event to attend without knowing where the other will be. Lee will receive 10 utils (a measure of happiness) if he ends up at the baseball game with Ally and 5 utils at the baseball game without her. Ally will receive 8 utils if she finds Lee at the baseball game and 6 utils at the baseball game without him. Lee will receive 12 utils at the soccer game with Ally and 4 utils at the soccer game without her. Ally will receive 10 utils at the soccer game with Lee and 3 utils at the soccer game without him.

    (a) Complete the payoff matrix above to reflect the utility levels that Ally and Lee will receive in each scenario.
    (b) Where would Ally and Lee go if they were able to coordinate their strategies? Explain.
    (c) Does Lee have a dominant strategy in this game? Explain.
    (d) Identify every set of strategies in this scenario that represents a Nash equilibrium.

3. When one person receives a flu shot, many other people benefit, because they no longer bear the risk of catching the flu from the shot recipient.

    (a) Graph the supply and demand for flu shots, indicating both the private and the social marginal benefit. Label the equilibrium price and quantity and the socially optimal quantity of flu shots.
    (b) What policy would you recommend to help bring about the socially optimal number of flu shots? Explain how your recommendation would remedy the situation.

STOP
END OF EXAM

Chapter 16
Microeconomics Practice Test: Answers and Explanations

MICROECONOMICS PRACTICE TEST ANSWER KEY

Section I

1.	B	21.	A	41.	E
2.	C	22.	C	42.	D
3.	D	23.	B	43.	B
4.	B	24.	D	44.	E
5.	E	25.	E	45.	D
6.	C	26.	C	46.	B
7.	A	27.	B	47.	E
8.	D	28.	E	48.	D
9.	C	29.	C	49.	C
10.	E	30.	A	50.	B
11.	C	31.	B	51.	C
12.	B	32.	D	52.	B
13.	A	33.	C	53.	A
14.	E	34.	E	54.	A
15.	B	35.	C	55.	D
16.	A	36.	A	56.	C
17.	B	37.	A	57.	C
18.	A	38.	A	58.	D
19.	E	39.	E	59.	B
20.	E	40.	A	60.	B

SECTION I

1. **B** Here are the fundamental questions for economic systems to answer. What goods and services will be produced? How will they be produced? For whom will they be produced? When and where are lesser concerns not typically discussed among the primary economic questions.

2. **C** These are all examples of factors of production. They are not public goods because some are excludable and rival in consumption. They are not inferior, which would mean that one would purchase fewer of them as income increased. They are inputs rather than outputs. And they are not substitutes in production, which would mean that one would have to choose which of them to produce using the same resources.

3. **D** Consumer surplus is the value obtained from the purchase of a good in excess of what is paid for it. Graphically, this makes it the difference between the price line and the demand curve up to the quantity purchased. In the figure, this is the area ABC. BCD is supplier or producer surplus, and OACE is total utility (in terms of dollars).

4. **B** The law of diminishing marginal utility states that as you consume more and more of the same good during a given period, your enjoyment gained from each additional unit of the good decreases. This is why consumers are willing to spend less for each additional unit of a good and the demand curve has a negative slope, thus the law of demand. The law of supply is based on increasing marginal costs. Likewise, total cost, production possibilities, and the marginal product of capital are unrelated to marginal utility.

5. **E** Returns to scale depend on the response of output to changes in all inputs. Because only one input is changed here, there is not enough information provided to determine returns to scale. The wisdom of hiring five workers depends on the price and the wage rate, in addition to marginal product. If the price of Gyros is high enough and the wage rate is low enough, the fifth worker might be a bargain. Diminishing marginal returns begin when an additional worker contributes less to total output than the workers before him or her. The marginal (additional) contributions of the first five workers are 4, 6, 7, 5, and 3 respectively, so it is when the fourth worker is hired that diminishing marginal returns begin.

6. **C** Economic profit is calculated by subtracting all costs from revenues, including opportunity costs. Because opportunity costs are what could be made in the next best alternative situation, earning zero economic profit means earning the most that could be made elsewhere. Zero economic profits are also called normal profits, and they are what all firms earn in the long run in a competitive industry. They do not indicate any resource allocation errors.

7. **A** Given the same market demand and cost curves, a competitive industry will produce more of a good at a lower price than a monopoly. Since monopolies produce lower quantities of a good, the consumer and producer surplus is lower. A lack of competition can also result in goods of inferior quality. While both market structures produce at the quantity where MR = MC, monopolies charge a price above MC while competitive firms charge a price equal to MC, resulting in allocative efficiency in competitive markets.

8. **D** For a good to have an elastic demand, the quantity of the good demanded must be sensitive to the price. The quantity of a good demanded is completely insensitive to price changes (perfectly inelastic) when the demand curve is vertical. Because cigarettes are addictive, and life-sustaining pills are necessary, the quantities of these goods demanded are likely to be relatively insensitive to price (inelastic). This brings us down to a choice between all soda pop and Sprite. Because there are far more substitutes available for Sprite than there are for all types of soda pop, the demand for Sprite will be more elastic than the demand for all soda pop.

9. **C** A new procedure that reduces the cost of making Frisbees will not affect the value of Frisbees to consumers, so it will not cause the demand curve to shift at all. Because firms are willing to supply more Frisbees at any given price when they cost less to produce, the supply curve will shift to the right.

10. **E** A perfectly competitive firm sells all of its output at the same price. Thus, marginal revenue and average revenue are both constant at the market price. Total revenue is a straight line from the origin with a constant slope equal to the market price.

11. **C** Both a decrease in the number of buyers and expectations of future surpluses would decrease demand. A decrease in the demand for a substitute in production (say, magazines) would decrease the price of magazines and increase the supply of textbooks, because paper resources would be shifted from magazines to textbooks as the price magazines could garner dropped. A decrease in taxes on textbook suppliers would decrease the cost of supplying textbooks and thus increase their supply, which is based on the marginal cost of provision. An increase in printing costs would increase the cost of textbook production and decrease textbook supply.

12. **B** Demand curves should be added vertically to find the total demand for public goods, but not for the other items. Prices are too high (higher than marginal cost, which is the benchmark for allocative efficiency) as the result of imperfect competition. Quantities may be too high when negative externalities exist, but are too low when there are positive externalities and for public goods. An excess of pollution results only from negative externalities and perhaps imperfect information. All of these items are sources of market failure, which occurs when resources are not allocated efficiently.

13. **A** Typical marginal product, average product, and marginal cost curves have both negatively and positively sloped sections. A typical total product curve has an increasing slope at the beginning (due to increasing marginal returns), and then a decreasing but positive slope (due to diminishing marginal returns) before it flattens out and the slope becomes negative. The line shown is a typical total cost curve, with decreasing and then increasing positive slope resulting from decreasing and then increasing marginal cost.

14. **E** Firms with every type of market structure maximize profits by producing where marginal cost equals marginal revenue, if at all. Producing more will increase costs more than revenues, and producing less will fail to take advantage of opportunities to sell additional units when the additional revenue exceeds the additional cost.

15. **B** Country A gives up 1 chair per shirt, and country B gives up $\frac{2}{3}$ of a chair per shirt. We know this because if country B goes from producing all chairs to producing all shirts, it gives up 20 chairs for 30 shirts, so it loses $\frac{20}{30}$, or $\frac{2}{3}$ as many chairs as it makes shirts. Because the opportunity cost of shirts is higher in country A, country B has the comparative advantage in shirts. That rules out (A) and (D). Because country A has an absolute advantage in shirts and chairs (it can produce more with the same resources), (C) and (E) are ruled out, and the answer must be (B). The first part of (B) is correct because it costs country A 1 chair per shirt and it costs country B $\frac{3}{2}$ chairs per shirt.

16. **A** The Wagner Act gave workers the right to organize. The other four are landmark antitrust acts designed to limit attempts by firms to obtain excessive market power.

17. **B** The drought will decrease the supply of pineapples and the medical discovery will increase the demand. A decrease in supply increases equilibrium price and decreases equilibrium quantity, while an increase in demand increases equilibrium price and increases equilibrium quantity. Because both changes increase price, it is clear that the new equilibrium price will be higher. However, because the decrease in supply decreases quantity and the increase in demand increases quantity, the new equilibrium quantity may be higher, lower, or the same, depending on the relative sizes of the shifts in supply and demand.

18. **A** The marginal product "pulls" average product up or down depending on whether it is above or below average product. If the MP—the output of the last or marginal worker hired—is above the average, the average will increase. If the MP is below the average, it will fall. MP intersects AP at the maximum of AP, not MP. AP and MP are sometimes both rising, sometimes both falling, and sometimes going in opposite directions, as when MP is above AP and falling and AP is rising.

19. **E** Total utility is the combined benefit derived from all units of a good, and marginal utility is the benefit from the last unit consumed. Because consumers purchase goods until the marginal utility equals the price, the good with the lowest price will provide the lowest marginal utility. With air being free, we consume it until the marginal benefit is zero. At the same time, the total utility of air is very large, and surpasses the total utility from the other items because air is the only good listed that is required to keep all of us alive.

20. **E** By adding supply curves horizontally, the quantities each firm will provide at each price are combined into a total quantity supplied by the market at each price. Vertical summation is going in the wrong direction, adding prices for given quantities. Marginal revenue curves depend on demand, not supply, so it would be inappropriate to use them to find a market supply curve.

21. **A** The firm in this situation is not covering its average variable costs. Not only is it losing money, but it is also not earning enough to help pay for any of its fixed costs. It minimizes its losses by shutting down immediately, thus eliminating its variable costs and having to pay only for its fixed costs.

22. **C** This situation involves a negative externality—noise from the party traveling where it isn't wanted. The most efficient parties are held until the marginal benefit (MB) equals the marginal social cost (MSC), which is the marginal private cost (MPC) plus the marginal external cost (MEC). Banning parties might not be efficient, because the marginal benefit from the first few parties might exceed the marginal social cost. Permitting any and all parties might not be efficient because the number of parties might exceed the number for which MB = MSC. Permitting parties on Tuesdays and Saturdays or charging a tax equal to the party value does not weigh MB against MSC and may result in too many or too few parties. The best choice is to impose a tax equal to the value of lost sleep from a party. This tax equals the marginal external cost, so when deciding whether or not to hold a party, the potential party hosts will consider all of the costs, both private and external, in addition to the benefits.

23. **B** Although using Process of Elimination would work here to find the answer, the easiest approach is simply to draw the graph. Treating the existing equilibrium as that for 2002, the only way to draw a new equilibrium at the same quantity and a lower price is to shift demand to the left and supply to the right.

24. **D** In the absence of a price ceiling, either a monopoly or a perfectly competitive firm can legally charge any price it wants, but in both cases prices that are too high can result in losses or zero sales. A perfectly competitive firm has a horizontal marginal revenue and demand curve. Both can be expected to have an upward sloping total revenue curve.

25. **E** Fixed costs are those that do not change as more output is produced, so the cost of sauce does not qualify. Variable costs are those that do change with output, and marginal cost is the cost of producing one more unit of output, so sauce costs are part of each of these. Total costs are total fixed costs plus total variable costs, so sauce costs are a component of total costs as well.

26. **C** To achieve the socially optimal outcome, the government should set the price where the marginal cost curve intersects the demand curve. That way, consumers will purchase more of the output until another unit would create less additional benefit than the marginal cost of producing it. The equation of marginal revenue and marginal cost determines the profit-maximizing quantity for a firm, but not the socially optimal outcome for a natural monopoly. Setting price where the average total cost curve intersects the demand curve permits a fair return but not a socially optimal outcome. There is no reason to set price where marginal revenue or average revenue equal zero.

27. **B** An increase in the number of trained tuba makers will increase the labor supply curve (shift it to the right) and decrease the wage. An increase in the price of tuba lessons will decrease the demand for tubas—a complementary good—and thus decrease the price of tubas. Because the demand for tuba makers is derived from the demand for tubas, when tuba demand goes down, tuba maker demand goes down and thus wages go down. A tax on tubas will similarly decrease the demand for tubas and tuba makers and decrease their wages. An effective price ceiling will lower the price and marginal revenue and thus the marginal revenue product ($MRP_L = MP_L \times MR$), which is the value of an additional worker and the basis for labor demand. When labor demand decreases, equilibrium wage goes down. On the other hand, an increase in the price of tubas will increase MRP_L and thus increase the demand for workers and the wage rate.

28. **E** The law of demand relates price and quantity demanded, not income and quantity demanded. A joint product is produced as a result of production of another good, like leather and beef. Complementary goods are those one purchases more of when the price of another other goes down, like hotel stays and airfare. A normal good is one that the consumer buys more of when income increases (like ice cream in this situation). Thus, the correct answer is an inferior good—one that the consumer purchases less of when income increases.

29. **C** When price discrimination is possible, market segments with relatively elastic demand pay lower prices and those with relatively inelastic demand pay higher prices. Price discrimination does not indicate horizontal or vertical demand curves. Because consumer surplus is the difference between what most consumers would pay, and the price, and price discrimination allows firms to charge consumers prices that are closer to or exactly the most they would pay, consumer surplus decreases.

30. **A** When a perfectly competitive labor market is in equilibrium, individual firms face a horizontal labor demand curve and are considered price takers. Everyone who wants to work at the market wage rate can do so, resulting in an unemployment rate of zero.

31. **B** Marginal cost is the additional cost of producing one more unit. With a total fixed cost of 100, the marginal cost is 3, 2, 4, and 5 for producing the first four basketballs. Note that these numbers fall and then rise. These numbers are found by subtracting the total cost of producing one fewer from the total cost of producing the current number. For example, to produce 1, the marginal cost is $103 - 100 = 3$. The marginal cost of the fourth basketball is $114 - 109 = 5$. Total variable cost is total cost minus total fixed cost, or $109 - 100 = 9$, when three units are produced.

32. **D** Efficiency and utility maximization can occur with a curved or straight PPF, as long as the economy operates on the PPF and not within it. The substitutability of the goods in consumption has no bearing on their production, and just because the marginal product functions are straight lines, that does not prevent the PPF from being curved. The curvature of PPFs results from increasing opportunity costs arising from the use of resources that are less and less specialized for the production of a particular good. If the resources used to make the two goods are not specialized, opportunity costs are constant and the PPF is a straight line.

33. **C** Both competitive and monopolistically competitive industries have a relatively large number of competitors. A monopoly consists of only one firm. A duopoly has two competitors, so an industry with 3 firms as described would most accurately be called an oligopoly.

34. **E** Public goods are defined as things such as national defense that benefit everyone. These are all associated with public goods.

35. **C** The marginal products of the first five workers are 5, 4, 3, 2, and 1 respectively. With a constant selling price of $2 per unit of output, their marginal revenue products are 10, 8, 6, 4, and 2 dollars. A firm's demand curve for labor is equivalent to its marginal revenue product curve for labor, and a wage-taking firm should hire until the MRP_L equals or exceeds the wage. Thus, Loony Spoons should hire three workers. The fourth and subsequent workers bring in less money in sales than they must be paid in wages.

36. **A** An effective price ceiling must be below the equilibrium price; requiring firms to charge no more than a price above the equilibrium price would have no effect on their behavior because they wouldn't want to charge more than the equilibrium price anyway. Increases in the quantity of the good supplied and surpluses in the supply of the good would result from a price floor, not a ceiling. The quantity of the good supplied would decrease rather than increase. Additionally, price ceilings do not cause the demand or supply curves to shift.

37. **A** The income elasticity of demand is the percentage change in quantity demanded divided by the percentage change in income, or $\frac{15}{10} = 1.5$. For normal goods, demand decreases when income decreases; For Alec, vitamins are an inferior good. Necessities are those that have a price elasticity of demand less than one.

38. **A** Marginal returns are those gained when only one input is varied and the other is fixed. For example, holding the number of workers fixed at four and increasing the number of shovels from 0 to 3, the marginal returns decrease from 4 with the first shovel to 2 (6 − 4) with the second shovel and then stay constant at 2 (8 − 6) with the third shovel. All of the rows and columns exhibit some decreasing marginal returns, so it is incorrect to say that all of the relevant numbers in the table are consistent with either constant or increasing marginal returns. Economies of scale exist when the long-run average cost is decreasing as output increases, as would be the case with increasing returns to scale. Along the diagonal 3 to 6 to 9 trees, we see that output increases in proportion to the amounts of each of the inputs. For example, when each of the inputs is doubled, the number of trees doubles from 3 to 6. This is called constant returns to scale.

39. **E** Dominant strategies, dominant strategy equilibria, and Nash equilibria are easily found using the "circle" method explained in the game theory section of this book. Briefly, for each possible strategy for Bob, you circle the payoff for the best move for Tom and vice versa. If Tom has two payoffs circled in the same column (or row if you put him on the left rather than the top) as he does in the "high" column, then

"high" is a dominant strategy for Tom—he should do it regardless of what Bob does. If Bob has two payoffs circled in the same row (or column if he's on top) then the strategy represented by that row is dominant for Bob. A dominant strategy equilibrium exists when both players have a dominant strategy. The box with two circles in it indicates the dominant strategy equilibrium if it exists. However, because Bob should go high if Tom goes low and Bob should go low if Tom goes high, Bob does not have a dominant strategy and a dominant strategy equilibrium does not exist.

40. **A** There is no reason to expect a monopolistically competitive firm to face a horizontal or vertical demand curve. It will face a downward sloping demand curve because its product is differentiated, but in the long run, the lack of barriers to entry will allow similar firms to compete away demand until economic profits are zero.

41. **E** A bumper crop of oranges and the ability to pay orange pickers less would shift the supply curve to the right. Tang is a substitute for orange juice, so if its price decreases, people will buy more Tang and less orange juice, shifting the demand curve for orange juice to the left. Expectations of lower future prices for orange juice might lead people to put off some of their purchases of orange juice until the price drops, thus decreasing demand (shifting it to the left). Expectations of higher future incomes among juice drinkers would lead some of them to make more purchases now. This is called consumption smoothing.

42. **D** The demand for labor is determined by the marginal revenue product of labor, which is the product of the marginal product of labor and the marginal revenue from the output produced by the labor. Thus, if the marginal product of labor decreases, so does the demand for labor. An increase in the price of the good would increase the demand for labor, as would an increase in demand for the good. An increase in the wage rate would cause a movement along the labor demand curve rather than a shift in the curve.

43. **B** There is not enough information provided to make conclusions about profits or losses. Increasing-cost industries are those that make up a large proportion of the demand for an input, meaning that expansion of these industries is likely to bid up the prices of those inputs and cause average production costs to increase. Decreasing-cost industries experience decreasing average production costs as output increases, perhaps because mass production of inputs becomes feasible with increased input demand. On the basis of the information provided, the best conclusion is that army figures are made in a constant cost industry, meaning that it uses a small enough proportion of the input (plastic) so that it does not bid up the input price as the industry expands.

44. **E** Firms maximize profit by producing where MR = MC, unless price is below AVC, in which case they should shut down. MR = MC at a quantity of 80.

45. **D** The n-firm concentration ratio is the sum of the market shares of the largest n firms in an industry. Because a monopoly holds 100 percent of the market share, regardless of the value of n, the concentration ratio is 100.

46. **B** A Nash equilibrium is a term from game theory that indicates that each party in a strategic game wants to stick with its strategy, given what the other party is doing. After applying the "circle" method explained in this book, a Nash equilibrium occurs whenever two circles appear in the same square of a payoff matrix.

47. **E** Technical efficiency and efficiency in production are two names for the same type of efficiency, which requires that the ratio of the marginal products of the inputs equals the ratio of their costs per unit. Distributive efficiency and efficiency in exchange are also two names for the same type of efficiency, which requires that the price ratio for outputs equals the ratio of the marginal utilities for the outputs. The condition that P = MC is the direct requirement for allocative efficiency. Even if you did not remember this, you might note that allocative efficiency is the only unique type of efficiency among the answer choices—the other two types are listed twice under different names. Because there can be only one correct answer, it must be the one with only one listing.

48. **D** Price discrimination involves charging customers or groups of customers different prices based on their willingness to pay. The goal is to increase profits, so item IV is incorrect. The firm must have market power, meaning that it faces a downward sloping demand curve and it is not a price taker. This rules out item I. The other three items are the conditions for price discrimination as explained in the text of this book.

49. **C** A perfectly competitive firm's demand curve is horizontal at the price determined by the market equilibrium. Thus, each firm can sell as many units as it wants at the market price, and marginal revenue equals the price. It is the need to lower the price in order to sell more units that causes firms with market power to have marginal revenue levels that fall below price levels.

50. **B** The marginal revenue curve is below the demand curve for a monopoly, because the monopoly must lower its price on all units sold in order to sell one more. This results in additional revenue that is less than the price on the demand curve by the amount of losses on units previously sold at a higher price. Similarly, the marginal factor cost curve is above the labor supply curve for a monopsony, because it must increase its wage in order to hire one more unit of labor. Thus, the marginal factor cost is larger than the wage rate reflected on the labor supply curve by the additional amount paid to workers previously earning lower wages.

51. **C** Choices (A), (B), (D), and (E) provide solutions for imperfect competition, incomplete information, and negative and positive externalities respectively. A free rider problem arises when people try to benefit from a public good without paying for it. The government can avoid this by taxing everyone and providing the public good itself, as it does for highways and national defense.

52. **B** Monopolies are common among public utilities due to economies of scale. Marginal cost does not rely on price. Monopolies are able to maintain market power due to barriers to entry. And both monopolies and monopolistically competitive firms must lower their price in order to sell more units of their output. The correct answer is (B). The marginal revenue curve is below the demand curve for monopolies because they must lower their price in order to sell more. Because they lower the price in order to sell one more unit, the marginal revenue is not the price as indicated on the demand curve, but that price minus the lost earnings on all of the previous units that are now selling at a lower price.

53. **A** When the seventh carrot is produced, production of tomatoes goes from 10 to 8, so the opportunity cost is 2 tomatoes. The slope of the PPF is the change in carrots over the change in tomatoes, $-\frac{1}{2}$, which is the negative inverse of the opportunity cost of carrots. The absolute value of the slope is the opportunity cost of producing the horizontal axis good (tomatoes).

54. **A** The labor demand curve is independent of the labor supply curve. A decrease in the price of output or a decrease in the marginal product of labor will shift the labor demand curve to the left. Because the market demand curve for labor is the horizontal summation of individual firm labor demand curves, when the number of firms increases, the market demand curve for labor will shift to the right.

55. **D** These items are all barriers to entry that create market power and allow firms to maintain economic profits into the long run. None of them are required for a firm to earn short-run profits, which can occur even in a competitive industry. The requirements for price discrimination are market power, consumers with differing and separable demand elasticities, and the ability to prevent resale.

56. **C** For a firm in a perfectly competitive market, P = MR = AR, all of which can be read from the demand curve, which is horizontal at the market equilibrium. Like so many of the questions, the answer here can be found immediately by drawing the relevant graphs.

57. **C** Cross-price elasticity is the only type of elasticity that considers two particular goods, which rules out (A) and (D). A horizontal demand curve simply means that the one good has a perfectly elastic demand, and says nothing about its relationship with another particular good, thus ruling out (B). The cross-price elasticity is the percentage change in the quantity demanded of one good divided by the percentage change in the price of another good. If an increase in the price of one good (movie tickets) causes an increase in the quantity of the other good (movie rentals) demanded, the cross-price elasticity is positive and the goods are substitutes. If an increase in the price of one good (gasoline) causes a decrease in the quantity of the other good demanded (sports utility vehicles), the cross-price elasticity is negative and the two goods are complements.

58. **D** The spillover effects described here are one type of externality. When externalities are positive, subsidies are required to bring the marginal benefit to the creator(s) of the externalities up to the marginal social benefit. Otherwise, these goods and services will be underconsumed. Increasing marginal utility and inelastic supply are not characteristic of education or other sources of positive externalities.

59. **B** When a negative externality (such as pollution) exists, output exceeds the social optimum. Subsidies, government purchases, free markets, and minimums will either increase or have no effect on the quantity produced. The quantity can be restricted by quantity limits as noted here. Other solutions to negative externalities include taxes and restrictions on problem-causing production methods and emissions.

60. **B** The market labor demand curve is derived by taking the sum of individual firm demand curves; the derivation is not the other way around. The supply curve for labor does not determine labor demand. The equilibrium wage determines the quantity of labor demanded but not the shape of the demand curve for labor. Rather, labor demand is a function of the marginal product of labor and the price of the output, which is derived from the demand for the output produced by labor.

SECTION II

Below are the fully correct answers. However, remember that you can still earn points on the free-response questions if you give only a partially correct answer. So, use the response below to see how much you got right and estimate how well you would do on the real AP exam.

1.

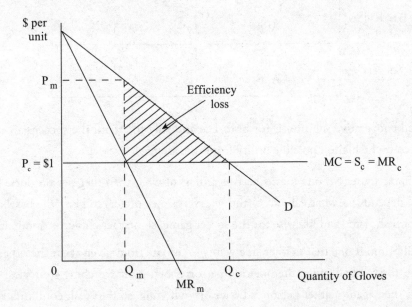

(a) The figure you drew should look similar to the figure above. A monopoly would charge P_m , which is above the marginal cost of $1, and produce the lower quantity Q_m as indicated in the figure.

(b) The marginal cost and competitive supply curve are horizontal at $1 and the competitive equilibrium price and quantity are P_c and Q_c , respectively.

(c) The section above the competitive price line and below the demand curve represents consumer surplus under perfect competition. With the lower quantity and higher price in the monopolized market, the shaded portion of consumer surplus is entirely lost. The portion between P_c and P_m on the vertical axis and between 0 and Q_m on the horizontal axis is transferred from consumer surplus to monopoly profits. Because price is above marginal cost for a monopoly, the allocative efficiency condition that P = MC is violated.

(d) A competitive firm can sell all that it wants at the market price, so its marginal revenue is constant at the market price. A monopoly must lower its price in order to sell another unit of its product, so its marginal revenue is the price minus the lost revenues from units previously sold at a higher price. Thus, the marginal revenue is less than the price, as indicated by line MR_m.

2.

(a)

	Ally	
	Baseball	Soccer
Lee Baseball	L: 10 A: 8	L: 5 A: 3
Soccer	L: 4 A: 6	L: 12 A: 10

(b) The preferred cooperative solution is for both Lee and Ally to attend the soccer game, because each of them will receive the highest possible utility from that strategy.

(c) No. A dominant strategy is one that is best regardless of what the other person does. In this case, Lee's best strategy depends on what Ally does, and vice versa. Lee prefers to be at the baseball game if Ally is there but not if she isn't, and likewise for the soccer game, so neither choice is dominant.

(d) A Nash equilibrium is one that neither side wants to deviate from given what the other person is doing. If both are at the baseball game, then neither person is better off switching strategies. If both are at the soccer game, then again neither person is better off switching, so the Nash equilibria are both go to the baseball game and both go to the soccer game.

3.

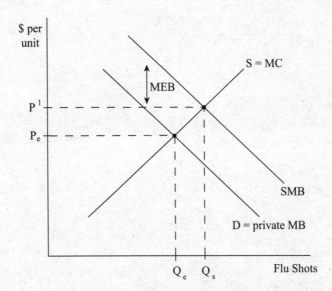

(a) The figure above illustrates the supply and demand for flu shots. The demand will reflect the private marginal benefit, while the social marginal benefit is the private marginal benefit plus the marginal external benefit. The equilibrium price and quantity are P_e and Q_e, and the socially optimal quantity is Q_s.

(b) I would recommend that flu shots be subsidized by the amount of the marginal external benefit. An alternative policy would be to make flu shots mandatory for Q_s people. With a subsidy equal to the MEB, people would be willing to pay up to the social marginal benefit per shot, which equals their private marginal benefit plus the subsidy. The SMB curve would effectively become the demand curve, and the quantity purchased would be Q_s at a price of P^1.

Chapter 17
Macroeconomics
Practice Test

AP® Economics
Macro Exam

SECTION I: Multiple-Choice Questions

DO NOT OPEN THIS BOOKLET UNTIL YOU ARE TOLD TO DO SO.

At a Glance

Total Time
1 hour, 10 minutes
Number of Questions
60
Percent of Total Grade
66.7%
Writing Instrument
Pencil required

Instructions

Section I of this examination contains 60 multiple-choice questions. Fill in only the ovals for numbers 1 through 60 on your answer sheet.

Indicate all of your answers to the multiple-choice questions on the answer sheet. No credit will be given for anything written in this exam booklet, but you may use the booklet for notes or scratch work. After you have decided which of the suggested answers is best, completely fill in the corresponding oval on the answer sheet. Give only one answer to each question. If you change an answer, be sure that the previous mark is erased completely. Here is a sample question and answer.

Sample Question   Sample Answer

Chicago is a

(A) state
(B) city
(C) country
(D) continent
(E) village

Use your time effectively, working as quickly as you can without losing accuracy. Do not spend too much time on any one question. Go on to other questions and come back to the ones you have not answered if you have time. It is not expected that everyone will know the answers to all the multiple-choice questions.

About Guessing

Many candidates wonder whether or not to guess the answers to questions about which they are not certain. Multiple-choice scores are based on the number of questions answered correctly. Points are not deducted for incorrect answers, and no points are awarded for unanswered questions. Because points are not deducted for incorrect answers, you are encouraged to answer all multiple-choice questions. On any questions you do not know the answer to, you should eliminate as many choices as you can, and then select the best answer among the remaining choices.

GO ON TO THE NEXT PAGE.

This page intentionally left blank.

GO ON TO THE NEXT PAGE.

MACROECONOMICS
Section I
Time—70 Minutes
60 Questions

Directions: Each of the questions or incomplete statements below is followed by five suggested answers or completions. Select the one that is best in each case and then fill in the corresponding oval on the answer sheet.

1. Which of the following is included in U.S. GDP?

    I. The market value of movies made in Africa by U.S. citizens
    II. The market value of olive oil made in Italy and sold in the United States
    III. The market value of blue jeans made in the United States and sold in Japan
    IV. The market value of wine made in the United States by Canadian citizens

    (A) II, III, and IV only
    (B) I and III only
    (C) II and IV only
    (D) IV only
    (E) III and IV only

2. Assume commercial banks save no excess reserves and the reserve requirement is 20 percent. How much money is created in new loans from all banks after this bank receives a deposit of $1,000 ?

    (A) $800
    (B) $1,000
    (C) $4,000
    (D) $5,000
    (E) $20,000

3. In a given period, the average price level in the country of Sherwood tripled, and Robin's income increased from $30,000 to $60,000. What happened to Robin's nominal and real income?

	Nominal Income	Real Income
(A)	Increased	Decreased
(B)	Increased	Increased
(C)	Decreased	Decreased
(D)	Increased	Stayed the same
(E)	Decreased	Increased

4. The upward sloping section of the aggregate supply curve can be explained by

    (A) excess capacity that allows output to increase without upward pressure on prices
    (B) the physical limit on output that prevents additional output from being produced
    (C) wages and other input prices that adjust more slowly than output prices
    (D) accurate information within firms about how their prices compare to the overall price level
    (E) a rational desire to produce more at higher price levels because the prices received for items sold will in turn allow the sellers to purchase more output from others

5. Which of the following is a direct, accurate link within the circular flow?

    (A) Goods and services are exchanged for inputs via the factor markets.
    (B) Wages and rents are exchanged for income via the product markets.
    (C) Household expenditures result in revenues for firms via the product markets.
    (D) Household income results in revenues via the factor markets.
    (E) Firms exchange revenues for land, labor, and capital via the product markets.

6. Which of the following would be an example of fiat money?

    (A) Cigarettes used as money in prisons
    (B) Dollar bills
    (C) Gold coins
    (D) Arrowheads used as a medium of exchange
    (E) Chickens used for bartering

GO ON TO THE NEXT PAGE.

7. Assume Astobia and Bonavia are countries that exercise free trade. If the real interest rate in Astobia decreases in comparison to Bonavia's real interest rate, then for Bonavia which of the following would be true of capital flow, the value of its currency, and its exports?

	Capital Flow	Currency	Exports
(A)	outflow	appreciation	decrease
(B)	outflow	appreciation	increase
(C)	inflow	depreciation	decrease
(D)	inflow	depreciation	decrease
(E)	inflow	appreciation	decrease

8. Expansionary fiscal policy would best be prescribed to

(A) eliminate a recessionary gap
(B) reduce inflation
(C) reduce the interest rate
(D) eliminate an inflationary gap
(E) avoid crowding out

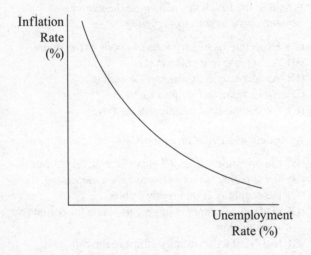

9. The figure above illustrates a/an

(A) demand curve
(B) Phillips curve
(C) production possibilities frontier
(D) aggregate supply curve
(E) Lorenz curve

10. The aggregate demand curve is

(A) a horizontal summation of market demand curves
(B) a horizontal summation of firm demand curves
(C) a simple aggregation of demand curves for individual goods
(D) a vertical summation of firm demand curves
(E) not found by adding product demand curves horizontally or vertically

11. Assuming there is no statistical discrepancy, a trade surplus must be offset elsewhere in the

(A) current-account balance only
(B) financial-account balance only
(C) merchandise balance of trade only
(D) current-account or financial-account only
(E) merchandise balance of trade or current-account only

12. Kevin wants shoes and grows turnips. Lisa wants turnips and makes sheet metal. Bob wants sheet metal and makes shoes. Which function of money will cater most directly to the situation at hand?

(A) Store of value
(B) Unit of account
(C) Medium of exchange
(D) Means of deferred payment
(E) Standard measure

13. Classical economists believe

(A) in the quantity theory of money—that both the velocity and the quantity of goods and services sold per period are fairly stable
(B) there is a serious risk of a liquidity trap because the demand curve for money is relatively flat
(C) that the government should make every effort to fine-tune the economy
(D) that the aggregate supply curve is L-shaped
(E) that an increase in the money supply has a small and indirect effect on total spending

GO ON TO THE NEXT PAGE.

14. The aggregate supply curve will shift to the right in response to

   (A) a decrease in the labor supply
   (B) an increase in investment in capital
   (C) an increase in corporate taxes
   (D) a decrease in the availability of education and training
   (E) natural disasters

15. A fixed output level in the long run at full-employment output corresponds with which of the following shapes of the long-run Phillips curve?

   (A) Horizontal
   (B) Convex to the origin
   (C) Concave to the origin
   (D) Vertical
   (E) Linear with a slope of 1

16. Every choice results in a foregone best alternative, which economists call the

   (A) accounting cost
   (B) switching cost
   (C) inferior cost
   (D) average cost
   (E) opportunity cost

17. The aggregate demand curve has a negative slope in part because when the price level increases

   (A) the value of cash increases
   (B) imports become relatively more expensive
   (C) the real quantity of money increases
   (D) the interest rate increases
   (E) exports increase

18. When the value of the U.S. dollar appreciates relative to other currencies, which of the following is the most likely to occur?

   (A) Imports into the United States will decrease.
   (B) Exports from the United States will increase.
   (C) U.S. residents will take more vacations in foreign countries.
   (D) More foreign visitors will travel to the United States.
   (E) Investments in U.S. securities will increase.

19. Among those hurt by inflation are

   I.   borrowers at fixed interest rates
   II. individuals on fixed incomes
   III. those with savings earning fixed interest rates
   IV. restaurant owners

   (A) I and II only
   (B) II and III only
   (C) II and IV only
   (D) II only
   (E) II, III, and IV only

20. A difference between M1 and M2 is that

   (A) M1 is a first mortgage and M2 is a second mortgage
   (B) M2 is M1 plus assets that are more liquid
   (C) M2 includes savings deposits
   (D) M1 is larger than M2
   (E) M2 is always double M1

21. Which of the following will cause the aggregate demand curve to shift to the left?

   (A) Expectations of surpluses of goods in the future
   (B) A decrease in income taxes
   (C) An increase in government spending
   (D) An increase in foreign income
   (E) Expectations of inflation in the future

22. According to Keynesian economists,

   (A) the investment demand curve is relatively elastic
   (B) fiscal policy is more effective than monetary policy
   (C) the economy is inherently stable
   (D) inadequate supply is largely to blame for periods of stagnation
   (E) real GDP will naturally adjust to the full-employment level

GO ON TO THE NEXT PAGE.

23. Which of the following results from stagflation?

    (A) Unemployment decreases.
    (B) The price level decreases.
    (C) The aggregate supply curve shifts to the right.
    (D) The Phillips curve shifts to the right.
    (E) Real GDP increases.

24. Which of the following will shift the demand curve for the Mexican peso to the left?

    (A) Speculation that the peso will increase in value
    (B) An increase in interest rates in Mexico relative to other countries
    (C) A lower rate of inflation in Mexico relative to other countries
    (D) An increase in incomes elsewhere relative to in Mexico
    (E) A decrease in the international demand for Mexican-made textiles

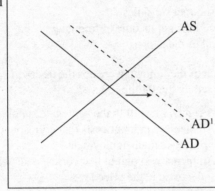

Price Level

AS

AD¹

AD

Real GDP

25. Which of the following is illustrated in the figure above?

    I.   Stagflation
    II. Cost-push inflation
    III. Supply-side inflation
    IV. Demand-pull inflation

    (A) I and II only
    (B) II and III only
    (C) II and IV only
    (D) IV only
    (E) I and IV only

26. The government of a country decides to increase government spending and taxes by the same amount in order to keep a balanced budget. The MPC is 0.75. Which of the following is true of this situation?

	Policy Direction	Expenditure Multiplier	Tax Multiplier
(A)	expansionary	4	3
(B)	expansionary	4	–3
(C)	contractionary	4	3
(D)	contractionary	4	–3
(E)	contractionary	5	4

27. Having a fractional reserve banking system means that

    (A) no single loan can be larger than 20 percent of the bank's holdings
    (B) the central bank reserves the right to audit any bank at any time
    (C) the central bank holds a certain fraction of GDP on reserve at all times
    (D) the central bank must approve loans over $1 million
    (E) a bank cannot lend out all of its deposits

28. If technology makes production less expensive and at the same time exports decrease, which of the following will result with certainty?

    (A) Real GDP will increase.
    (B) Real GDP will decrease.
    (C) The price level will increase.
    (D) The price level will decrease.
    (E) Real output will remain the same.

29. Which of the following must exist to allow for mutual benefit from specialization and trade between two countries?

    (A) Comparative advantage in the production of a good or service
    (B) Absolute advantage in the production of a good or service
    (C) Increasing marginal returns in production
    (D) Absolute and comparative advantage in the production of a good or service
    (E) Absolute advantage and increasing marginal returns in production

GO ON TO THE NEXT PAGE.

30. The GDP Deflator differs from the CPI in that the GDP Deflator

    (A) is thought to slightly overestimate the inflation rate
    (B) uses base year quantities in its calculations
    (C) incorporates both current year prices and base year prices
    (D) incorporates current year quantities in its calculations
    (E) is the favored price index of the U.S. government

31. It is a monetarist point of view that

    (A) monetary policy should be used to fine-tune the economy
    (B) crowding out is not a problem
    (C) the money supply should be increased steadily
    (D) the velocity of money is unstable
    (E) the economy is inherently unstable

32. Which group of people will suffer the most from a rising price level?

    (A) Debtors with fixed interest rates
    (B) People with fixed money incomes
    (C) Investors in gems, coins, and stamps
    (D) Property owners
    (E) Lenders of adjustable-rate mortgage loans

33. Droughts, technical glitches, and restrictions on the use of resources can all result in

    (A) a vertical Phillips curve
    (B) supply shocks
    (C) structural shocks
    (D) demand-pull inflation
    (E) deflation

34. On a bank's balance sheet, which of the following is considered a liability?

    (A) Required reserves
    (B) Excess reserves
    (C) Loans
    (D) Deposits
    (E) Reserve ratio

35. Suppose yesterday the euro was trading on the foreign exchange market at $1.36 U.S. and today it is trading at $1.40 U.S. Which of the following is true?

    (A) The U.S. dollar has appreciated.
    (B) The euro has depreciated.
    (C) Interest rates in the United States have decreased.
    (D) The demand for U.S. products has decreased.
    (E) The euro has appreciated.

36. In order to reduce or eliminate crowding out, expansionary fiscal policy can be accompanied by

    (A) an increase in government spending
    (B) a decrease in investment
    (C) expansionary monetary policy
    (D) contractionary monetary policy
    (E) an increase in the interest rate

37. In order to go from national income to GDP, one must

    (A) add depreciation expenses
    (B) add indirect taxes
    (C) subtract subsidies
    (D) add the net income of foreigners
    (E) all of the above

38. Which of the following creates the trade-off depicted by the Phillips curve?

    (A) A rightward shift in the aggregate supply curve
    (B) An increase in input costs that corresponds with an increase in unemployment
    (C) An increase in output that corresponds with a decrease in the price level
    (D) A leftward shift in the aggregate supply curve
    (E) A rightward shift in the aggregate demand curve

GO ON TO THE NEXT PAGE.

39. The natural rate of unemployment

    (A) includes structural and frictional unemployment
    (B) includes cyclical and frictional unemployment
    (C) includes structural and cyclical unemployment
    (D) includes structural, frictional, and cyclical unemployment
    (E) is around 1 percent

40. According to Say's law,

    (A) when price goes up, supply goes up
    (B) it is better to give than receive
    (C) demand creates its own supply
    (D) supply creates its own demand
    (E) demand and supply are mutually independent

41. A budget deficit exists when

    (A) the total amount that the government owes at a given time is positive
    (B) government spending exceeds tax collections for a given period
    (C) exports exceed imports in a given year
    (D) imports exceed exports in a given year
    (E) the total amount that the government owes at a given time is negative

42. The money supply will increase as a result of which of the following?

    (A) A decrease in the required reserve ratio
    (B) An increase in the discount rate
    (C) The selling of bonds by the Federal Reserve
    (D) An increase in the fraction of deposits that must be held by banks
    (E) An increase in income taxes

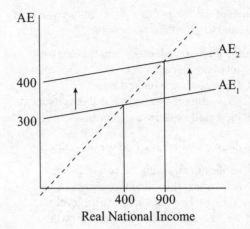

43. According to the aggregate expenditure graph above, what is the value of the expenditure multiplier?

    (A) 2
    (B) 2.25
    (C) 3
    (D) 4
    (E) 5

44. A dark room technician who develops film into photographs loses his job because few people use film cameras any more. This is an example of which of the following?

    (A) Frictional unemployment
    (B) Structural unemployment
    (C) Cyclical unemployment
    (D) Seasonal unemployment
    (E) Discouraged workers

45. Country A has a current account surplus; this means that

    (A) Country A also has a financial account surplus
    (B) Country A has a financial account deficit
    (C) Country A must borrow from its foreign reserves
    (D) Country A is operating in a recessionary gap
    (E) Country A is operating in an inflationary gap

GO ON TO THE NEXT PAGE.

46. Which of the following is the most likely to be a deterrent to growth in the economy?

    (A) Spending on education and training
    (B) Increases in capital
    (C) Increases in the interest rate
    (D) Expenditures on research and development
    (E) Increased capacity utilization

47. The domestic purchasing power of a currency

    (A) varies directly with the cost of living
    (B) is inversely related to the savings rate
    (C) is inversely related to the price level
    (D) varies directly with economic growth
    (E) is inversely related to the level of aggregate supply

48. Julia would spend $30 per week even if she made no income. Her weekly income is $1,000 and her marginal propensity to consume is 0.5. How much does Julia save per week?

    (A) $500
    (B) $ 35
    (C) $530
    (D) $ 80
    (E) $470

49. Classical economists generally believe that

    I. wages fluctuate quickly
    II. Say's law does not hold
    III. input and output prices will stay in line with each other
    IV. the government should not worry about maintaining aggregate demand at an adequate level

    (A) II and IV only
    (B) I , III, and IV only
    (C) I and IV only
    (D) II and III only
    (E) I, II, and III only

50. When a bank's balance sheet shows that the bank has excess reserves

    (A) the bank's reserves exceed the bank's assets
    (B) the bank can make additional loans
    (C) the bank's actual reserves are less than its required reserves
    (D) the bank is required to change its interest rate
    (E) the bank has fallen below the required reserve ratio

51. The real interest rate is

    (A) what one sees when looking at bank literature
    (B) the nominal interest rate divided by the inflation rate
    (C) the nominal interest rate plus the anticipated inflation rate
    (D) the nominal interest rate plus the compound interest rate
    (E) the nominal interest rate minus anticipated inflation

52. The formula for the money multiplier is

    (A) $\dfrac{1}{(1-\text{MPC})}$

    (B) $\dfrac{1}{(1-\text{Required reserve ratio})}$

    (C) $\dfrac{\text{MPC}}{\text{Required reserve ratio}}$

    (D) $\dfrac{1}{\text{Required reserve ratio}}$

    (E) $\dfrac{(1-\text{MPC})}{\text{MPC}}$

53. Which of the following would shift the aggregate demand curve to the right?

    (A) An increase in the price level
    (B) Depreciation in the international value of the dollar
    (C) An increase in personal income tax rates
    (D) An increase in interest rates
    (E) A decrease in the price level

GO ON TO THE NEXT PAGE.

54. Which of the following is true when expansionary fiscal and expansionary monetary (easy money) policy are used at the same time?

 (A) Unemployment will increase.
 (B) Real GDP will decrease.
 (C) Interest rates will remain relatively constant.
 (D) Inflation will decrease dramatically.
 (E) Investment will be crowded out.

55. Suppose an economy is in long-run equilibrium at the full-employment level of output. If government spending then increases,

 (A) an inflationary gap is created because the aggregate demand curve shifts to the right
 (B) an inflationary gap is created because the aggregate supply curve shifts to the right
 (C) an inflationary gap is created because potential GDP shifts to the left
 (D) a recessionary gap is created because the aggregate supply curve shifts to the left
 (E) a recessionary gap is created because the aggregate demand curve shifts to the left

56. Suppose that Tiger Woods buys a golf ball in England for $1 and the marginal propensity to consume in England is 0.75. What is the total increase in England's real GDP resulting from Mr. Woods's purchase?

 (A) $1
 (B) $1.25
 (C) $1.75
 (D) $4
 (E) $7.50

57. If prices are expected to rise more slowly in the future,

 (A) the Phillips curve will shift to the right
 (B) the actual rate of inflation will increase
 (C) the actual inflation rate will remain steady unless supply shocks set in
 (D) the government will carry out contractionary fiscal policy to prevent this occurrence
 (E) these expectations will become reality

58. A decrease in real investment stemming from higher interest rates due to government purchases is most commonly called

 (A) crowding out
 (B) zero policy effectiveness
 (C) the Laffer effect
 (D) fiscal defeat
 (E) fiscal imbalance

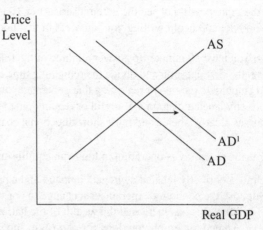

59. According to the theory of rational expectations, an increase in government spending to increase AD as illustrated in the figure above will be met with which of the following?

 (A) A sustainable increase in real GDP
 (B) An increase in AS
 (C) A countervailing decrease in AD
 (D) A decrease in AS
 (E) Apathy and inaction

60. A use of easy money (expansionary) policy by the Fed could result in which of the following?

 (A) An increase in net exports
 (B) A decrease in net exports
 (C) An increase in the real interest rate
 (D) An increase in the nominal interest rate
 (E) Crowded out investment

END OF SECTION I

GO ON TO THE NEXT PAGE.

MACROECONOMICS
Section II
Planning time—10 minutes
Writing time—50 minutes

You will have 10 minutes to read the exam questions. Spend this time reading through all of the questions, practicing graphs, noting possible problem-solving approaches, and otherwise planning your answers. It's fine to make notes on the green question insert, but be sure to write your answers and anything else that might be worth partial credit in the pink answer booklet—the graders will not see the green insert. After 10 minutes you will be told to break the seal on the pink Free-Response booklet and begin writing your answers in that booklet.

Directions: You have 50 minutes to answer all three of the following questions. It is suggested that you spend approximately half your time on the first question and divide the remaining time equally between the next two questions. In answering the questions, you should emphasize the line of reasoning that generated your results; it is not enough to list the results of your analysis. Include correctly labeled diagrams, if useful or required, in explaining your answers. A correctly labeled diagram must have all axes and curves clearly labeled and must show directional changes. Use a pen with black or dark blue ink.

1. Assume the economy is operating in long-run equilibrium at the full-employment level of output.

    (a) Draw a correctly labeled aggregate demand and aggregate supply graph that represents this scenario.
    (b) Suppose the economy experiences a change in consumer spending due to a sharp increase in stock market indices and that this has increased the wealth of the nation.
      (i)   Amend the graph you drew for part (a) to show the results of this change.
      (ii) Show the new equilibrium output and price level on your graph.
      (iii) What type of gap exists in this economy?
      (iv) Explain the effect of this change on the unemployment rate.
    (c) Recommend a fiscal policy action that could move the economy back to full-employment output.
    (d) Explain the effect of the recommended fiscal policy action on
      (i)   Aggregate demand
      (ii) The price level
      (iii) Real GDP
    (e) Explain how the following will influence the effect of the fiscal policy you recommended.
      (i)   Crowding out
      (ii) Changes in net exports

GO ON TO THE NEXT PAGE.

2. Suppose the reserve requirement is 10 percent and the National Bank of Austin holds no excess reserves. Then Alexandra deposits $1,000 in her checking account at the National Bank of Austin.

  (a) Incorporate the following three terms into a general explanation of how a bank can create money: deposits, required reserves, excess reserves.
  (b) After Alexandra's $1,000 deposit and prior to any other deposits or withdrawals, what is the largest amount that the National Bank of Austin can lend out?
  (c) Determine the money multiplier in this economy. Show your work.
  (d) What is the maximum value of additional deposits that can be created as the result of Alexandra's $1,000 deposit?
  (e) What policy change by the Federal Reserve would double the size of the money multiplier?

3. Suppose that Cyber Sara, the Bill Gates of the new millennium, takes technology to new heights with robots that provide widespread cost savings in the production of goods and services.

  (a) Use a correctly labeled aggregate demand and aggregate supply diagram to explain the direct effect of this increase in productivity on output and the price level in the United States.
  (b) If Cyber Sara's technology is available only in the United States, use a new, correctly labeled aggregate demand and aggregate supply diagram to illustrate the effect of the robots on exports.
  (c) Explain how the change in exports identified in part (b) will affect the value of the dollar relative to foreign currencies.

STOP

END OF EXAM

———————————

Chapter 18
Macroeconomics
Practice Test:
Answers and
Explanations

MACROECONOMICS PRACTICE TEST ANSWER KEY

Section I

1.	E	21.	A	41.	B
2.	C	22.	B	42.	A
3.	A	23.	D	43.	E
4.	C	24.	E	44.	B
5.	C	25.	D	45.	B
6.	B	26.	B	46.	C
7.	E	27.	E	47.	C
8.	A	28.	D	48.	E
9.	B	29.	A	49.	B
10.	E	30.	D	50.	B
11.	D	31.	C	51.	E
12.	C	32.	B	52.	D
13.	A	33.	B	53.	B
14.	B	34.	D	54.	C
15.	D	35.	E	55.	A
16.	E	36.	C	56.	D
17.	D	37.	E	57.	E
18.	C	38.	E	58.	A
19.	E	39.	A	59.	D
20.	C	40.	D	60.	B

SECTION I

1. **E** U.S. GDP is the total market value of all final goods and services produced in a year within the United States. Because the movies and olive oil were produced elsewhere, they can be ruled out. GDP includes net exports (exports minus imports), so even though they were exported, the blue jeans are included in GDP since they were made in the United States. The wine is included as well, because although Canadians make it, it fits the criteria of being produced within the United States.

2. **C** This bank must keep 20 percent, which is $200, and can lend out the remaining $800. The answer is (C), because the money multiplier is the reciprocal of the reserve requirement, or $\frac{1}{0.2}$ = 5. When the money multiplier takes effect, $800 5 = $4000.

3. **A** Robin's nominal income is the number of dollars he received, which increased from $30,000 to $60,000. Robin's real income is the buying power of the dollars he receives. Because prices have tripled while his nominal income doubled, prices have increased by more than income. He will be able to buy less with his $60,000 now than when he received half of this income but prices were one-third what they are now. Thus, real income has decreased.

4. **C** Choice (A) explains the horizontal section of the AS curve. Choice (B) explains the vertical section of the AS curve. Inaccurate information within firms about how their prices compare to the overall price level can fool firms into producing more at higher prices if they don't realize that the prices for everything else are going up at the same time. Higher price levels will not allow sellers to purchase more output from other sellers because an increase in the price level means that, on the average, prices for output in general have increased. Thus, just as sellers are receiving more for their goods, they must also pay more for goods that they purchase. Wages and other input prices that adjust more slowly than output prices can provide a profit incentive for firms to produce more at higher price levels because their revenues increase by more than their costs. When output and price level increase at the same time, this results in an upward sloping section of the AS.

5. **C** As illustrated in the circular flow diagram, goods and services are exchanged for dollars in the product markets. Wages and rents are exchanged for inputs in the factor markets. Household income funds expenditures, which result in revenues via the product markets. And firms exchange revenues for goods and services. The correct answer is that household expenditures do result in revenues for firms via the product markets.

6. **B** Fiat money has no intrinsic value, and its value in exchange comes as the result of government order, or "fiat." Cigarettes, gold, arrowheads, and chickens all have value beyond their usefulness as money, so they cannot be considered fiat money. A dollar bill, on the other hand, is a piece of paper that has value as money only because the government says it does.

7. **E** Because Astobia's interest rate is now lower than Bonavia's, it would be more profitable for investors to invest in Bonavia's economy. Therefore, there would be an inflow of capital as more money comes into the country. This will cause Bonavia's currency to appreciate, which will increase the demand for Bonavia's currency. However, as Bonavia's currency appreciates, it will be more expensive for people from other countries to buy products from Bonavia, and therefore their exports will decrease. The answer is (E).

8. **A** Expansionary fiscal policy will increase aggregate demand and aggregate expenditure. It is thus likely to increase the price level and the interest rate, and cause crowding out. It will cause an inflationary gap to get bigger, but will help to eliminate a recessionary gap.

9. **B** The curve describing the relationship between inflation and unemployment is called a Phillips curve. A demand curve would have price or dollars on the vertical axis and quantity on the horizontal axis. The other curves listed will have different shapes and different axes.

10. **E** The aggregate demand curve is not a simple aggregation of individual demand curves for goods or firms. These demand curves indicate what happens when the price of one good changes relative to the price of other goods. The AD curve reflects changes in demand when the average price level for all goods increases or decreases.

11. **D** A trade surplus occurs in the merchandise balance of trade, which is part of the current-account balance. It must be offset elsewhere in the current-account or financial account balances.

12. **C** The difficulty of this situation is that there is not a double coincidence of wants. That is, no one can get what he or she wants by simply exchanging his or her product for another's product. Although money serves all of the functions listed, their problem will be solved directly by the use of money as a medium of exchange. They can each purchase what they want from one person and sell what they have to another person using money without concern for the mismatched product interests of the people they are dealing with.

13. **A** The liquidity trap concept is a concern of Keynesian economists. Classical economists worry that efforts by the government to fine-tune the economy will backfire. They believe that aggregate supply is vertical, and that an increase in the money supply has a significant and direct effect on total spending. Classical economists do indeed believe in the quantity theory of money.

14. **B** The aggregate supply curve will shift to the right when inputs become cheaper, more productive, or more plentiful. This would result from an increase in the labor force, an increase in education and training, or an increase in investment. With more investment in capital, workers have more equipment to work with and more output can be produced, shifting the AS curve to the right. Natural disasters and government policies that increase production costs will shift AS to the left.

15. **D** If output in the long run is fixed at full employment output, this implies that the unemployment rate is the same regardless of the price level. Thus, the Phillips curve is vertical.

16. **E** The value of the next-best alternative foregone when a choice is made is called the opportunity cost. Accounting costs do not include opportunity costs. Switching and inferior costs are not common terms in economics, and the average cost is the total cost of producing a number of goods or services divided by that number.

17. **D** When the price level increases, the value of cash decreases and imports become relatively less expensive. Exports decrease because they become relatively more expensive. The real quantity of money decreases, thus increasing the interest rate and decreasing investment and real GDP.

18. **C** When the U.S. dollar appreciates relative to other currencies, this means that each dollar will purchase more of other currencies and it takes more of other currencies to purchase a dollar. Thus, imports into the United States are less expensive and will increase. Exports from the United States become more expensive and will decrease. Trips to the United States and U.S. securities also become relatively more expensive. On the other hand, because dollars buy relatively more in other countries, U.S. residents will take more vacations in foreign lands.

19. **E** Borrowers with fixed interest rates are actually helped by inflation because the value of what they must pay back goes down. Individuals on fixed incomes are hurt by inflation, because the purchasing power of their income decreases. Savers earning fixed interest rates are hurt because the value of their holdings and interest income goes down. Finally, restaurant owners are among those hurt because they incur menu costs—the cost of printing new menus with higher prices.

20. **C** M1 and M2 are different but overlapping measures of the money supply. M1 is the sum of currency, checking deposits, and travelers' checks. M2 is M1 plus savings deposits and some other less-liquid assets. Because M1 is part of M2, M1 cannot be larger than M2. At the same time, there is no reason why M2 would always be double M1.

21. **A** Decreases in taxes, increases in government spending or foreign income, or expectations of future inflation will shift the AD curve to the right. If consumers expect surpluses of goods in the future, they will purchase less now—shifting AD to the left—and purchase more in the future when the surpluses are expected to lead to lower price levels.

22. **B** Keynesian economists believe that investment demand is relatively inelastic, and thus unresponsive to changes in interest rates. They believe the economy is inherently unstable, that inadequate demand is largely to blame for periods of stagnation, and that real GDP needs a boost to reach the full-employment level. They also believe that the money supply has little effect on interest rates due to a relatively flat money demand curve, and that changes in interest rates have little effect on investment due to a

relatively inelastic investment demand curve. For these reasons they see little use for monetary policy and prefer fiscal policy instead.

23. **D** Stagflation results from the aggregate supply curve shifting to the left, which increases unemployment and the price level and decreases real GDP. Because unemployment increases for a given inflation rate, the Phillips curve shifts to the right.

24. **E** Speculation that the peso will increase in value will increase the demand for the peso, shifting the demand curve to the right. If Mexico offers higher interest rates, investors will demand more pesos in order to put their funds in Mexican financial institutions. A lower rate of inflation in Mexico will draw additional consumption of Mexican goods, thus increasing peso demand. An increase in incomes elsewhere will lead foreign consumers to spend more and demand pesos. But a decrease in the international demand for Mexican-made textiles will decrease the demand for pesos used to purchase those textiles.

25. **D** Stagflation is the combination of a rising price level, rising unemployment, and stagnant or falling real GDP. This results from cost-push inflation, which is also called supply-side inflation because it results from a shift in the AS curve to the left. The figure in the question illustrates demand-pull inflation, which does not result in stagflation. With demand-pull inflation, the AD curve shifts to the right, raising the equilibrium price level and fueling inflation.

26. **B** Increasing government spending is expansionary; however, the increase in taxes is contractionary. Government spending is a component of aggregate demand/aggregate expenditure, and therefore a change in government spending will change aggregate expenditure by that amount. The increase in taxes will cause a decrease in consumption; however, consumption will not change by the same amount as the tax increase, as people will change their consumption based on the MPC. In this case the MPC is 0.75, so consumption will change only by 75 percent of the amount of tax change. Thus, the overall effect in this situation is expansionary. Cross out (C), (D), and (E). The equation for the expenditure multiplier is $\frac{1}{1-\text{MPC}}$, which equals $\frac{1}{0.25}$, or 4. The tax multiplier is always one less than the expenditure multiplier and negative, so it is −3. The answer is (B).

27. **E** Under a fractional reserve banking system, a fraction of total deposits must be held on reserve and the rest can be lent out. This prevents a bank from lending out all of its deposits.

28. **D** The improvement in technology will shift the AS curve to the right, which decreases the price level and increases real GDP. The decrease in exports will shift the AD curve to the left, decreasing the price level and decreasing real GDP. Because the two events have opposing influences on real GDP, the net result is uncertain. However, both events decrease the price level, so it is certain that the price level drops.

29. **A** Neither an absolute advantage nor increasing marginal returns in the production of a good are necessary to allow mutual benefit from specialization and trade. The opportunity for two countries to benefit from specialization and trade rests only on the existence of a comparative advantage in the production of a good or service.

30. **D** The CPI uses base year quantities, is favored by the U.S. government, and is thought to slightly overestimate the inflation rate. Both indexes incorporate both current year and base year prices. The GDP Deflator differs from the CPI in its use of current year quantities in its calculations.

31. **C** Monetarists suggest that the use of monetary policy to fine-tune the economy could be destabilizing. They also believe that the crowding out of private investment due to increased interest rates substantially weakens fiscal policy. They see velocity and the economy in general to be relatively stable. Monetarists favor steadily increasing the money supply at a rate equal to the growth in real output rather than active fiscal or monetary policy.

32. **B** People with fixed money incomes will suffer because the purchasing power of their fixed incomes will fall as the price level rises. Debtors will benefit because the purchasing power of the money they must pay back falls as the price level rises. Investors in gems, coins, stamps, and property can expect the prices of the items they own to increase with the price level. Lenders of adjustable-rate mortgages are protected from inflation because the interest rates they receive increase with the price level.

33. **B** Each of these events would shift the AS curve to the left, increasing inflation and unemployment. A vertical Phillips curve implies that unemployment is constant, so that is ruled out, as is deflation. Demand-pull inflation is caused by an increase in aggregate demand, not a decrease in aggregate supply. Structural shocks result from changes in the structure of aggregate demand. These events described are all sources of supply shocks.

34. **D** Reserves are assets of the bank, as are loans, which must be repaid to the bank. Because depositors and not the bank own deposits, deposits are liabilities that must eventually be returned to the owners.

35. **E** Because the euro is now worth more in dollars, it has appreciated. The correct answer is (E).

36. **C** Crowding out occurs when an increase in government spending (which constitutes expansionary fiscal policy) increases the interest rate and decreases investment. Thus, an increase in government spending, a decrease in investment, or an increase in the interest rate would all make the problem continue. Contractionary monetary policy would only increase the interest rate more, but expansionary monetary policy could relieve upward pressures on the interest rate and diminish the crowding out effect.

37. **E** Depreciation expenses are subtracted from corporate profits before the NI calculation, so they must be added to capture the value of output needed to replace or repair worn-out buildings and machinery. Indirect taxes are part of the expenditure on goods and services (GDP) but they do not become income for suppliers of productive services (NI) so they must be added to NI to find GDP. Subsidy payments are part of NI but are not made in exchange for goods and services so they must be subtracted from NI to find GDP. Finally, GDP includes the income of foreigners working within the country whose GDP is being calculated but not the income of citizens working abroad. Thus, the net income of foreigners must be added to NI to obtain GDP.

38. **E** The Phillips curve depicts a trade-off between inflation and unemployment—when one increases, the other decreases. Shifts in the aggregate supply curve result in inflation and unemployment both increasing or both decreasing. An increase in input costs will shift AS to the left and increase the price level; the corresponding increase in unemployment creates a positive relationship between inflation and unemployment, not a trade-off. An increase in output decreases unemployment. When this is accompanied by a decrease in the price level, again no trade-off between inflation and unemployment results. It is a shift in the AD curve that causes inflation to increase and unemployment to decrease or vice versa.

39. **A** The natural rate of unemployment, which historically in the United States has been around five percent, is the sum of structural and frictional unemployment.

40. **D** Classical economists believe in Say's law, which suggests that when supplying goods, workers earn money to spend or save, and savings end up being borrowed and spent. Thus, they say that supply creates its own demand.

41. **B** The total amount that the government owes at a given time has to do with the national debt, not the balance of the budget. Exports compared with imports have to do with the trade surplus or deficit. Whether a budget deficit exists is based on the difference between government spending and tax collections for a given period (usually a year). If the government spends more than it collects in taxes, there is a deficit. If it spends less than it collects in taxes, there is a surplus. If it spends the same amount that it collects, then the budget is said to be "balanced."

42. **A** A decrease in the required reserve ratio will allow banks to loan out more of their deposits and increase the money multiplier, thus increasing the money supply. Each of the other actions will decrease the money supply, with the exception of the income tax increase, which results in a transfer of money from individuals to the government.

43. **E** The expenditure multiplier is found by dividing the change in income by the change in spending, so $500 \div 100 = 5$. The multiplier says that when a component of aggregate expenditure is increased, the real national income/output will increase by more, according to the multiplier. The answer is (E).

44. **B**   Structural unemployment occurs when someone cannot find a job because his or her type of labor is no longer demanded. Structural unemployment is usually related to outdated technologies (such as telegraphs, typewriters, etc.) or jobs that are no longer as common (such as switchboard operators and typists).

45. **B**   Current account and financial account must always be balanced; therefore if one is positive, the other must be negative by the same amount. The answer is (B).

46. **C**   Spending on education and training leads to skilled and productive workers that help the economy grow. Increases in capital give workers more equipment to work with and enable them to expand output. Research and development leads to improvements in technology that assist in the production process. Increased capacity utilization brings production levels from within the production possibility frontier to points closer to the frontier itself, increasing output and growth. Increases in the interest rate, however, deter investment in capital among other sources of growth.

47. **C**   After an increase in the price level, a given amount of a currency will purchase fewer goods and services, so its purchasing power has decreased. The purchasing power is thus inversely related to the price level.

48. **E**   Julia's autonomous consumption is $30 and she spends half of each additional dollar she earns, so she spends a total of $30 + $500 = $530. This leaves $1,000 − $530 = $470 for her savings.

49. **B**   Classical economists believe in Say's law. They also believe that wages and other input prices fluctuate quickly to stay in line with output prices. For both of these reasons, they feel that the economy is inherently stable and the government does not need to intervene in order to influence aggregate demand.

50. **B**   When a bank has excess reserves, it can make additional loans because the bank's actual reserves are greater than its required reserves. In other words, it has exceeded the required reserve ratio. The amount by which actual reserves exceed required reserves can be lent out to bank customers.

51. **E**   What one sees in bank literature is the nominal interest rate. The effective annual yield, which accounts for compound interest, is also a nominal rate. The real interest rate is the nominal interest rate minus anticipated inflation.

52. **D**   The money multiplier does not involve the marginal propensity to consume, which rules out (A), (C), and (E). The correct answer is $\dfrac{1}{\text{Required reserve ratio}}$.

53. **B**   Depreciation in the international value of the dollar will decrease imports and increase exports as American goods are now less expensive and imports are now more expensive, thereby shifting aggregate demand to the right (which constitutes an increase in aggregate demand). Changes in the price level cause movements along a fixed aggregate demand curve rather than a complete shift of it. An increase in personal income taxes would decrease consumption spending, a component of aggregate demand. An increase in interest rates would decrease investment, which is also a component of aggregate demand.

54. **C** Expansionary fiscal policy will increase interest rates by increasing the transaction demand for money in money market accounts, or decreasing the supply of loanable funds in the loanable funds market while increasing the demand for loanable funds. The interest rates, in that case, will remain constant. The answer is (C).

55. **A** An inflationary gap exists when the short-run equilibrium of aggregate supply and aggregate demand falls to the right of full-employment output. Starting in long-run equilibrium, an increase in government spending would increase aggregate demand and bring the short-run equilibrium to the right, thus creating an inflationary gap.

56. **D** The autonomous spending multiplier is the number by which an initial amount of new autonomous spending (spending that does not depend on income) should be multiplied to find the resulting increase in real GDP. The autonomous spending multiplier is $\dfrac{1}{(1 - \text{MPC})}$, which in this case is $\dfrac{1}{(1 - 0.75)} = \dfrac{1}{0.25} = 4$. Thus, Tiger Woods's \$1 purchase will result in an increase in England's real GDP of 4 \$1 = \$4.

57. **E** Expectations about inflation are self-fulfilling. If individuals expect price levels to rise more slowly, they will build these expectations into their wage and price demands and thereby cause prices to rise more slowly. Because inflation will decrease for any given unemployment rate, the Phillips curve will shift to the left. If the government were to carry out contractionary fiscal policy, price levels would increase even more slowly.

58. **A** Crowding out occurs when the demand for funds to finance government purchases increases the interest rate and thereby decreases real investment. The resulting decrease in aggregate demand is typically smaller than the increase due to the government spending, so the intended fiscal policy is not fruitless.

59. **D** According to the theory of rational expectations, people learn to anticipate government policies designed to influence the economy, and build the policies' effects into their wage and price demands. Thus, anticipating the AD shift and the subsequent increase in the price level, people will demand higher prices and wages and shift AS back to the left. The net result of the government policy is thus inflation with no increase in real GDP.

60. **B** Expansionary monetary policy will decrease interest rates, which will induce a capital inflow and increase investment and consumption. As a result, there will be increased inflation, which will cause the relative price to be high for foreign nations, which will decrease net exports, so the answer is (B).

SECTION II

Below are the fully correct answers; however, remember that you can still earn points on the free-response questions if you give only a partially correct answer. So, use the responses below to see how much you got right to estimate how well you would do on the real AP exam.

1.

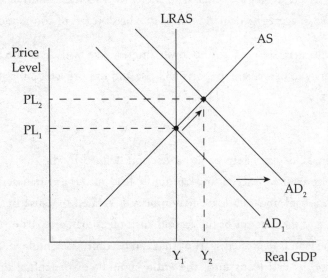

(a)–(b)(ii): Answers are shown on the graph above.

(b) (iii) Because prices have risen, this is an inflationary gap.

(iv) The unemployment rate will fall because it will take more employment to produce the new, higher level of real GDP. The full-employment level of output produced in the beginning corresponded with the natural rate of unemployment. Thus, after the change, the unemployment rate will fall below the natural rate.

(c) Contractionary fiscal policy, meaning some combination of a decrease in government spending, an increase in taxes, and a decrease in transfer payments, would help the economy move back to the full-employment output level.

(d) (i) As possible elements of contractionary fiscal policy, an increase in taxes or a decrease in transfer payments will dampen consumption—a component of aggregate demand—and shift the aggregate demand curve to the left. A decrease in government spending will shift aggregate demand to the left as well.

(ii) The decrease in aggregate demand will lead to a lower equilibrium price level.

(iii) The decrease in aggregate demand will also lead to a lower equilibrium level of real GDP.

(e) (i) Deficit spending creates the need for the government to borrow funds, which increases the overall demand for loanable funds, increases the interest rate, and decreases, or "crowds out," investment spending. With contractionary fiscal policy, higher taxes or lower government expenditures decrease the need for government borrowing, thus reversing the crowding out effect. Interest rates decrease, allowing investment and therefore aggregate demand to increase. This increase in aggregate demand will offset some of the decrease in aggregate demand that is the direct result of contractionary fiscal policy.

(ii) Net exports will increase, because the lower interest rate will deter foreign investment and cause the domestic currency to depreciate. Exports will rise and imports will fall as the result of a depreciated currency.

2.

(a) When customers make deposits into banks, a fraction defined by the reserve requirement, in this case 10 percent, becomes required reserves and cannot be lent out. The remainder is excess reserves and can be lent out. When a bank makes a loan, new money is created, because both the amount of the first customer's deposit and the amount of the second customer's loan are part of the M1 money supply. As the money from the loan is deposited, part of that can become a second loan, and the process continues with successive deposits and loans until the entire amount of the initial deposit is held as required reserves in banks.

(b) Ten percent of the deposit, or $100, becomes required reserves. The remaining $900 can be lent out.

(c) The money multiplier is $\dfrac{1}{\text{reserve requirement}} = \dfrac{1}{0.1} = 10$.

(d) With a money multiplier of 10, Alexandra's $1,000 deposit can result in a total of $10,000 in deposits, $1,000 of which is Alexandra's deposit and $9,000 of which is created as the result of Alexandra's deposit.

(e) The Federal Reserve sets the reserve requirement for banks, which determines the money multiplier. By lowering the reserve requirement to 5 percent, the Fed would cause the money multiplier to become $\dfrac{1}{0.05} = 20$.

3.

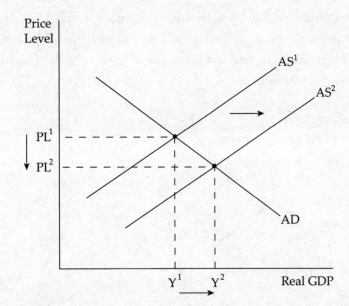

(a) The widespread cost savings in the production of goods and services will translate directly into an increase (shift to the right) in the aggregate supply curve, as illustrated in the figure above. That is, firms will be willing to supply more goods and services at any given price level because they are cheaper to produce. Output will increase and the price level will decrease.

(b) The decreased price level resulting from the shift of aggregate supply from AS1 to AS2 in the figure shown in part (a) will make prices in the United States relatively less expensive than prices elsewhere. This will lead to an increase in exports and a decrease in imports, both of which shift the AD curve to the right as illustrated in this figure:

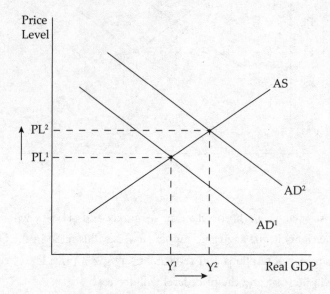

(c) The increase in exports will lead to an increase in the demand for dollars with which to purchase those exports. The increased demand for dollars will shift the dollar demand curve to the right and increase the value of the dollar relative to foreign currencies. This effect is illustrated in the following figure in the context of the dollar-euro market. The effect will be similar in other currency markets.

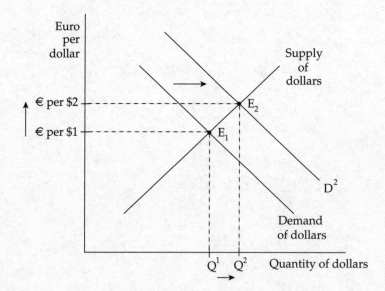

Appendix:
Formula Sheets

Microeconomics

Allocative Efficiency Condition	P = MC, or more precisely, Marginal Social Benefit (MSB) = Marginal Social Cost (MSC)
Average Fixed Cost	$\text{AFC} = \dfrac{\text{Total Fixed Cost (TFC)}}{\text{Quantity of Output (Q)}}$
Average Product	$\text{AFP} = \dfrac{\text{Total Product}}{\text{Quantity of Input}}$
Average Profit	$\text{Average Profit} = \dfrac{\text{Total Profit}}{\text{Quantity}}$
Average Revenue	$\text{Average Revenue} = \dfrac{\text{Total Revenue}}{\text{Quantity}}$
Average Total Cost	$\text{ATC} = \dfrac{\text{Total Cost (TC)}}{\text{Quantity of Output (Q)}}$
Average Variable Cost	$\text{AVC} = \dfrac{\text{Total Variable Cost (TC)}}{\text{Quantity of Output (Q)}}$
Cross-Price Elasticity of Demand	$\dfrac{\text{Percentage Change in Quantity Demanded of Good X}}{\text{Percentage Change in Price of Good Y}}$
Distributive Efficiency Condition	$\dfrac{\text{MU}_F}{\text{P}_F} = \dfrac{\text{MU}_C}{\text{P}_C}$
Elasticity of Supply	$\dfrac{\text{Percentage Change in Quantity Supplied}}{\text{Percentage Change in Price}}$ (Use the point or arc formula as indicated below for the price elasticity of demand, substituting the quantity supplied for the quantity demanded.)
Factor of Production Hiring Rule: Hire Until	MRP = MFC (in other books, MFC is sometimes called MRC)

Gini Coefficient	$$\dfrac{\text{shaded area}}{\text{area of triangle ABC}}$$
Marginal Cost	$MC = \dfrac{\Delta TC}{\Delta Q} = \dfrac{\Delta TVC}{\Delta Q}$
Marginal Product of Labor	$MP_L = \dfrac{\Delta TP}{\Delta L}$
Marginal Revenue	$MR = \dfrac{\Delta TR}{\Delta Q}$
Marginal Revenue Product of Labor (MRP$_L$)	$MRP_L = MP_L \quad MR_{output}$
Optimal Combination of Resources Condition	$\dfrac{MP_L}{w} = \dfrac{MP_K}{r}$
Optimal Consumption Rule	$\dfrac{MU_X}{P_X} = \dfrac{MU_Y}{P_Y}$

Price Elasticity of Demand

Simple "Point" Formula	$\dfrac{\%\Delta Q_d}{\%\Delta P} = \dfrac{\dfrac{\Delta Q_d}{Q}}{\dfrac{\Delta P}{P}} = \dfrac{\dfrac{Q_{new} - Q_{old}}{Q_{old}}}{\dfrac{P_{new} - P_{old}}{P_{old}}}$
More Precise "Arc" Formula	$\dfrac{\dfrac{Q_{new} - Q_{old}}{\left(\dfrac{Q_{new} + Q_{old}}{2}\right)}}{\dfrac{P_{new} + P_{old}}{\left(\dfrac{P_{new} + P_{old}}{2}\right)}}$

Price for a Competitive Firm	$P = MR = AR$
Production Efficiency Condition	$\frac{w}{r} = \frac{MP_L}{MP_K}$ or $\frac{MP_K}{r} = \frac{MP_L}{w}$ or $p = \min ATC$
Profit	$Profit = TR - TC$
Profit-Maximizing Output Level (if output should be produced at all), rule for finding	$MR = MC$
Slope	$\frac{Rise}{Run}$
Slope of the Total Product Curve	$\frac{Rise}{Run} = \frac{\text{Change in Total Product}}{\text{Change in the Number of Unites of an Input}} = \text{Marginal Product}$
Socially Optimal Level of Output	$MSB = MSC$
Total Costs	Total Costs = Total Fixed Costs + Total Variable Costs, $TC = TFC + TVC$

Macroeconomics

Aggregate Expenditure in a Simple Model Without Government or Foreign Sectors	$AE = C + I$
Allocative Efficiency Condition	$P = MC$, or more precisely, Marginal Social Benefit (MSB) = Marginal Social Cost (MSC)
Autonomous Spending Multiplier	$\text{Multiplier} = \frac{1}{1 - MPC} = \frac{1}{MPS}$
Balanced Budget Multiplier	Balanced Budget Multiplier = $\frac{1}{1 - MPC} + \left(\frac{-MPC}{1 - MPC}\right) = \frac{1 - MPC}{1 - MPC} = 1$
Bank's Reserve Ratio	$\text{Reserve Ratio} = \frac{\text{Bank Reserves}}{\text{Total Deposits}}$
Budget Deficit	Budget Deficit = Federal Government Spending – Tax Collections (A negative deficit indicates a surplus.)
Financial Account Balance	Financial Account Balance = Foreign Purchases of Home Assets – Home Purchases of Foreign Assets
Consumer Price Index	$CPI = \frac{\text{Base Year Quantities} \times \text{Current Year Prices}}{\text{Base Year Quantities} \times \text{Base Year Prices}} \times 100$
Consumption Function	$C = C_a + MPC(Y)$

Current-Account Balance	Current-Account Balance = Trade Balance + Services Balance + Unilateral
Distributive Efficiency Condition	$\dfrac{MU_F}{P_F} = \dfrac{MU_C}{P_C}$
Equality of Leakages and Injections	$S + T + M = I + G + X$
Equation of Exchange	$MV = PQ$
Gross Domestic Product	$GDP = C + I + G + (X - M)$ $GDP = NI + Depreciation + Indirect\ Taxes - Subsidies + Net\ Income$ of Foreigners
Gross Domestic Product Deflator	$GDP\ Deflator = \dfrac{Current\ Year\ Quantities \times Current\ Year\ Prices}{Current\ Year\ Quantities \times Base\ Year\ Prices} \times 100$
Income in a Simple Model Without Government or Foreign Sectors	$Y = C + S$
Inflation Between Two Years	Inflation Between Years Y and Z = $\left[\dfrac{CPI\ in\ Year\ Z}{CPI\ in\ Year\ Y} - 1\right] \times 100$
Marginal Propensity to Consume	$MPC = \dfrac{Change\ in\ Consumption}{Change\ in\ Income}$
Marginal Propensity to Save	$MPS = \dfrac{Change\ in\ Saving}{Change\ in\ Income}$
Marginal Propensity to Save and Marginal Propensity to Consume Sum	$MPC + MPS = 1$
Merchandise Trade Balance	Merchandise Trade Balance = Value of Merchandise Exports – Value of Merchandise Imports
Nominal Interest Rate	Nominal Interest Rate = Real Interest Rate + Anticipated Inflation
Okun's Law	% increase in unemployment above natural rate 2 = % decrease in output (The 2 in the equation is an approximation.)
Production Efficiency Condition	$\dfrac{w}{r} = \dfrac{MP_L}{MP_K}$

Real GDP	$\dfrac{\text{Nominal GDP}}{\text{CPI* for the same year as the nominal figure}} \times 100$ *CPI or GDP deflator
Real Interest Rate	Real Interest Rate = Nominal Interest Rate − Anticipated Inflation
Rule of 70	Doubling time $= \dfrac{70}{\%\text{ change per year}}$ With 10% inflation, prices double in $\dfrac{70}{10} = 7$ years.
Slope	$\dfrac{\text{Rise}}{\text{Run}}$
Tax Multiplier	Tax Multiplier $= -\dfrac{\text{MPC}}{\text{MPS}}$
Total Amount of Deposits Resulting from an Initial Deposit That Is Ultimately Held as Reserves	Simple Money (or Deposit) Multiplier $= \dfrac{1}{\text{Required Reserve Ratio}}$
Unemployment Rate	$\dfrac{\text{Unemployed}}{\text{Labor Force}}$

The Princeton Review®

1. YOUR NAME:
(Print)   Last   First   M.I.

SIGNATURE: _____ DATE: _____ / ___ / ___

HOME ADDRESS: _____
(Print)   Number and Street

_____
            City   State   Zip Code

PHONE NO. : _____
(Print)

IMPORTANT: Please fill in these boxes exactly as shown on the back cover of your test book.

2. TEST FORM

_____

6. DATE OF BIRTH

Month	Day	Year
○ JAN		
○ FEB		
○ MAR	⓪ ⓪	⓪ ⓪
○ APR	① ①	① ①
○ MAY	② ②	② ②
○ JUN	③ ③	③ ③
○ JUL	④	④ ④
○ AUG	⑤	⑤ ⑤
○ SEP	⑦	⑦ ⑦
○ OCT	⑧	⑧ ⑧
○ NOV	⑨	⑨ ⑨
○ DEC		

3. TEST CODE   **4. REGISTRATION NUMBER**

⓪	Ⓐ	⓪	⓪	⓪	⓪	⓪	⓪	⓪	⓪	⓪
①	Ⓑ	①	①	①	①	①	①	①	①	①
②	Ⓒ	②	②	②	②	②	②	②	②	②
③	Ⓓ	③	③	③	③	③	③	③	③	③
④	Ⓔ	④	④	④	④	④	④	④	④	④
⑤	Ⓕ	⑤	⑤	⑤	⑤	⑤	⑤	⑤	⑤	⑤
⑦	Ⓖ	⑦	⑦	⑦	⑦	⑦	⑦	⑦	⑦	⑦
⑧		⑧	⑧	⑧	⑧	⑧	⑧	⑧	⑧	⑧
⑨		⑨	⑨	⑨	⑨	⑨	⑨	⑨	⑨	⑨

7. SEX
○ MALE
○ FEMALE

The Princeton Review®

5. YOUR NAME

First 4 letters of last name				FIRST INIT	MID INIT
Ⓐ Ⓐ Ⓐ Ⓐ				Ⓐ	Ⓐ
Ⓑ Ⓑ Ⓑ Ⓑ				Ⓑ	Ⓑ
Ⓒ Ⓒ Ⓒ Ⓒ				Ⓒ	Ⓒ
Ⓓ Ⓓ Ⓓ Ⓓ				Ⓓ	Ⓓ
Ⓔ Ⓔ Ⓔ Ⓔ				Ⓔ	Ⓔ
Ⓕ Ⓕ Ⓕ Ⓕ				Ⓕ	Ⓕ
Ⓖ Ⓖ Ⓖ Ⓖ				Ⓖ	Ⓖ
Ⓗ Ⓗ Ⓗ Ⓗ				Ⓗ	Ⓗ
Ⓘ Ⓘ Ⓘ Ⓘ				Ⓘ	Ⓘ
Ⓙ Ⓙ Ⓙ Ⓙ				Ⓙ	Ⓙ
Ⓚ Ⓚ Ⓚ Ⓚ				Ⓚ	Ⓚ
Ⓛ Ⓛ Ⓛ Ⓛ				Ⓛ	Ⓛ
Ⓜ Ⓜ Ⓜ Ⓜ				Ⓜ	Ⓜ
Ⓝ Ⓝ Ⓝ Ⓝ				Ⓝ	Ⓝ
Ⓞ Ⓞ Ⓞ Ⓞ				Ⓞ	Ⓞ
Ⓟ Ⓟ Ⓟ Ⓟ				Ⓟ	Ⓟ
Ⓠ Ⓠ Ⓠ Ⓠ				Ⓠ	Ⓠ
Ⓡ Ⓡ Ⓡ Ⓡ				Ⓡ	Ⓡ
Ⓢ Ⓢ Ⓢ Ⓢ				Ⓢ	Ⓢ
Ⓣ Ⓣ Ⓣ Ⓣ				Ⓣ	Ⓣ
Ⓤ Ⓤ Ⓤ Ⓤ				Ⓤ	Ⓤ
Ⓥ Ⓥ Ⓥ Ⓥ				Ⓥ	Ⓥ
Ⓦ Ⓦ Ⓦ Ⓦ				Ⓦ	Ⓦ
Ⓧ Ⓧ Ⓧ Ⓧ				Ⓧ	Ⓧ
Ⓨ Ⓨ Ⓨ Ⓨ				Ⓨ	Ⓨ
Ⓩ Ⓩ Ⓩ Ⓩ				Ⓩ	Ⓩ

Section 1   Start with number 1 for each new section.
If a section has fewer questions than answer spaces, leave the extra answer spaces blank.

1. Ⓐ Ⓑ Ⓒ Ⓓ Ⓔ   31. Ⓐ Ⓑ Ⓒ Ⓓ Ⓔ
2. Ⓐ Ⓑ Ⓒ Ⓓ Ⓔ   32. Ⓐ Ⓑ Ⓒ Ⓓ Ⓔ
3. Ⓐ Ⓑ Ⓒ Ⓓ Ⓔ   33. Ⓐ Ⓑ Ⓒ Ⓓ Ⓔ
4. Ⓐ Ⓑ Ⓒ Ⓓ Ⓔ   34. Ⓐ Ⓑ Ⓒ Ⓓ Ⓔ
5. Ⓐ Ⓑ Ⓒ Ⓓ Ⓔ   35. Ⓐ Ⓑ Ⓒ Ⓓ Ⓔ
6. Ⓐ Ⓑ Ⓒ Ⓓ Ⓔ   36. Ⓐ Ⓑ Ⓒ Ⓓ Ⓔ
7. Ⓐ Ⓑ Ⓒ Ⓓ Ⓔ   37. Ⓐ Ⓑ Ⓒ Ⓓ Ⓔ
8. Ⓐ Ⓑ Ⓒ Ⓓ Ⓔ   38. Ⓐ Ⓑ Ⓒ Ⓓ Ⓔ
9. Ⓐ Ⓑ Ⓒ Ⓓ Ⓔ   39. Ⓐ Ⓑ Ⓒ Ⓓ Ⓔ
10. Ⓐ Ⓑ Ⓒ Ⓓ Ⓔ   40. Ⓐ Ⓑ Ⓒ Ⓓ Ⓔ
11. Ⓐ Ⓑ Ⓒ Ⓓ Ⓔ   41. Ⓐ Ⓑ Ⓒ Ⓓ Ⓔ
12. Ⓐ Ⓑ Ⓒ Ⓓ Ⓔ   42. Ⓐ Ⓑ Ⓒ Ⓓ Ⓔ
13. Ⓐ Ⓑ Ⓒ Ⓓ Ⓔ   43. Ⓐ Ⓑ Ⓒ Ⓓ Ⓔ
14. Ⓐ Ⓑ Ⓒ Ⓓ Ⓔ   44. Ⓐ Ⓑ Ⓒ Ⓓ Ⓔ
15. Ⓐ Ⓑ Ⓒ Ⓓ Ⓔ   45. Ⓐ Ⓑ Ⓒ Ⓓ Ⓔ
16. Ⓐ Ⓑ Ⓒ Ⓓ Ⓔ   46. Ⓐ Ⓑ Ⓒ Ⓓ Ⓔ
17. Ⓐ Ⓑ Ⓒ Ⓓ Ⓔ   47. Ⓐ Ⓑ Ⓒ Ⓓ Ⓔ
18. Ⓐ Ⓑ Ⓒ Ⓓ Ⓔ   48. Ⓐ Ⓑ Ⓒ Ⓓ Ⓔ
19. Ⓐ Ⓑ Ⓒ Ⓓ Ⓔ   49. Ⓐ Ⓑ Ⓒ Ⓓ Ⓔ
20. Ⓐ Ⓑ Ⓒ Ⓓ Ⓔ   50. Ⓐ Ⓑ Ⓒ Ⓓ Ⓔ
21. Ⓐ Ⓑ Ⓒ Ⓓ Ⓔ   51. Ⓐ Ⓑ Ⓒ Ⓓ Ⓔ
22. Ⓐ Ⓑ Ⓒ Ⓓ Ⓔ   52. Ⓐ Ⓑ Ⓒ Ⓓ Ⓔ
23. Ⓐ Ⓑ Ⓒ Ⓓ Ⓔ   53. Ⓐ Ⓑ Ⓒ Ⓓ Ⓔ
24. Ⓐ Ⓑ Ⓒ Ⓓ Ⓔ   54. Ⓐ Ⓑ Ⓒ Ⓓ Ⓔ
25. Ⓐ Ⓑ Ⓒ Ⓓ Ⓔ   55. Ⓐ Ⓑ Ⓒ Ⓓ Ⓔ
26. Ⓐ Ⓑ Ⓒ Ⓓ Ⓔ   56. Ⓐ Ⓑ Ⓒ Ⓓ Ⓔ
27. Ⓐ Ⓑ Ⓒ Ⓓ Ⓔ   57. Ⓐ Ⓑ Ⓒ Ⓓ Ⓔ
28. Ⓐ Ⓑ Ⓒ Ⓓ Ⓔ   58. Ⓐ Ⓑ Ⓒ Ⓓ Ⓔ
29. Ⓐ Ⓑ Ⓒ Ⓓ Ⓔ   59. Ⓐ Ⓑ Ⓒ Ⓓ Ⓔ
30. Ⓐ Ⓑ Ⓒ Ⓓ Ⓔ   60. Ⓐ Ⓑ Ⓒ Ⓓ Ⓔ

The Princeton Review®

Completely darken bubbles with a No. 2 pencil. If you make a mistake, be sure to erase mark completely. Erase all stray marks.

1. YOUR NAME:
(Print)
Last   First   M.I.

SIGNATURE: _____ DATE: ___/___/___

HOME ADDRESS: _____
(Print)
Number and Street

_____
City   State   Zip Code

PHONE NO. : _____
(Print)

IMPORTANT: Please fill in these boxes exactly as shown on the back cover of your test book.

2. TEST FORM

5. YOUR NAME

First 4 letters of last name				FIRST INIT	MID INIT
Ⓐ	Ⓐ	Ⓐ	Ⓐ	Ⓐ	Ⓐ
Ⓑ	Ⓑ	Ⓑ	Ⓑ	Ⓑ	Ⓑ
Ⓒ	Ⓒ	Ⓒ	Ⓒ	Ⓒ	Ⓒ
Ⓓ	Ⓓ	Ⓓ	Ⓓ	Ⓓ	Ⓓ
Ⓔ	Ⓔ	Ⓔ	Ⓔ	Ⓔ	Ⓔ
Ⓕ	Ⓕ	Ⓕ	Ⓕ	Ⓕ	Ⓕ
Ⓖ	Ⓖ	Ⓖ	Ⓖ	Ⓖ	Ⓖ
Ⓗ	Ⓗ	Ⓗ	Ⓗ	Ⓗ	Ⓗ
Ⓘ	Ⓘ	Ⓘ	Ⓘ	Ⓘ	Ⓘ
Ⓙ	Ⓙ	Ⓙ	Ⓙ	Ⓙ	Ⓙ
Ⓚ	Ⓚ	Ⓚ	Ⓚ	Ⓚ	Ⓚ
Ⓛ	Ⓛ	Ⓛ	Ⓛ	Ⓛ	Ⓛ
Ⓜ	Ⓜ	Ⓜ	Ⓜ	Ⓜ	Ⓜ
Ⓝ	Ⓝ	Ⓝ	Ⓝ	Ⓝ	Ⓝ
Ⓞ	Ⓞ	Ⓞ	Ⓞ	Ⓞ	Ⓞ
Ⓟ	Ⓟ	Ⓟ	Ⓟ	Ⓟ	Ⓟ
Ⓠ	Ⓠ	Ⓠ	Ⓠ	Ⓠ	Ⓠ
Ⓡ	Ⓡ	Ⓡ	Ⓡ	Ⓡ	Ⓡ
Ⓢ	Ⓢ	Ⓢ	Ⓢ	Ⓢ	Ⓢ
Ⓣ	Ⓣ	Ⓣ	Ⓣ	Ⓣ	Ⓣ
Ⓤ	Ⓤ	Ⓤ	Ⓤ	Ⓤ	Ⓤ
Ⓥ	Ⓥ	Ⓥ	Ⓥ	Ⓥ	Ⓥ
Ⓦ	Ⓦ	Ⓦ	Ⓦ	Ⓦ	Ⓦ
Ⓧ	Ⓧ	Ⓧ	Ⓧ	Ⓧ	Ⓧ
Ⓨ	Ⓨ	Ⓨ	Ⓨ	Ⓨ	Ⓨ
Ⓩ	Ⓩ	Ⓩ	Ⓩ	Ⓩ	Ⓩ

3. TEST CODE   **4. REGISTRATION NUMBER**

⓪	Ⓐ	⓪	⓪	⓪	⓪	⓪	⓪	⓪	⓪	⓪
①	Ⓑ	①	①	①	①	①	①	①	①	①
②	Ⓒ	②	②	②	②	②	②	②	②	②
③	Ⓓ	③	③	③	③	③	③	③	③	③
④	Ⓔ	④	④	④	④	④	④	④	④	④
⑤	Ⓕ	⑤	⑤	⑤	⑤	⑤	⑤	⑤	⑤	⑤
⑦	Ⓖ	⑦	⑦	⑦	⑦	⑦	⑦	⑦	⑦	⑦
⑧		⑧	⑧	⑧	⑧	⑧	⑧	⑧	⑧	⑧
⑨		⑨	⑨	⑨	⑨	⑨	⑨	⑨	⑨	⑨

6. DATE OF BIRTH

Month	Day		Year	
○ JAN				
○ FEB				
○ MAR	⓪	⓪	⓪	⓪
○ APR	①	①	①	①
○ MAY	②	②	②	②
○ JUN	③	③	③	③
○ JUL		④	④	④
○ AUG		⑤	⑤	⑤
○ SEP		⑦	⑦	⑦
○ OCT		⑧	⑧	⑧
○ NOV		⑨	⑨	⑨
○ DEC				

7. SEX
○ MALE
○ FEMALE

The Princeton Review®

Section ① Start with number 1 for each new section.
If a section has fewer questions than answer spaces, leave the extra answer spaces blank.

1. Ⓐ Ⓑ Ⓒ Ⓓ Ⓔ
2. Ⓐ Ⓑ Ⓒ Ⓓ Ⓔ
3. Ⓐ Ⓑ Ⓒ Ⓓ Ⓔ
4. Ⓐ Ⓑ Ⓒ Ⓓ Ⓔ
5. Ⓐ Ⓑ Ⓒ Ⓓ Ⓔ
6. Ⓐ Ⓑ Ⓒ Ⓓ Ⓔ
7. Ⓐ Ⓑ Ⓒ Ⓓ Ⓔ
8. Ⓐ Ⓑ Ⓒ Ⓓ Ⓔ
9. Ⓐ Ⓑ Ⓒ Ⓓ Ⓔ
10. Ⓐ Ⓑ Ⓒ Ⓓ Ⓔ
11. Ⓐ Ⓑ Ⓒ Ⓓ Ⓔ
12. Ⓐ Ⓑ Ⓒ Ⓓ Ⓔ
13. Ⓐ Ⓑ Ⓒ Ⓓ Ⓔ
14. Ⓐ Ⓑ Ⓒ Ⓓ Ⓔ
15. Ⓐ Ⓑ Ⓒ Ⓓ Ⓔ
16. Ⓐ Ⓑ Ⓒ Ⓓ Ⓔ
17. Ⓐ Ⓑ Ⓒ Ⓓ Ⓔ
18. Ⓐ Ⓑ Ⓒ Ⓓ Ⓔ
19. Ⓐ Ⓑ Ⓒ Ⓓ Ⓔ
20. Ⓐ Ⓑ Ⓒ Ⓓ Ⓔ
21. Ⓐ Ⓑ Ⓒ Ⓓ Ⓔ
22. Ⓐ Ⓑ Ⓒ Ⓓ Ⓔ
23. Ⓐ Ⓑ Ⓒ Ⓓ Ⓔ
24. Ⓐ Ⓑ Ⓒ Ⓓ Ⓔ
25. Ⓐ Ⓑ Ⓒ Ⓓ Ⓔ
26. Ⓐ Ⓑ Ⓒ Ⓓ Ⓔ
27. Ⓐ Ⓑ Ⓒ Ⓓ Ⓔ
28. Ⓐ Ⓑ Ⓒ Ⓓ Ⓔ
29. Ⓐ Ⓑ Ⓒ Ⓓ Ⓔ
30. Ⓐ Ⓑ Ⓒ Ⓓ Ⓔ
31. Ⓐ Ⓑ Ⓒ Ⓓ Ⓔ
32. Ⓐ Ⓑ Ⓒ Ⓓ Ⓔ
33. Ⓐ Ⓑ Ⓒ Ⓓ Ⓔ
34. Ⓐ Ⓑ Ⓒ Ⓓ Ⓔ
35. Ⓐ Ⓑ Ⓒ Ⓓ Ⓔ
36. Ⓐ Ⓑ Ⓒ Ⓓ Ⓔ
37. Ⓐ Ⓑ Ⓒ Ⓓ Ⓔ
38. Ⓐ Ⓑ Ⓒ Ⓓ Ⓔ
39. Ⓐ Ⓑ Ⓒ Ⓓ Ⓔ
40. Ⓐ Ⓑ Ⓒ Ⓓ Ⓔ
41. Ⓐ Ⓑ Ⓒ Ⓓ Ⓔ
42. Ⓐ Ⓑ Ⓒ Ⓓ Ⓔ
43. Ⓐ Ⓑ Ⓒ Ⓓ Ⓔ
44. Ⓐ Ⓑ Ⓒ Ⓓ Ⓔ
45. Ⓐ Ⓑ Ⓒ Ⓓ Ⓔ
46. Ⓐ Ⓑ Ⓒ Ⓓ Ⓔ
47. Ⓐ Ⓑ Ⓒ Ⓓ Ⓔ
48. Ⓐ Ⓑ Ⓒ Ⓓ Ⓔ
49. Ⓐ Ⓑ Ⓒ Ⓓ Ⓔ
50. Ⓐ Ⓑ Ⓒ Ⓓ Ⓔ
51. Ⓐ Ⓑ Ⓒ Ⓓ Ⓔ
52. Ⓐ Ⓑ Ⓒ Ⓓ Ⓔ
53. Ⓐ Ⓑ Ⓒ Ⓓ Ⓔ
54. Ⓐ Ⓑ Ⓒ Ⓓ Ⓔ
55. Ⓐ Ⓑ Ⓒ Ⓓ Ⓔ
56. Ⓐ Ⓑ Ⓒ Ⓓ Ⓔ
57. Ⓐ Ⓑ Ⓒ Ⓓ Ⓔ
58. Ⓐ Ⓑ Ⓒ Ⓓ Ⓔ
59. Ⓐ Ⓑ Ⓒ Ⓓ Ⓔ
60. Ⓐ Ⓑ Ⓒ Ⓓ Ⓔ

NOTES